Uncommon **Boston**

Uncommon Boston

a guide to hidden spaces and special places
Updated Edition

SUSAN BERK with JILL BLOOM

Illustrations by Linda A. Wielblad

ADDISON-WESLEY PUBLISHING COMPANY, INC.
Reading, Massachusetts • Menlo Park, California • New York
Don Mills, Ontario • Wokingham, England • Amsterdam
Bonn • Sydney • Singapore • Tokyo • Madrid • San Juan

Library of Congress Cataloging-in-Publication Data

Berk, Susan.
  Uncommon Boston: a guide to hidden spaces and special places/
Susan Berk with Jill Bloom; illustrations by Linda A. Wielblad. —
Updated ed.
    p. cm.
  Includes bibliographical references.
  ISBN 0-201-52363-9
  1. Boston (Mass.) — Description — 1981– — Guide-books. I. Bloom,
Jill. II. Title.
F73.18.B47 1990
917.44'610443 — dc20   89-29298
                                                                              CIP

Cover design by Victoria Blaine
Text design by Carson Design
Set in 10 point Palatino by Compset, Inc., Beverly, MA

Addison-Wesley books are available at special discounts for bulk purchases for
sales promotions, premiums, fund-raising, or educational use. For details,
contact:

Special Markets Department
Addison-Wesley Publishing Company, Inc.
Reading, MA 01867
617-944-3700 × 2431

ABCDEFGHIJK-AL-943210
First printing, February 1990

Contents

Introduction

In colonial times, a common was a piece of land held "in common ownership" by a community, hence the name still used for the tempting green public space in the center of the city of Boston. But "common" has another connotation in the twentieth century — it means "ordinary, or without special distinction." And that's the last thing we would want to say about our city.

Since its founding in 1982, Uncommon Boston, Ltd., a tour company dedicated to revealing what is unique and special in Boston, has shown that this city is far from ordinary — or even predictable. Where else do you have a street that abruptly changes its name from Summer to Winter? Or a major church literally floating on wooden support columns? Or a state emblem that changes direction according to the political party in power? Only in Boston . . . so we couldn't resist the double pun when we named our company. We hope you appreciate our somewhat unorthodox approach toward introducing you to this city.

Uncommon Boston is not an ordinary guidebook. It doesn't simply list the names, places, and dates of the sites you'd expect to find in a book about Boston. Not only have we discovered some unusual sites, off the beaten path even for long-time residents, we've also tried to present the tried-and-true tourist attractions in a new light, by telling little-known stories about them, approaching them from a different architectural angle, or by making museums, monuments, and mansions come alive with a glimpse of the personalities who have helped form Boston's rich and impressive history.

The result is a fascinating, informative book, compiled in a lively yet practical manner, that is as much a pleasure to read at leisure as it is to use to guide you as you proceed through the city. The tours are organized by theme — from a Literary Lions tour to a Chocowalk, Kidtreks to Amiable Antiques. You can mix-and-match the tours according to your own needs and interests.

But an uncommon guidebook needs more than uncommon references to make it work; it also needs an uncommon reader.

This is not only a book for tourists, conventioneers, and business travelers coming to Boston for the first time. It's for people who are thinking of making an extended visit, whether for college, business, or family reasons, and who really want to get to know their new home. It's for residents who want to show out-of-town guests something that really catches Boston's flavor in a special way. And it's for those folks who have lived in Jamaica Plain, the North End, or Brighton all their lives and have never really explored Beacon Hill, the South End, or Back Bay. In short, this book is for anyone who wants to go behind the red brick façade of the city and find out what really makes its heart beat.

For practical reasons, we've limited the majority of our tours to Boston only. Although we're the first to get excited about sites and experiences farther afield (and recommend day trips whenever you can manage them), this book would simply be too unwieldy if we tried to encompass everything. Occasionally, we break our rule and venture outside Boston proper — but not too far, or too often. By limiting ourselves to Boston, we were able to offer you a manageable itinerary without overwhelming you. We couldn't completely exclude Cambridge, of course, but we've mercilessly — albeit reluctantly — kept our journeys across the Charles to a minimum. Since the tours conducted by Uncommon Boston, Ltd., usually last about two and a half hours, we've used that as a reasonable if arbitrary time limit. We find that people usually need a break by then, whether it's for a meal, a rest, or just some time to wander aimlessly and discover their own uncommon bit of the city.

Even within the narrow confines of the city limits, it was harder deciding what to leave out than what to include. Sometimes we simply had to stop when the allotted tour time ran out; other times we made the decision based on what was readily available from other sources, or could be found without the use of a book at all. In general, we let our personal preference, knowledge, and experience be our guide.

At the end of each tour, we provide the necessary practical details to help you plan your trip. There you will find information about each stop listed (indicated in the text by **boldface** type). The entries include addresses, phone numbers, whether or not there is a fee, and other appropriate information. Since hours of operation change often, these are not included. It's always wise to call ahead.

All phone numbers are in the 617 area code, unless otherwise noted. Additional lists at the ends of chapters include other tidbits that will enliven your trip, such as recommended reading lists and additional resources.

We feel confident that you will discover something uncommon on nearly every page, because we think that Boston is an uncommonly exciting city. And please, wander as far from the paths we describe as your own creativity, imagination, and sense of adventure will allow. Find people to talk to, investigate hidden nooks and crannies, and strike out on your own whenever you can. We welcome your feedback and suggestions for future editions, so if you happen upon something you'd like to share with us, please let us know. One of the nicest things about Boston is that it holds delights and surprises for even the most seasoned traveler, as you will soon see for yourself.

Boston

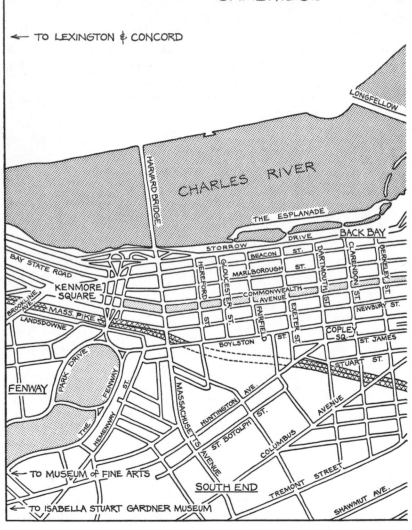

CAMBRIDGE

← TO LEXINGTON & CONCORD

LONGFELLOW

HARVARD BRIDGE

CHARLES RIVER

THE ESPLANADE

STORROW DRIVE   BACK BAY

BAY STATE ROAD

BEACON ST.
HEREFORD   MARLBOROUGH   ST.   DARTMOUTH
GLOUCESTER ST.   CLARENDON   BERKELEY ST.
KENMORE SQUARE   COMMONWEALTH AVENUE
BROOKLINE AVE.   FAIRFIELD   EXETER ST.   ST.
MASS PIKE   NEWBURY ST.
LANDSDOWNE   BOYLSTON ST.   COPLEY SQ.   ST. JAMES

PARK DRIVE
STUART ST.

FENWAY   THE FENWAY   ST.   MASSACHUSETTS AVENUE   HUNTINGTON AVE.   AVENUE
HEMENWAY   ST. BOTOLPH ST.
COLUMBUS

← TO MUSEUM of FINE ARTS

SOUTH END   TREMONT STREET

← TO ISABELLA STUART GARDNER MUSEUM   SHAWMUT AVE.

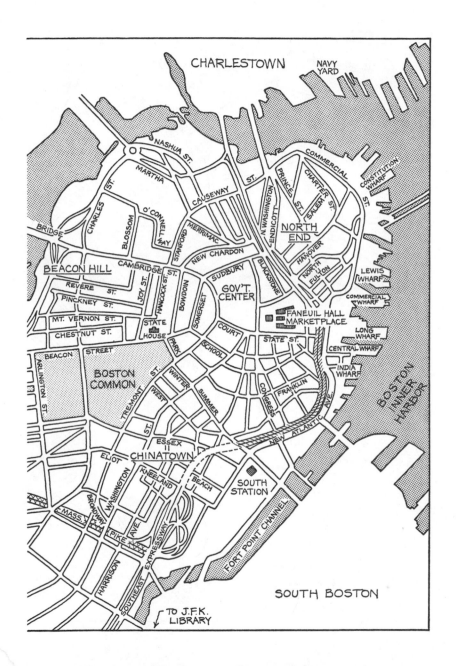

Cambridge

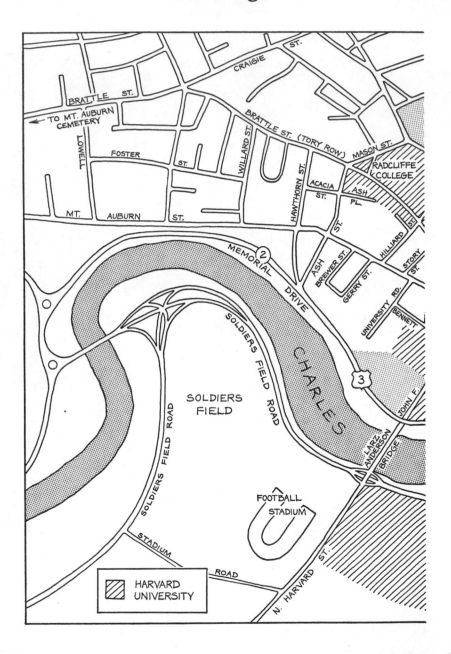

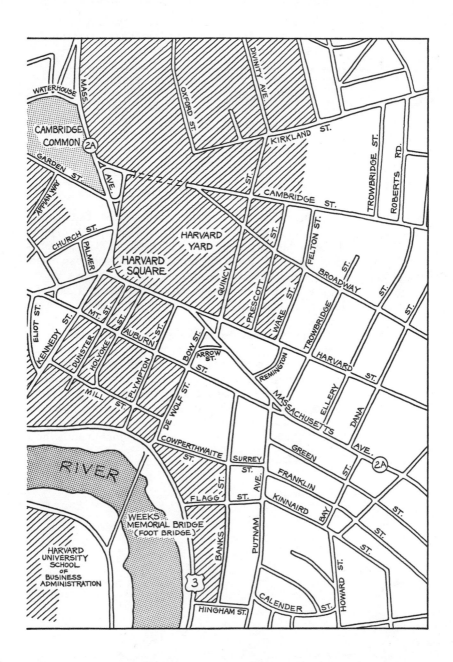

> To my husband, Lee, and my daughters, Nancy and Lucy.
> For their patience and understanding, with love.
> To my parents, family, and friends.

Acknowledgments

Special thanks to: Hannah Benoit; Fred Bouchard; Jean Cook; Peter Drummey; Andrew Houghton; Sherry Houghton; Cyrisse Jaffee; Malcolm Johnson; Fred Kirsch; Leslie MacPherson; Betsy Malloy; Robin Manna; Marcia Monosson; Barbara Moore; Barbara Ohstrom; Emily Prigot; Joan Waldman; John White; Alan Winecour; and our heartfelt thanks to the hundreds of people who were interviewed, taped, queried, and called for information, verification, and opinions. Without their cooperation, none of this would have been possible.

This second time around, I'd like to express my gratitude for the wonderful assistance of Sally Kydd, resident and tour guide on Beacon Hill; Sherry Bishins, indefatigable hospitality greeter; and Lisa Luboff, journalist, transplanted writer, and my summer 1989 intern from UCLA. We haven't space to mention each of the tourism chiefs, hotel workers, shopkeepers, curators, and private citizens who joined us in our attempt at accuracy and shared their knowledge with warmth and humor. Thanks also to editor John Bell, who was helpful from the beginning and whose philosophy was to improve rather than cut.

Uncommon Boston

CHAPTER ONE

Historic Boston

Boston proper, excluding the neighboring communities of Roxbury, Dorchester, and Charlestown, is actually quite a small place. It was originally only 880 acres, and even with the extensive landfill project that created the South End and Back Bay in the early nineteenth century, it has barely doubled to 1900 acres.

But what a lot of action is packed into that small, tidy package! This city has seen more from its bricked and cobbled hills than any other American city, and few European cities of its size can rival Boston's rich political, social, and cultural heritage.

> *Boston is a great city of firsts: the first public library in America, the first subway, the first college, and the first public school are all here. Boston is even responsible for the first lighthouse and the first Christmas card ever produced in America.*

Boston is a birthplace of the famous, including three vice presidents and three presidents. Benjamin Franklin was also born here, in spite of what Philadelphia would have you believe. Famous songs were composed here — "John Brown's Body," at the fort on George's Island in the harbor in 1861, and "America," for a Sunday service at Park Street Congregational Church in 1832.

3

"If bricks could talk," one of our guides is fond of saying, "what great stories we could hear about our past!" Fortunately, bricks *can* talk, or very nearly so. A walk along the Freedom Trail, through the old churches and graveyards and across Beacon Hill, is about as close as you can get to an ambling visual history of the birth of this country. All you need to do is "listen."

We've divided this chapter into three tours. The last two — Graveyards and Churches and Bulfinch's Boston — show you Boston's past from a new angle. For the first tour, however, we've broken our own rule and behaved in a typically Boston fashion by observing tradition. In Boston Basics you get an overview of all the usual historic hot spots. We'd be remiss if we left these places out purely in the interest of "uncommonness," and you'd be missing some of the best Boston has to offer. Although our Boston Basics tour may not be unconventional, it includes everything that makes Boston such an uncommon city in the first place. So, just this once, forswear Yankee individualism and join the hordes traveling Boston's Freedom Trail. And remember that this trail was blazed by people who did everything *but* follow the crowd!

Boston Basics

The only logical place to start a historic tour of Boston is at the beginning. Illogically, this places you not in downtown Boston, but in Charlestown, which is across the Charles River in the northeast corner of the city. But no matter, because in Charlestown you are afforded the opportunity to get a bird's-eye view of the city before plunging into its long and tangled history.

Charlestown is actually set on a peninsula, jutting out into the harbor. It was here that the settlers arriving from Salem first landed. Finding no fresh water available to them, they traveled farther, across the Charles to the place the Indians called "Shawmut" — later known as Boston.

By the time of the Revolutionary War, however, Charlestown was a thriving community, and it was here, near Bunker Hill, that one of the bloodiest battles of that war was fought. It's also here, in Monument Square on Bunker Hill, that you'll find the **Bunker Hill Monument,** which offers that great bird's-eye view we mentioned earlier.

Actually, the monument's name is a misnomer. It is on Breed's Hill where the battle itself was fought on June 17, 1775. The British were the only side to keep records, and they thought the battle took place on Bunker Hill. Thus, that name had perpetuated itself in our history books. During the night the Americans had fortified 70-foot-high Breed's Hill, rather than 110-foot-high Bunker Hill, for strategic reasons. It lay on the route between the harbor where the British could land reinforcements and the higher hill. Even though the colonists lost the battle, it was a tactical victory because it showed the British and the rest of the country that the colonists were ready, willing, and able to fight.

The monument was designed by Solomon Willard and constructed between 1824 and 1842 with funds raised by public subscription. General Lafayette came all the way from France to lay its cornerstone in 1825.

> *One of the largest contributors to the Bunker Hill Monument was a Jewish patriot named Judah Touro, for whom the oldest synagogue in the country, in Newport, Rhode Island, was named.*

Journey back into the past for lunch or dinner in the oldest continuously operating tavern in America. Built in 1780, the **Warren Tavern,** with its low beamed ceilings and stucco walls, reverberates with memories of visits by George Washington and Paul Revere, whose handpierced lanterns decorate the walls. It was on this site that Dr. Joseph Warren devised the plan to send Paul Revere and William Dawes to arouse the countryside when he realized that the British troops were gathering on the Boston Common. Unfortunately, the good doctor died in the Battle of Bunker Hill. Once you have found the tavern at 2 Pleasant Street in Charlestown, you are in for some good old American food with an international flair in a spot that echoes the camaraderie and casual elegance of an earlier day.

From Bunker Hill you can walk to City Square or take public transportation to the Charlestown Navy Yard, where young Navy enlistees will give you a guided tour through the famous battleship, the USS *Constitution*. There is no charge for this tour, but the lines are often lengthy, so leave a member of your party holding your place and visit the excellent gift shop and the **USS *Constitution* Museum.** The tour is interesting, but tends to be too long, and the stairs on board are steep, so senior citizens, small children, and the handicapped should be aware of that.

The Constitution *is nicknamed "Old Ironsides," because the cannonballs allegedly bounced off her thick wooden sides during naval battles. But there are other legends attached to this hearty ship. Occasionally, and very much against the rules, wives of officers were allowed on board. Once or twice, pregnant wives went into labor, and had to be delivered hastily. The best (and least obtrusive) place to do this was apparently in the bulkhead near the cannons — hence the expression, "son of a gun"!*

It is little known, except to those that are at the USS *Constitution* at 8 A.M. or sunset, that the cannons are fired for the ceremonial raising and lowering of the flag each day.

Those cannons go into more conventional service every July Fourth, when the anniversary of America's independence is celebrated by a twenty-one-gun salute with forty-four cannons. The ship is also turned around every year on that date, both as a commemorative gesture of her former seaworthy glory and to prevent her wood from warping on one side.

At last there is a place to have a snack or lunch near the ship in the former Navy testing facility. During the season from April to October, standard American fare is served cafeteria style at the **Shipyard Galley** with seating both indoors and out.

For take-out or self-service, try **Blossom's Café and Catering.** After choosing from a seasonal menu, you can await your order in the charming European-style restaurant. For more elegant dining, or if you would enjoy sitting on an outside deck overlooking the USS *Constitution*, try **Barrett's,** which features American cuisine.

Walk past the scale station to the **Boston Marine Society** to see their collections of paintings and models of sailing and steamships, along with artifacts from the sea. The large mural painted for them by Samuel F. Evans to commemorate the Bicentennial in 1976 depicts the history of the harbor and the society, which was founded in 1724 to support the families of the captains hurt or lost at sea.

To understand the early city of Boston, it is essential to understand its topography. When Governor John Winthrop first brought his settlers here in 1630, he was confronted by a peninsula two miles long and one mile wide — almost an island. Three hills, not one, dominated it, and its uneven shoreline was riddled with coves and swamps. The original land access was along a single narrow road (now Washington Street).

Since those days, two of the hills (and part of the third) have been leveled and used as fill to create the modern shoreline. Although eventually the residential and governmental center of the city moved to Beacon Hill, the earliest and only continuously occupied part of Boston is the North End, where the ships of commerce that made the city's fortune first docked.

So from Charlestown, cross back into Boston's North End and head for the **Old North Church** on Salem Street, the oldest church building in the city. Built in 1723, the Old North (a.k.a. Christ Church, Episcopal) sports the famous steeple from which sexton Robert Newman hung the two lanterns to warn Paul Revere that the British were coming by sea.

Beneath the church are the bodies of some 1500 non-Puritan souls who, because of the religious control of the city, were not allowed burial in the town-owned burial grounds. One body is said to be that of Major John Pitcairn, who commanded five companies of His Majesty's Marines at Bunker Hill and bled to death from battle wounds in 1775. Major Pitcairn's family wanted his body returned to England, but it seems someone may have made a mistake, and sent another body in its place! To this day, the mystery of the whereabouts of Major Pitcairn's body remains unsolved.

The Museum and Gift Shop next door to the church was built as a separate sanctuary in 1918 for an Italian Protestant congregation who could not understand the service in the main church. Today it contains a famous painting of the ride of Paul Revere.

From the church, walk through Paul Revere Mall onto Hanover Street. Cross Prince Street, turn right, and you'll be at the **Paul Revere House,** the only seventeenth-century house still standing within the original city limits. Built about 1680, after the great fire of 1676, using the "memory style" of architecture (the builders worked from their memories of English city houses), the house was already about ninety years old when Paul Revere moved into it with his family in 1770. It must have been quite crowded, for Revere had sixteen children by two wives, and his mother-in-law lived with him as well. Probably one of the reasons Paul was able to sneak out for the midnight ride was because his home was already too jam-packed to provide barracks for British soldiers who were commandeering space at the time, so there was no one to check on his whereabouts. The house was restored at the turn of the century, and the interior depicts life as it would have been in Revere's day.

Pass under the expressway, and after wandering through Haymarket and the historic Blackstone Block (see page 65) you'll come to **Faneuil Hall,** known as the birthplace of American democracy. Built in 1742 by Peter Faneuil (pronounced "Funnel," as his gravestone in the Old Granary Burial Ground reads), the building was given to the town for use as a public meeting space and market. When it was built, it was at the head of nearby Long Wharf, which was subsequently filled in. Charles Bulfinch enlarged the building in 1805, and the upper story, which he added, is still used as a public speaking hall, although the first floor has been restored to its original use as an English-style market. Public figures from Samuel Adams to J.F.K. have taken the podium in Faneuil Hall. It's also home of the museum of the Ancient and Honorable Artillery Company, the oldest volunteer militia in North America (circa 1638).

Quincy Market/Faneuil Hall Marketplace, across the plaza from Faneuil Hall, was originally designed as a market by Alexander Parris in 1824. The central hall, along with the North and South Markets, was used as warehouse and retail space for 150 years. It was named for the second mayor of Boston, Josiah Quincy, who was in office at the time, and he was able to build it at no cost to the taxpayers. The markets fell into disuse until 1968 when the Rouse Company restored them and opened them as a series of small shops and concessions selling everything from gourmet peanut butter to prized antiques. Today, the Quincy Market/Faneuil Hall Marketplace draws twenty-five million people a year through its doors. A few of the businesses, such as M. Berenson meats and Doe Sullivan's Old Market, have been in operation in the market since the 1800s. Across the street, in the forecourt of the Bostonian Hotel, is a fountain that depicts the original outline of colonial Boston before the bays were filled in along the shoreline.

Crossing back under the expressway, head south to Commercial Wharf, home of the **Boston Tea Party Ship Museum.** This is not the site of that famous revolutionary act on December 16, 1773, but it's close enough. The original site, Griffin's Wharf, is now landfill that is probably directly under the expressway. The original boat no longer exists either, but the *Beaver II*, a close replica, was built in Denmark and sailed to Boston in 1973. On board the ship you can see an audio-visual presentation, drink tea, and throw a bale of it overboard.

Most of us are familiar with the story of the Boston Tea Party — how the rebelling colonists, dressed as Indians, sneaked aboard the ship in the dead of a winter night and dumped three hundred chests of costly tea from England into the harbor to protest the high tax placed on it by the British. But few people now realize just how costly tea was then — the colonists used to keep it locked up with their valuables — and how infuriating it must have been for them to have a restrictive tax placed on this most precious of necessities. It's interesting to note that only after the tea protest did the thirteen colonies finally decide to band together and form the first Continental Congress. Tea was the tie that bound them at last.

If you're in town on December 16, don't miss the annual re-enactment of this historic act of rebellion, which begins at the **Old South Meeting House,** reached by crossing back beneath the Central Artery. The rest of the year the Meeting House is worth a visit to use the self-guided tour, to hear a re-enactment of the debate leading up to the Tea Party, and to see a model of how Boston looked in colonial times.

Walk east along Washington Street to the **Old State House** on State Street. This brick National Historic Landmark, built in 1712, was once the most prominent building on the Boston skyline. It was built to house the Governor of the Massachusetts Bay Colony, and it was in front of this building that the Boston Massacre of 1770 occurred, a skirmish between a few angry townspeople and some nervous British soldiers which served to push the colonies closer to revolution. It was also from the balcony of the Old State House that John Adams read the Declaration of Independence for the first time in public. In July of 1976, two hundred years after that famous reading, during the Bicentennial, Queen Elizabeth II stood on the same balcony to bring greetings to Boston. The Royal Lion and Unicorn that grace the gambrel roof were removed during the Revolution, but have since been restored. They are the symbols of the British crown from pre-Revolutionary times. After the War of Independence, the building served as the seat of government until the new State House was erected in 1798.

Directly across the street at number fifteen is the headquarters of the **National Park Service.** This little-known resource can provide you with excellent tours of Boston's **Freedom Trail,** as well as general information. The Boston National Historic Park is a unique interpretation of America's past in an urban setting. It is a cooperative venture between the city, private industry, nonprofit organizations that administer the various sites, and the Park Service. Rangers are also located at Dorchester Heights Monument in South Boston, where George Washington was able to drive the British from their long occupation of Boston.

Now up State Street to Tremont Street and the **Boston Common,** which was purchased from William Blaxton in 1634 for use by the town as a cow pasture and militia drill ground. The Reverend Blaxton, later Blackstone, was an early squatter in Boston, preceding the first settlers by several years. Some say the phrase "Boston Brahmin," meaning a member of one of Boston's oldest and most notable families, derives directly from him. Apparently this eccentric man was known to own — or ride around on — a Brahma bull. (A more reasonable explanation for the phrase is its reference to the high caste of India.)

Once the city acquired the land, public punishments and occasional executions took place here, as did many public gatherings and fairs. Livestock grazing was allowed, and cows weren't outlawed until 1830. The Frog Pond, where children still wade all summer long, was the site of the Great Water Celebration of 1864, which marked the opening of the first freshwater aqueduct, and meant that residents of Boston were no longer dependent on wells. The Greater Boston Convention and Visitor's Center booth on the east side of the Common is a good place to find out more about the city and the various sites open to tourists. The Park Street Subway Station below the Common, a hub of the oldest subway system in America (1897), is also worth a look.

Walk diagonally across the Common from the station to the set of steps at the foot of Joy Street. Follow the street to the other side of Beacon Hill, where you will find the Boston African-American National Historic site and the **Museum of Afro-American History.** In the **Abiel Smith Schoolhouse,** at 46 Joy Street, you can pick up a map for a self-guided tour. Better yet, call ahead for a guided tour.

Massachusetts was the first state in the union to abolish slavery. The largest free black community in the nation lived on the north slope of Beacon Hill. The 54th Regiment, formed from this community, was the first black regiment to go to battle during the Civil War, and William Carney of the 54th received the Medal of Honor for bravery at Fort Wagner, South Carolina.

The children of the community were educated in the Abiel Smith Schoolhouse for about twenty years until parents protested this segregation. The children were then moved to the Phillips School, the first integrated school in America.

Since blacks could attend but not participate in the life of the local churches, the **African Meeting House** was built. During excavations around the site and in the apartment in the basement of the church, archeologists found many ceramic plates that had belonged to Domingo Williams. His business was to cater fashionable parties, assemblies, and social entertainments. He was obviously more than just a "waiter," as he was listed in the city directory.

Across Charles Street from the Common is the Public Garden (not to be confused with the Boston Garden, a sports arena near the North End; see page 226). Half the size of the Common, the Garden was established as a botanical preserve in 1837 and dedicated in 1859 with great fanfare. The Garden boasts what is proudly billed as the world's smallest suspension bridge, and has variously housed an open air zoo, a tropical park with palm trees and cacti, and the astounding array of flowers, trees, and shrubs that you see today — all maintained by the Boston Department of Parks and Recreation with the help of The Friends of the Public Garden, a private group. Don't miss a ride on the lovely, famed Swan Boats, which circle the Lagoon from mid April to late September. That concession has been held by the Paget family for three generations, since 1877. (See Chapter 8.)

Walk west down Boylston Street to Copley Square, and you can end your tour with another bird's-eye view of Boston from the top of the John Hancock Tower, that glittering wedge of glass and steel. (The panes no longer fall out as they did when the building was first erected in the early 1970s, when sidewalks had to be cordoned off to protect passersby from glass panels sucked out of the frame by wind currents.) The **John Hancock Observatory** on the top floor affords a stunning wraparound panorama of the city, and informative exhibits and videos describe the various views. You can use the free binoculars to zero in on some of the Boston Basics you've already seen, or to find something new and exciting yet to explore.

Tour Sites

Boston Marine Society
Charlestown Navy Yard
Boston, MA 02129
242-0522
242-0181

Boston Tea Party Ship Museum
Congress Street Bridge
Boston, MA 02110
338-1773

Bunker Hill Monument
Monument Square
Charlestown, MA 02129
242-5641

Bunker Hill Pavilion
55 Constitution Rd.
Charlestown, MA 02129
241-7575

John Hancock Observatory
Hancock Place
Boston, MA 02116
247-1977
Admission fee.

Museum of Afro-American
    History
Abiel Smith Schoolhouse
46 Joy St.
Boston, MA 02114
742-1854 for tours of
    meetinghouses.
742-5415 Rangertours, National
    Park Service.

Old North Church
193 Salem St.
Boston, MA 02113
523-6676

Old State House
206 Washington St.
Boston, MA 02109
242-5655

Paul Revere House
19 North Square
Boston, MA 02113
523-2338

Quincy Market/Faneuil Hall
    Marketplace
Near Government Center
Entertainment daily.

USS *Constitution* Museum
Visitors Information
Boston Naval Shipyard
Charlestown, MA 02129
426-1812
Admission fee.

ADDITIONAL BOSTON BASICS

Bunker Hill Museum
43 Monument Square
Charlestown, MA 02129
241-8220

Tea Party Ship
Congress Street Bridge
Boston, MA 02110
338-1773
Admission fee.

GENERAL TOURIST INFORMATION

Cape Cod Chamber of Commerce
Hyannis, MA 02601
508-362-3225

Charlestown Navy Yard
  Visitor Center
Charlestown, MA 02129
242-5601

City Hall Visitor Center
1 City Hall Square
Boston, MA 02108
536-4100

Greater Boston Convention and
  Visitor's Center
Prudential Plaza West
Boston, MA 02199
Call for visitor information or to
  receive their guide to Boston.
536-4100

Martha's Vineyard Chamber
  of Commerce
Martha's Vineyard, MA 02568
508-693-0085

Massachusetts Bay Transit
  Authority (MBTA)
Boston
722-3200 or 1-800-392-6100
Bus, subway, and commuter rail
  information.

Massachusetts Department
  of Tourism
100 Cambridge Street
Boston, MA 02202
727-3201

Nantucket Chamber of Commerce
Nantucket, MA 02554
508-228-1700

National Park Service
  Visitor Center
15 State St.
Boston, MA 02109
242-5642

RESTAURANTS

Barrett's
2 Constitution Plaza
Charlestown, MA 02129
242-9600

Blossom's Café and Catering
Charlestown Navy Yard
Boston, MA 02129
242-1911

Constitution Commissary
   Convenience Store
Charlestown Navy Yard
Boston, MA 02129
242-6089

Warren Tavern
2 Pleasant St.
Boston, MA 02129
241-8142

Shipyard Galley
Charlestown Navy Yard
Boston, MA 02129
421-5660

Graveyards, Churches, and Synagogues

Boston has always been a mecca for the spirit, from the arrival of the first religious freedom fighters (the Puritans) to the heyday of the mystical transcendentalists (read Henry James's *The Bostonians* for a scathing insight into this arcane philosophy). Consequently, the city's religious structures have always been of primary importance to its inhabitants — in both the here and the hereafter — and a tour of the city's old churches and burial grounds can provide an enjoyable history lesson as well as a good two-hour walk.

One block west of the Old North Church, on Hull Street in the North End, is the **Copp's Hill Burial Ground,** the second oldest burial ground in the city. Probably incorporated in 1659, Copp's Hill contains the bodies of Cotton Mather and his father, Increase. Cotton was the strict Puritan clergyman who wrote about the famous Salem witch trials. Also buried here is Daniel Malcolm, a patriot whose tomb was used by the British for target practice. Look for the chips where the bullets bounced off the slate! Copp's Hill also contains an obelisk commemorating Prince Hall, one of the few black men to fight in the Battle of Bunker Hill. As many as a thousand pre-Revolutionary black freemen are buried here as well, a testament to the early black presence in the city (see Black Heritage Trail, page 28).

> *Don't be too concerned about treading on founding fathers (and mothers) as you visit the Copp's Hill Burial Ground. As in all colonial graveyards, the tombstones, for the most part, are not over the original graves. They were placed helter-skelter wherever there was room, and the only reason the graveyard looks tidy is that during the Depression, one of the WPA projects was to rearrange the stones and line them up in an orderly fashion.*

Passing by the Old North Church and down the Revere Mall, with its statue of the famous midnight rider, we come to **St. Stephen's Church** on Hanover Street, the only Charles Bulfinch–designed church still existing in Boston. When completed in 1804, St. Stephen's was used as a Unitarian church. But with the influx of Irish Catholics into the area in the middle of the nineteenth century, it was purchased by the Catholic diocese. Shortly after, in 1870, it was elevated six feet and moved back twelve feet in order to accommodate the widening of Hanover Street. In the hope of attracting Italian worshipers, it was also renovated to resemble an ornate Italian palazzo, as the pictures in the foyer reveal. In 1960, Cardinal Cushing ordered the church restored to its original Bulfinch design, and lowered six feet again. The work was done by the same architectural firm that handled the first renovation, proving that in Boston, the more things change, the more they remain the same.

Walking through Quincy Market to Washington Street will bring you to the **Old South Meeting House** at Washington and Milk Streets. This structure was built in 1729, on the site of the original 1670 cedar building. Ben Franklin, who was born across the street at 17 Milk Street, was baptized in the Old South in 1705. And it was here that thousands of colonists gathered before the Boston Tea Party in 1773. During the Revolution, the British showed their contempt for American religious beliefs by using the structure as a stable and riding academy. During the Great Fire of 1872, which burned 65 acres of the city, the church was saved by

EBENEZER
son of
Nathan & Mary
Born ... 17..
Died.... 176...

the arrival of the first steam-propelled pressurized water pumper, brought by rail from New Hampshire to battle the blaze. Finally, in 1877, the Old South became the headquarters of the Old South Association, a Boston historical society, and the congregation moved to the third, or "new," Old South in Copley Square.

It's interesting to note that the first minister of the Old South, the Reverend Thomas Thatcher, wrote the first medical treatise published in North America. Its subject was "the treatment of measles and smallpox for the common peoples of New Englande." Thatcher's household included what must have been a whimsical indulgence in Puritan times — a pet parrot — which was listed in the inventory of his estate along with "other olde things." The treatises and inventory are both on view at the **Massachusetts Historical Society,** 1154 Boylston Street.

From Washington Street, walk up School Street to Tremont Street where **King's Chapel** graces the corner. Founded in 1688 as an Anglican place of worship for British officers, the original small wooden structure was naturally unpopular with the colonists. When the present building was constructed in 1749, it was built around the original, which was then demolished and tossed out the windows stick by stick. After the Revolution decimated the Anglican congregation, King's Chapel became the first Unitarian church in America. The reason there is no steeple is quite practical — the congregation simply ran out of money!

Next to King's Chapel is the **King's Chapel Burial Ground,** the first organized burial ground in the city. John Winthrop, the first governor of the Massachusetts Bay Company, and William Dawes, Paul Revere's companion rider, are buried here. You can tell the Puritan graves by their skull-and-crossbone motifs, for the

Puritans looked upon death as dourly as they did life. But the graves of the French Huguenots with their angels and cherubs display a much more cheery attitude.

In colonial times, King's Chapel, as well as other historical burial grounds, was rented to local farmers. There were two benefits — cropped grass and some income.

Cross Tremont Street and follow it south to the **Old Granary Burial Ground,** where you will find the remains of, among others, Paul Revere, John Hancock, and Elizabeth VerGoose, the reputed author of the Mother Goose rhymes. Ben Franklin erected a now-refurbished monument to his parents here, although that devoted son is buried in Philadelphia. The cemetery was established in 1660, making it the third oldest in the city. As the name implies, the graveyard was built on the site of an old wooden granary, where sails were sewn for the *Constitution.*

Because these old gravestones are so fragile, stone rubbings have been banned in Boston since the 1970s. However, if you wish to do more than just take note of the weeping willows, urns, and etchings that grace old gravestones, you can go to historic locations outside of Boston, such as Lexington and Concord, where rubbing is still allowed. You can get information and the tools for the job at **Oldstone Enterprises,** a hobby store at 186 Lincoln Street, Boston.

Next to the Old Granary is the **Park Street Church** (Congregational), designed by Englishman Peter Banner and completed in 1810. The church had a wonderful clock installed in its steeple so that Bostonians could know what time it was in the days before electricity and digital watches. The church is also known as Brimstone Corner, allegedly because of the hot-tongued abolitionist speeches preached from its pulpit. (William Lloyd Garrison gave his first public address against slavery here on July 4, 1829.) But there may be another reason for the name: during the War of 1812, gunpowder was reportedly secretly stored in the basement. In 1831, the song "America," probably better known by its first line, "My country 'tis of thee," was sung for the first time by Sunday school children standing on the church's steps. Legend has it that those famous words were hastily penned in honor of the Fourth of July celebration by the twenty-four-year-old author, Samuel Francis Smith, half an hour before the recital!

Continuing down Tremont Street, opposite the Common is **St. Paul's Cathedral** (Episcopal). St. Paul's was designed in 1819 by Alexander Parris, who introduced Greek Revival architecture in the monumental style to Boston both here and again later at Quincy Market. **The Central Burying Ground,** closest to the corner of Boylston and Tremont Streets and across from the Colonial Theater, dates from the eighteenth and nineteenth centuries, and holds the remains of painter Gilbert Stuart and Revolutionary War–era composer William Billings. (He wrote "Chester," the most popular tune played by the Revolutionary soldiers.) Stuart, now revered as the greatest American portraitist, died in penury in 1828 and was buried here in an unmarked vault belonging to friends (Tomb #61).

Now cross the Common to Charles Street and make your way to the **Church of the Advent** (Episcopal) on the corner of Mount Vernon and Brimmer Streets. This is the spot on which the British — seven hundred of them — boarded boats on April 18, 1775, to sail across the Charles River on their march to Lexington and Concord (only later was the land filled in), whereupon Robert Newman hung two lanterns in the steeple of the Old North Church to warn the patriots that the British were advancing toward Lexington and Concord by sea. Built between 1875 and 1883, the Church of the Advent boasts a fine peal of bells, which each year accompanies the Boston Pops at the appropriate time during their July Fourth rendition of the *1812* Overture. And on the corner of Mt. Vernon and Charles is the Charles Street Meeting House, built by Asher Benjamin in 1807 (see page 25). The church now houses several retail establishments and offices.

By crossing the Public Garden, you'll find yourself on the corner of Arlington and Boylston Streets, site of the **Arlington Street Church.** Built between 1859 and 1861 by architect Arthur Gilman, this is often considered the mother church of the New England–originated Unitarian sect, and was the first public building erected in the Back Bay after it was filled with landfill in 1856. A statue of noted Unitarian minister and abolitionist William Ellery Channing stands across the street from the church, whose members have been noted since the Civil War era for their outspoken stand on the social and moral issues of foreign and domestic policy.

Turn left onto Newbury Street, one block north of Arlington

Street, to the **Emmanuel Church.** Built in the Rural Gothic style in 1864, this church is locally known as the "music church," because of the fine concerts it sponsors, covering everything from organ music to avant-garde jazz. And the **Church of the Covenant,** at the corner of Berkeley and Newbury Streets, is familiarly known as the "art church" because it houses the Gallery Naga, a cooperative of contemporary Boston artists offering original art at reasonable prices. This church claims to have the largest collection of Tiffany ecclesiastical stained-glass windows in the world. The sanctuary lantern, a great hanging sculpture, was first created by Tiffany for the Columbian Exhibition of 1893 in Chicago. Donated by R. H. White of White's Department Store, this was the first public electric chandelier in the United States. Finally, take note of the glorious organ, the last designed by the Welt-Tripp Company.

Down Berkeley Street, at the corner of Marlborough, is the **First and Second Unitarian Church,** recognizable by the burned-out remains of the old structure, which has been cleverly worked into the design of the new. The architectural collaboration is the 1968 work of Paul Rudolph, after a fire destroyed the original 1867 structure. The church houses an excellent nursery school and is also the site of numerous local concerts.

At the corner of Commonwealth and Clarendon Streets is the **First Baptist Church,** designed by H. H. Richardson in 1871. The banding of bas-relief sculpture at the top of the church was designed by Frédéric Auguste Bartholdi, who was later responsible for the Statue of Liberty and also created the bald eagle atop the main building at South Station. The bas-relief, depicting angels blowing on their trumpets, has earned the church the iconoclastic nickname "Church of the Holy Beanblowers." Stand on Newbury Street and look up at the frieze: you can see Abraham Lincoln kneeling with his chin in his hand. The cornerstone at the base of the tower contains the only public signature of John Hancock, who gave the bells in the tower.

On Boylston Street near Copley Square is the Congregational **New Old South Church,** which reflects the enthusiasm of John Ruskin for the architecture and decorative aspects of medieval Venice. It was designed by the architectural firm of Cummings and Sears. The Italian Gothic style is evident in the pointed arches above the windows, the patterns of the stones, and the colors on the cupola. In the case of the New Old South, the ornamentation extended even to the tower, which was originally so high (246 feet) that it began to lean perilously. By 1931, it listed 26 inches to one side and had to be replaced with a more reasonably proportioned tower in 1940.

In Copley Square itself is **Trinity Church** (Episcopal), designed by H. H. Richardson and completed in 1877. This sandstone structure in the French Romanesque style weighs more than ninety million tons and is supported on its marshy landfill base by four thousand wooden pilings that must be kept constantly damp to avoid shrinkage and rot. The stained-glass window by John La Farge of "The Presentation of the Virgin" was presented by Charles McKim, one of the architects of the Boston Public Library across the way, to memorialize his beloved wife Julia Appleton, niece of Henry Wadsworth Longfellow. McKim chose the theme from a painting by Titian because he believed the Virgin resembled his wife. The flamboyant bachelor Phillips Brooks, the fifteenth rector of Trinity, was also author of the classic Christmas carol, "O, Little Town of Bethlehem." Reflected in the ultramodern façade of its neighbor, the Hancock Tower, the deep red sandstone of the church seems to float with a marvelous textural integrity. Together, these two buildings are often said to represent everything Boston stands for: from the solid old spirituality to the ever-upward expansion of the modern high-tech world.

Another of Boston's architectural and spiritual treasures is the **Christian Science Mother Church** on Massachusetts Avenue, west of Copley Square. This impressive assemblage of buildings houses not only the church itself, but also the editorial offices of the respected newspaper, the *Christian Science Monitor*. The complex also contains an I. M. Pei–designed reflecting pool and a lovely reading room. But the church's main attraction is the Mapparium — a huge three-dimensional stained-glass map of the world (as it was in the 1930s). You can stand in the midst of this unique echo-chamber and feel as if you truly are in the hub of the universe. Tours of the entire church buildings are offered to the public free of charge.

In this cultural and ethnic city, ecclesiastical bridges relay the long-standing tone of sharing and working together. Proof of one ecclesiastical bridge appears on an inscribed rock in front of **Temple Ohabei Shalom** on Beacon Street, one of the oldest Jewish temples in Boston. When a fire destroyed the First Presbyterian Church in Brookline in 1961, Ohabei Shalom invited the congregation to hold services and activities at the synagogue.

A new congregation from Ohabei Shalom became **Temple Israel,** located on the corner of the Riverway and Longwood Avenue in Boston. Formerly referred to as "The Meetinghouse," its congregation of more than 135 years plays an important role in Boston by supporting community projects such as Project Bread and the Walk for Hunger. Architecturally, the building is a mix of classical and contemporary with an important Louise Nevelson sculpture out front.

The spirit of community and sharing is also echoed by a transaction that occurred in 1966 between Mishkan Tefilah Congregation and the **Elma Lewis School of Fine Arts** for young black artists in Roxbury. Relocating to a new synagogue, the congregation sold the facilities to the school for only one dollar.

An architectural gem worth seeing is the **Charles River Park Synagogue** in Longfellow Place. This synagogue is reminiscent of the former Jewish community that existed on the back of Beacon Hill.

The last church we'll visit isn't a church at all anymore. The **Church Court Condominium** on the corner of Massachusetts Avenue and Beacon Street was originally the Mt. Vernon Church (named not for its location, but because Mt. Vernon was a pleasant sounding name). It was destroyed in 1978 by a fire of mysterious origin, but Cambridge architect Graham Gund purchased the burned-out shell and constructed the whimsical yet elegant complex you see there now. The remaining walls and tower were artfully incorporated into the building and the sequence of arches and angles calls to mind the structure's original ecclesiastic purpose. Even the Gene Cauthen sculpture of the bronze angel perched atop the building symbolizes the harmony between the old usage and the new. Despite the fact that many proper Bostonians cried sacrilege, and tried to prevent the remodeling, the Church Court complex has become a symbol of this city's desire to honor the past and preserve it into the future.

Tour Sites

Arlington Street Church
351 Boylston St.
Boston, MA 02116
536-7050

Copp's Hill Burial Ground
Hull, Charles, & Snowhill Sts.
Boston, MA 02113
298-8750

Central Burying Ground
Corner of Boylston and
    Tremont Streets
Boston, MA 02116

Elma Lewis School of Fine Arts
300 Walnut St.
Roxbury, MA 02119
442-8014

Charles River Park Synagogue
55 Martha Rd.
Boston, MA 02114
523-0453

Emmanuel Church of Boston
15 Newbury St.
Boston, MA 02116
536-3355

Christian Science Mother Church
1 Norway St.
Boston, MA 02115
262-2300

First and Second Unitarian
    Church of Boston
66 Marlboro St.
Boston, MA 02116
267-6730

Church Court Condominium
490 Beacon St.
Boston, MA 02215
353-0971

First Baptist Church of Boston
110 Commonwealth Ave.
Boston, MA 02116
267-3148

Church of the Advent
30 Brimmer St.
Boston, MA 02108
523-2377

King's Chapel and Burial Ground
64 Beacon St.
Boston, MA 02108
227-2155

Church of the Covenant
67 Newbury St.
Boston, MA 02116
266-7480

Massachusetts Historical Society
1154 Boylston St.
Boston, MA 02215
536-1608

New Old South Church
645 Boylston St.
Boston, MA 02116
536-1970

Old Granary Burial Ground
83–115 Tremont St.
Boston, MA 02108
298-8750

Old South Meeting House
Washington St. at Milk St.
Boston, MA 02108
482-6439

Oldstone Enterprises
186 Lincoln St.
Boston, MA 02111
542-4112

Park Street Church
1 Park St.
Boston, MA 02108
523-3383

St. Paul's Cathedral
138 Tremont St.
Boston, MA 02111
482-5800

St. Stephen's Church
401 Hanover St.
Boston, MA 02113
523-1230

Temple Israel
260 Riverway
Boston, MA 02215
566-3960

Temple Ohabei Shalom
1187 Beacon St.
Brookline, MA 02146
277-6610

Trinity Church
Copley Square
Boston, MA 02116
536-0944

Bulfinch's Boston

There's yet another way to appreciate Boston's history, and that's by looking at it through the work of one of its most illustrious and prolific architects. Charles Bulfinch, designer of the U. S. Capitol, was more responsible for shaping the face of this city in the

early nineteenth century than perhaps any other individual. More than that, his shapes conformed closely to their function, so that by walking through Bulfinch's Boston, you see not only the forms he created, but the institutions he helped to mold.

Charles Bulfinch, born in 1763, grew up in a spacious mansion on Bowdoin Square (number 6), now the offices of New England Telephone. You can see his handsome image on a bronze plaque set into the side of the building. His father was a self-taught physician, but his neighbors were the great merchants of the day — the Parkmans, the Lymans, and the Coolidges. Bulfinch attended Boston Latin School and was witness to the Battle of Bunker Hill. Although a devoted patriot, he was also a great admirer of the English and their architecture, and his buildings reflect that influence. Bulfinch, the scion of a wealthy family, eschewed the "pursuit of business," and most of his famous civic structures, which include two state capitols, three churches, two public monuments, and dozens of private structures, were done on his "gratuitous advice" — a luxury few architects can usually afford. (Bulfinch went bankrupt after a failed real estate development called the Tontine Crescent.)

Bulfinch's protégé and architectural heir was Asher Benjamin, who did not exhibit such economic largesse, and was able eventually to live in the house he built for himself, 9 West Cedar Street. Benjamin is best known for his introduction of wooden Greek motifs — pilasters and friezes — to ornament the plain brick façades then in style.

Our Bulfinch tour begins at the foot of Beacon Hill. The structure at 141 Cambridge Street is the first of three houses he designed for Harrison Gray Otis, the wealthy and bombastic third mayor of Boston. This one, designed in 1795, is now the headquarters for the **Society for the Preservation of New England Antiquities.** Its elegant brick façade and symmetrical floor plan are in the Federal manner, with two rooms on each side of the entrance hall and the kitchen in an attached ell. But the attention to detailing and the graceful proportions are all Bulfinch, who is credited with developing and perfecting the Federal style of architecture.

The SPNEA is now a National Historic Landmark — a far cry from a period in the 1830s when it was used as a ladies' Turkish bath! Most of the interior wallpapers are reproductions of the originals, the furnishings and decorative arts are all originals, and some actually belonged to Otis during his residence there. The SPNEA's excellent guided tours give visitors a good feel for eighteenth-century upper-class Boston life. The Society itself is worth some time if you're interested in antiques. Their archives and documentation center is unsurpassed in this country.

> *Be sure to take a look at the **Old West Church**, designed in 1806 by Asher Benjamin, another fine example of brick Federal architecture. Now a church once again, it was a branch of the Boston Public Library as recently as 1960, and was the polling place where John F. Kennedy voted in the presidential election that year. During April 1775, the British dismantled the spire of the original 1636 church. Since it was the highest in the city, they believed the colonials would use it to signal their movements to Lexington and Concord.*

The next stop is a somewhat unlikely one — the Massachusetts General Hospital. MGH boasts the **Bulfinch Pavilion and Ether Dome,** near Cambridge and Fruit Streets, which is as fascinating for its history as for its Bulfinch connection. In 1816, Bulfinch was sent by the hospital board to examine several hospitals in New York, Philadelphia, and Baltimore, and to come up with design ideas for the Boston structure. Their only requirement was that the building be constructed of local Chelmsford granite, which was quarried by the inmates of the state prison in Charlestown.

Some critics say the pavilion and dome don't look like Bulfinch's work, and it's true that Alexander Parris prepared the working drawings. (Parris later became well known in his own right when he designed Quincy Market using the same granite.) Still, the classically proportioned dome, with its operating theater under the skylit arch, is significant not only architecturally, but also because it housed a public demonstration of the first operation ever performed under an anesthetic.

The doctor was John Collins Warren, one of MGH's founders, and the patient, suffering from a tumor in his jaw, was Gilbert Abbott. The year was 1846, and the ether was administered by a dentist named Thomas Green Morton. The operation, in which Abbott's tumor was removed, was usually a difficult one because the doctor had to work fast before his patient died of shock from the terrible pain.

According to the story Morton almost missed the operation, having stayed up late the night before perfecting his ether inhaler. And the photographer who was to be present became faint and had to leave the theater. But the operation was a success. Upon waking, Abbott said he had "felt no pain," whereupon Dr. Warren turned to his watching colleagues and pronounced, "Gentlemen, this is no humbug."

Later, Dr. Warren went to Scotland to observe Dr. Joseph Lister using antiseptic surgery, and he introduced these techniques to his colleagues in the amphitheater. Both the amphitheater and the dome are National Historic Landmarks.

From Mass. General, walk south on Charles Street, the lifeline of Beacon Hill. After wending your way past the street's numerous antique shops (see pages 138–39), you'll find yourself in front of the **Charles Street Meeting House** at number 70. Asher Benjamin designed this in 1807, and it is clearly reminiscent of the Bulfinch style and the sensibilities that Bulfinch expressed in his work. Its history, too, has embodied the spirit of Boston ever since the Meeting House first opened its doors as the Third Baptist Church.

The site was originally alongside the Charles River, where baptisms were regularly performed, but by the middle of the century, the land had been filled in. Even while still a Baptist church, the Meeting House had a history that foreshadowed its later eminence. In the mid-1830s, the Third Baptist had as a member abolitionist Timothy Gilbert, who shocked the congregation by inviting black people into his pew for Sunday worship. Gilbert was summarily expelled, and along with other free-thinking members, founded the Tremont Temple in 1842, the first integrated house of worship in the city.

In 1876 the Meeting House was sold to the African Methodist Episcopal Church, which sold the property to the Unitarian Universalists after the Depression. But it is as a meeting house that the building gained its fame, since it was the center of political activity for noted abolitionists William Lloyd Garrison, Harriet Tubman, Frederick Douglass, and others, during the heyday of antislavery sentiment in Boston. Today, the Meeting House, lovingly restored to pristine Federalist condition by the architect John Sharratt, is an important stop on the **Black Heritage Trail,** which should definitely be included in your exploration of the city. The National Park Service has declared the trail a National Historic Site and provides a fine walking tour brochure published by the U. S. Department of the Interior. This guide is carried at the Abiel Smith Schoolhouse on Joy Street and the National Park Service Visitors Center on State Street.

From Charles Street, head up Mt. Vernon Street into the heart of Beacon Hill. Henry James once called this "the most prestigious address in America," and for the most part, it's still true today. But Mt. Vernon could as easily be called Bulfinch Street, because of its significant association with Mr. Bulfinch. Bulfinch even designed and built a home for himself there at 87 Mt. Vernon Street. Unfortunately, due to the altruism he practiced early in his career, he couldn't afford to live in it! It now houses the New England chapter of the Archives of American Art.

Number 85 Mt. Vernon Street, as you head up the hill, is the second of Bulfinch's homes for Harrison Gray Otis. The residence was designed in 1800, and Bulfinch hoped that it would be a blueprint for the character of the rest of the Mt. Vernon neighborhood. The gracious forty-five-foot-wide freestanding mansion with its spacious landscaped grounds was not, however, to become *de rigueur,* perhaps because the Brahmins who built on Mt. Vernon were too "frugal." The Bulfinch design was added to by Benjamin several years later because Otis wanted to modernize and match his neighbors, who were building more ornate structures. You may recognize the house from the movie *The Thomas Crown Affair* and the TV series "Banacek." (By the way, if you happen to be out on an icy day, you'll appreciate the iron railings installed in the nineteenth century as the gift of one Beacon Hill resident who understood the difficulties of negotiating the steep brick sidewalks in winter.)

The **Nichols House Museum,** at number 55 Mt. Vernon Street, was designed by Bulfinch in 1804 for Jonathan Mason, one of the Mt. Vernon Proprietors, and purchased in 1885 by the doctor father of Miss Rose Standish Nichols. A noted gardening author and landscape gardener, Nichols was an early supporter of the Women's International League for Peace and Freedom, and one of the organizers of the discussion groups that evolved into the Foreign Policy Association. Her portrait and memorabilia add a delightful personal touch to this Bulfinch property, which is open to the public. Resident curator Bill Pare will guide you on a witty tour through the home.

The Mt. Vernon Street neighborhood has many lovely restaurants, should you wish to pause and take in a meal. In a Beacon Hill townhouse, at **Another Season** (97 Mt. Vernon), chef Odette Berry prepares elegant nouvelle cuisine for you to enjoy. Less formal, but equally delightful, is the **Hungry I** nearby at 71½ Charles Street, where you can dine al fresco in a tiny courtyard hidden behind the brick façade.

Before continuing on to Beacon Street and more Bulfinch, take a stroll around historic Louisburg Square. If Mt. Vernon is the most prestigious address in America, then this elegant rectangle is surely its front parlor. The stately brick townhouses around the cobblestoned square share the serenity of the central green park surrounded by a handsome cast-iron fence. The square was "developed" by S. F. Fuller in 1826, although the first house wasn't built until 1834. The Louisburg Square Proprietors' Association is the oldest homeowners association in the country. Owners are charged for maintenance of the park, and when the trees are trimmed, the wood is divided into twenty-two equal portions and delivered to the owners to use as firewood. Today, the concept of "private community" ownership extends to the parking spaces around the Square, so don't even try to park there.

Back in the 1950s, the city planned to replace the brick sidewalks with more up-to-date concrete. The Brahmins revolted. En masse, they moved out on the sidewalks with chairs and benches and sat, arms folded, determined not to let any transformation occur. As you can see, the brick remains intact.

The third Harrison Gray Otis house is at **Number 45 Beacon Street.** Designed by Bulfinch in 1805, this Federal mansion was the last and largest of the homes he did for Mr. Otis, who by then was a very wealthy fellow indeed. Otis stayed here until his death in 1848, and is said to have breakfasted on pâté de fois gras every morning, which probably contributed to his terrible gout!

The house was the scene of a great many society functions in its day, and visitors used to crowd into the great ballroom, drawing room, and conservatory. Rumor has it that ten gallons of alcoholic punch were consumed every afternoon by the politicians and society ladies who gathered there to partake of Otis's lavish hospitality. In spite of this, it's interesting to note that there was absolutely no indoor water supply, no gas light or heat until the 1830s, and no toilet facilities. Waste was removed by "privy-vaults" each night and carried by "soil collectors," who dumped it in nearby Brighton. The noisome cargo came to be known as "the Brighton Artillery." The current tenant of the house is the American Meteorological Society, and they *do* have plumbing.

Number 55 Beacon Street is another Asher Benjamin design, this one built in 1808 for James Smith Colburn. Today the house is the Massachusetts headquarters for the **National Society of Colonial Dames,** a society dedicated to the preservation of colonial and Victorian porcelain, clothing, furniture, and artifacts. It's open to the public on Wednesdays and offers a delightful glimpse into the minutiae of the periods.

The George Parkman House, at number 33 Beacon Street, was built by Cornelias Coolidge, Housewright, in 1825. For generations, the house has served as the city's mayoral dwelling, although the last few mayors have used it only for civic functions.

At the top of Beacon Street is the new **State House,** the jewel in the crown of Bulfinch's Boston. The building was completed in 1797, and the famous wooden dome was covered in copper by Paul Revere in 1802. It was gilded in 1872 and has never stopped glistening except when it was painted dark gray during World War II to prevent easy identification of the city. The pine cone atop the dome represents the vast timberlands of Maine, then still a part of Massachusetts. A tour of the State House, with its Hall of Flags and Senate Chambers, is available through the **Office of the Secretary of State.**

Now cross the street, enter the Boston Common, and rest on a bench. You've had a long walk and deserve to sit back for a while. This is a good time to try to assimilate all the colonial and Revolutionary history you've learned, because in the next chapter you will leap forward a century and explore the city during the Victorian era.

Dr. George Francis Parkman lived at number 33 Beacon Street after the death of his father, also Dr. George Parkman, who was murdered in 1850 by Harvard professor John White Webster. The story has it that Dr. Parkman (senior) was a loan shark, and that Webster, a gambler, was in debt to him. Webster allegedly murdered him and buried him in a wall at Mass. General Hospital, where his body was found by a janitor. The scandal was so great that his son became a hermit and willed his millions to the city for the upkeep of the cursed house and of parks throughout the city.

Tour Sites

Black Heritage Trail
National Park Service
15 State St.
Boston, MA 02109
223-0058

Bulfinch Pavilion/Ether Dome
Massachusetts General Hospital
55 Fruit St.
Boston, MA 02114
726-8540

Charles Street Meeting House
121 Mt. Vernon St.
Boston, MA 02108
227-0094

National Society of Colonial
  Dames
55 Beacon St.
Boston, MA 02108
742-3190
Admission fee.

Nichols House Museum
55 Mt. Vernon St.
Boston, MA 02108
227-6993

The George Parkman House
33 Beacon St.
Boston, MA 02108

Office of the Secretary of State
State House
Beacon St.
Boston, MA 02133
727-3676

Society for the Preservation of
    New England Antiquities
    (SPNEA)
Harrison Gray Otis House
141 Cambridge St.
Boston, MA 02114
227-3956
Admission fee.

Old West Church
131 Cambridge St.
Boston, MA 02114
227-5088
Call for concert schedule.

RESTAURANTS

Another Season
97 Mt. Vernon St.
Boston, MA 02108
367-0880

The Hungry I
71½ Charles St.
Boston, MA 02114
227-3524

General Resources

TOUR ORGANIZATIONS

Boston by Foot
77 N. Washington St.
Boston, MA 02114
367-2345
Fee.
Ask about their program for little
    children — Boston by Little
    Feet.

Boston Walkabouts
Tapes available from
Uncommon Boston
437 Boylston St., fourth floor
Boston, MA 02116
731-5854
Cassette-recorded tour of the
    Freedom Trail, available for
    purchase in English, French,
    German, and Japanese.

Historic Neighborhoods
  Foundation
1 Devonshire Place
China Trade Building
Boston, MA 02109
426-1898
Offers various tours, such as
  "Eating Your Way Through
  Boston" and "Make Way for
  Ducklings."
Fee.

RECOMMENDED READING

Appleberg, Marilyn J. *I Love Boston Guide*. New York: Collier MacMillan, 1983.

Booth, Robert. *Boston's Freedom Trail*. Chester, Conn.: The Globe Pequot Press, 1984.

Car Free in Boston. Association for Public Transport. 1988.

Cushing, George M., Jr. *Great Buildings and Sights of Boston: A Photographic Guide*. Mineola, N. Y.: Dover Publications, 1982.

Hammel, Faye. *Frommer's 1985–1986 Guide to Boston*. New York: Frommer/ Pasmantier Publishers, 1985.

Harris, John. *Historic Walks in Old Boston*. Chester, Conn.: The Globe Pequot Press, 1982.

Howland, Llewellyn, and Isabelle Storey, eds. *A Book for Boston*. Boston: David R. Godine, 1980.

Kay, Jane Holtz. *Lost Boston*. Boston: Houghton Mifflin Co., 1982.

Lyndon, Donlon. *The City Observed — Boston. A Guide to the Architecture of the Hub*. New York: Random House, 1982.

McVoy McIntyre, A. *Beacon Hill: A Walking Tour*. Boston: Little, Brown & Co., 1975.

Ross, Corinne Madden. *To Market, To Market*. Boston: Charles River Books, 1980.

Southworth, Susan and Michael. *A. I. A. Guide to Boston Architecture*. Chester, Conn.: The Globe Pequot Press, 1984.

Vanderwarker, Peter. *Boston Then and Now*. Mineola, N. Y.: Dover Publications, 1983.

Whitehill, Walter Muir. *Boston: A Topographical History*. Cambridge, Mass.: Harvard University Press, 1968.

Whitehill, Walter M., and Knowles, Katherine. *Boston: Portrait of a City*. New York: Barre Publishers, 1964.

ADDITIONAL AND RELATED READING

Amory, Cleveland. *The Proper Bostonians*. Boston: Parnassus Press, 1984.
Notable essays on nineteenth-century Boston.

Forbes, Esther. *Johnny Tremain*. New York: Dell, 1969.
The award-winning story of a boy's experiences during the Revolutionary War; for children and young adults.

James, Henry. *The Bostonians*. New York: Penguin, 1984.

Marquand, John P. *The Late George Apley*. New York: Washington Square Press, 1982.
A portrait of a Boston gentleman at the turn of the century.

O'Connor, Edwin. *The Last Hurrah*. Boston: Little, Brown & Company, 1985.
A portrait of rambunctious Boston mayor James Michael Curley and his era.

Poe, Edgar Allan. *The Cask of Amontillado*. Mahwah, N. J.: Troll Associates, 1982.
Poe, who lived in the South End, was inspired to write this story by a rumor that the soldiers on Castle Island, in Boston Harbor, actually had a man buried in the castle's thick walls.

CHAPTER TWO

Victorian Boston

It's hard to believe that the elegant Back Bay, with its wide, tree-lined streets and imposing brick and stone buildings, was once a murky tidal marsh, home to nothing more than grass snakes and assorted amphibious creatures. But, as its name implies, the Back Bay was once exactly that — a huge wetlands separating Boston from what is now Brighton.

Economics, not aesthetics, dictated the twenty-five-year-long project that created the Paris-like section of the city, whose broad Commonwealth Avenue is sometimes compared to the Champs-Élysées. Uriah Cotting, the developer of India Wharf, was the originator of the project. He saw great potential in damming the Charles River's tidal flow by extending what is now Beacon Street beyond the Common and across the wetlands, and he wanted to build factories to use the harnessed water power.

The fortuitous invention of the steam shovel helped his plans along, but the factory project failed. The landfill, however, was a huge success. Trains made their round-the-clock runs to the gravel quarries in the Needham hills, and the newly created lots were auctioned as quickly as the fill settled.

Since it was created during the near-century-long Victorian era (1825 to 1900), the Back Bay is now the nation's largest and most impressive repository of Victorian architecture. What's even more satisfying is the fact that since land development proceeded from east to west in a quite orderly fashion we can see the evolution of the form as clearly as if we were thumbing through the pages of a manual of Victorian architecture. Virtually every Victorian structure of importance in Boston is not only still standing, but is still in use as either a residence, business, or public space. Four hundred and fifty acres of fill has rarely been put to such enduring use!

The evolution of the Victorian residential district now known as the Back Bay coincided with the advent of central heating, a technical innovation that allowed for more spacious rooms and higher ceilings, both quintessential Victorian stylings. And despite their reputations as stodgy and repressed, the Victorians were not the least bit shy about ornamentation in architecture. Just look at the masonry: stone canopies, elaborate entryways, shutters, and ironwork, balconies and oriels, bay windows and mansard roofs! These are a far cry from the austerity of the previous century's formal Federalism.

Looking at Boston's Victorian mansions and gardens is the best way to get the feel of Victorian Boston, and a sense of the city's cultural as well as architectural coming-of-age. We particularly like this tour, because it illustrates the evolution of Boston's people and their lifestyle, as the country — and the city — came into its own.

Victorian Mansions

We've often heard that a man's home is his castle. In the mansions of Boston, it might be said that a man's home was his wife's castle, since the woman of the affluent house was the absolute arbiter of taste and style. If, wandering through the ornate palaces of a century ago, you find yourself wondering how any simple living was ever accomplished amid such flamboyance, remember that the Victorians prided themselves on the complexity of their taste, manner, and moral tone. The Victorian age was a prosperous one, and it is apparent in the oversized Commonwealth Avenue residences.

We'll begin our tour at number 5 Commonwealth Avenue, the **Baylies Mansion.** Walter C. Baylies was a successful industrialist who came to Boston on the crest of the textile boom, married the daughter of a wealthy Boston family, and set himself up as a paragon of all things Brahmin and proper. Still, he did something unheard of by tearing down the 1861 house on the site and erecting his own structure in its place in 1904. The original number 5 was the mirror image of number 3 (still standing), a structure built to blend in nicely with the rest of the street on the sunny block between Arlington and Berkeley Streets. But Baylies was not content to live in a house just like the one next door. His house had to be noticeable — but tasteful.

Excitement and originality, the Victorians felt, were allowed in life — but only within an organized and predictable format. This was true of their homes as well as their lives. So the serene orderliness of the Baylies mansion was the scene of many a lavish party, as well as the less orderly upbringing of six children, and a pet squirrel who chewed on the brocade draperies, much to Mrs. Baylies's dismay. Comings-out, weddings, and musical soirées were held in the huge ballroom, added in 1912 for Baylies's daughter Charlotte's debut, where the musicians played from a small balcony. During the First World War, the room was pressed into service for bandage rolling. The house stayed in the Baylies family until Walter died in 1936 at the age of seventy-three.

> *The Hotel Vendome was the only place in Boston where Sarah Bernhardt would deign to stop. It was also the first hotel in the city to switch to electric lighting, which was provided by a small independent lighting plant designed by Edison himself in 1882. (The Jordan Marsh Company, the State House, the offices of the* Boston Herald, *and the Bijou Theatre were electrified the same year.)*

Since 1941, the Baylies house has been home to the **Boston Center for Adult Education** (which paid $23,000 for it back then). Fortunately, it is still filled with music, reading, and dancing. Since ballroom dancing has again become the rage, you can take advantage of the opportunity to learn how in the beautiful ballroom at the Center. Once you've mastered the steps, move on to the Tea Dances at the **Ritz-Carlton Hotel** to display your skills.

If you are in the mood for a small café with lace curtains and delicious French pastry or a cup of *café au lait*, try **Café de Paris** on Arlington across from the Public Garden. To experience the delight of an authentic high tea, sink back in a comfortable chair or sofa at the Bristol Lounge of the **Four Seasons Hotel** and gaze out the large window overlooking the Garden. The top tier of the serving tray contains scones with whipped cream and jam. Daintily rolled sandwiches and fruit tarts occupy the next level and sweet breads rest on the bottom. There is a wide selection of properly brewed tea and warmed nuts for your tasting pleasure. While you sip your tea and soak in the atmosphere, you can also relax to a pianist playing light classical and popular music.

At number 160 Commonwealth Avenue is the former **Hotel Vendome,** a palatial sprawl of marble erected in 1871. The Vendome, with its elegant façade, balustrades, bays, and pediments, was once the preeminent place for the fashionable to stay when visiting Boston. For a hundred years the guest register contained the names of presidents, foreign heads of state, artists, and social lions. A century after it opened in 1871, the Vendome was converted into offices and condominiums, also with an eye to preserving the structure's integrity. A visit to **Pearson's** restaurant, in the basement level of the building, can provide you with a delicious, filling lunch and an opportunity to experience this Victorian splendor.

Across Commonwealth Avenue, at 306 Dartmouth Street, stands the **Ames-Webster House,** one of the most spectacular mansions in the Back Bay. Like so many of the area's structures, this one was built as a single-family home in 1872, from a design by Peabody and Stearns. A decade later it was enlarged by John Sturgis. The wrought-iron gate on the Dartmouth Street side of the house was where guests arrived in their carriages. Gentlemen would alight here and enter through the doorway to the left. In the meantime, the ladies would be driven through the *porte-cochère* (coach door) to a rear entrance, where they ascended by elevator to a second-floor powder room. After freshening up, they were able to make an impressive entrance to the first floor by means of the elaborately carved grand staircase. Victorian manners, like Victorian architecture, often made use of such genteel artifice.

By the middle of this century, however, the Ames-Webster house had lost its elegance and was in danger of being consumed by student housing or rooming house compartmentalization. But in 1969, it was converted into office space, with an absolute minimum of changes, setting a felicitous precedent for other conversions. No fluorescent lights are allowed, and an unobtrusive brass plaque is the only sign permitted to announce the occupants. But do take note of the outstanding greenhouse on Commonwealth Avenue, filled with plants and especially spruced up at Christmastime with poinsettias.

If you're interested in staying at a small, intimate lodging that steps back to Victorian times, try the nine-room hotel called **267 Commonwealth,** located at that address. The 1880 building was restored by Bob Vila, formerly the host of public television's "This Old House" series. Even if you don't stay, ask the manager for a tour. The suites are enhanced by working fireplaces, beautiful woodwork, and floral print papers that are similar to the originals.

On the opposite side of Commonwealth Avenue is number 314, known to architecture buffs as the **Burrage Mansion** but better known in the neighborhood as the home of the Boston Evening Clinic. The Burrage seems to be Victorian Boston's one exception to the rule that any sort of New York flamboyance be avoided like the plague. This limestone palace is more than eye-catching. It must have been positively show-stopping a century ago. Like the

Vanderbilt mansion in New York, which was its obvious inspiration, this building was patterned after a French chateau — Chenonceau — and is full of luxurious French Gothic detail, inside and out. There are two turreted towers, decorative chimneys, and even gargoyles.

Burrage was quite an eccentric in his time. He was an avid gem and mineral collector and had special vaults built to house his collections. Today, the building serves an equally unusual purpose. It is the home of one of the oldest public clinics in the country, begun in 1927 with the express purpose of providing care during "off" hours for working people. The service and care are excellent, by the way, should you need it.

From this point on Commonwealth Avenue, walk two blocks toward the Charles River to Beacon Street. Near the corner of Clarendon Street on the river side is the **Goethe Institute,** the German Cultural Center, at number 170 Beacon Street. This Italian Renaissance–style edifice was built for E. H. Gay in 1900, after the manner of the nearby Fuller mansion at number 150. The house was designed for Mr. Gay's extensive collection of Chippendale furniture, and the ornate interior, which has been preserved in near-mint condition, now serves as the perfect setting for the Goethe Institute's archives and cultural events.

A little farther up the street, at **150 Beacon Street,** the wealthy John Gardner lived. The house was originally built for the Gardners in 1861 by Mrs. Gardner's father-in-law but it was expanded when the couple bought number 152 next door and razed both buildings, constructing one grand home to make room for Mrs. Gardner's large musical soirées and growing collection of European art. The original structures were demolished in 1904.

The lady of the house was the famed and eccentric Isabella Stewart Gardner, the lioness of Boston Victorian society and the woman responsible for creating the lovely Gardner Museum. Mrs. Jack, as she was known to her public and the press (who loved to record her every move), had typically Victorian passions, albeit to a more-than-typical degree. She loved flowers, music, and art and — fortunately for us — had the funds to collect and commission it according to her considerable whim. During the last four decades of the nineteenth century, while living at the Beacon Street address, she amassed an impressive collection of Rubens and Titians, and commanded private concerts by Paderewski and the entire Boston Symphony Orchestra. She also established a reputation for eccentricity. Local residents who saw a woman walking a lion down Tremont Street could be pretty certain that they were looking at Mrs. Jack. She was seen at fancy dress balls with a pair of costly diamonds suspended above her head by wires, like butterfly antennae, and for a while she converted to Buddhism.

When her husband died, Mrs. Jack decided to move out of the Beacon Street house. The city honored her request that the number 152 never be used again on that street. It has not been.

But Mrs. Jack, although in mourning, wanted a fitting new home for both herself and her fabulous possessions. In 1902, she moved into the marble palace on the Fenway that bears her name. Although the **Isabella Stewart Gardner Museum** is a bit of a detour (Mrs. Gardner's friends were shocked when she moved out to the wilds of the Fens), we enthusiastically suggest that you make a visit. Mrs. Gardner's Venetian palazzo is both a mansion in the Victorian manner and the repository of one of the best Victorian-designed collections in the country.

> *Don't forget to pause in the third-floor Gothic Room, where the most famous of John Singer Sargent's several portraits of Mrs. Jack hangs. It depicts her in a form-hugging black dress, which caused quite a scandal in the Boston of 1889. In fact, it created such a furor that Mr. Gardner had it removed from its original exhibition place — the very proper and private all-male St. Botolph Club. Fortunately, Mrs. Jack kept the work at her "home," and now we can see it, and her, in the most magical of settings — the ultimate Victorian mansion.*

If the Gardner Museum's gray marble exterior seems austere, the interior fairly shouts with Mrs. Jack's passionate enthusiasm for the splendor of European and American paintings, sculpture, and textiles. All of the work you can see, including the stones of which the building is constructed, were collected by Mrs. Jack on fantastic shopping sprees funded by her own two million dollar inheritance (and later with her husband's legacy as well). It is hard to imagine someone actually living amidst all this splendor, as Mrs. Jack did until her death in 1924, but on becoming acquainted with the woman through her possessions, it's clear that she was up to the task.

One of the most striking aspects of the museum, called "Fenway Court" in Mrs. Jack's day, is the indoor garden that is abloom all year long with rare and fragrant trees, shrubs and flowers, just as it was in her time. The mosaic Roman floor tile, dating from the second century, adds to the textural opulence of stone and nature. Once your other senses have been gratified, stop at the Gardner Museum Café for a light meal in a charming area, with a view of the garden.

Mrs. Jack also established the tradition of concerts at the palace, which continues today as stipulated in her will. At the museum desk you will find a concert calendar, as well as a guide to the collection's art treasures, including the impressive collection of French impressionists, which were considered so avant-garde at the time.

Back on Beacon Street, head north to number 137, the **Gibson House.** Although the exterior of this structure can't hold a candle to Mrs. Jack's Victorian splendor, the interior is a virtual re-creation of Victorian family life. It is one of the earliest Back Bay homes, built in 1858 for Catherine Hammond Gibson, widow of John Gardiner Gibson, who, after making his fortune as a merchant in Cuba, returned to his native Boston and married his beloved. Two decades after his death, she had this home built. And ever since, the house with all its furniture and furbelows has been kept completely intact, thanks in large part to her grandson, Charles Hammond Gibson, who bequeathed it to the **Victorian Society in America** as a museum. The society offers walking tours and special programs about our Victorian heritage.

The house is dark, as many Victorian homes were, due to the heavy furniture and draperies (sunshine was considered "common" by the delicate ladies of the day). But on one floor, it appears that Catherine got tired of all that dark and had the walls painted a shocking white! In the basement kitchen is an impressive array of bells so that the servants could answer a summons from any room. (The only way they could tell *which* room, however, was by the difference in the tone of the bells.) The bathroom, with its huge tub, cane toilet, and natural air-conditioning system, is also an interesting relic — one of the first examples of total indoor plumbing in the Back Bay.

The museum offers an hour-long guided tour through the six floors of romantic Victoriana: filigreed picture frames, peacock feathers, fringed velvet upholstery, and embossed gilt wallpaper.

Extravagance and whimsy are everywhere in this Victoriana-lover's paradise.

The elegant granite bowfront mansion at number **118 Beacon Street** is also rather surprising, not for what it was, but for what it is. The former home of Henry King, built for him in 1903, is now used by Fisher College to prepare six hundred women annually for careers in secretarial, technical, fashion, and retail professions. Built in the Classic Revival style, the house boasts an elegant bowfront in the manner of eighteenth-century English mansions. The building was expensive even by late Victorian standards — it cost just over a million dollars to build. But both the interior and exterior have been well maintained by Fisher, which purchased the property in 1939 with the provision that the college remain dedicated to its care. It is one of the few old buildings purchased by local colleges that has not suffered extensive renovation, and the original stone and woodwork, as well as the furnishings and artwork, still grace rooms that now serve as classrooms, offices, and libraries. Tours are available.

At number 84 Beacon Street is the **Hampshire House,** built in the late nineteenth century for Bayard and Ruth Thayer by Ogden Codman, whose Brahmin blood ran as blue as his clients'. The mansion is now a restaurant with dining rooms on two floors, serving a continental menu. In the Oak Room Bar and Café, one can sink into the thick leather chairs, warm one's feet by the fire, and stare across the street at the Public Garden exactly as the Thayers and their guests might have done. In the basement is the **Bull & Finch Pub,** model for the "Cheers" television series. The Oak Room is much cozier, but feel free to give in to your curiosity and have a drink downstairs.

In true Victorian style, you might want to follow cocktails and dinner with a trip to the theater, and Boston has two lovely examples of late-Victorian architecture in the **Colonial Theater,** at 106 Boylston Street, diagonally across from the Public Garden, and the **Wilbur Theater,** at 246 Tremont Street. Both were designed by Clarence Blackhall after the turn of the century, but both — the Colonial in particular, with its rich icing of bas-relief, marble, mirrors, and brass — display a Victorian sensibility. They also house some excellent theater, including pre-Broadway, off-Broadway, and road shows.

Finally, exhausted by all this ornate splendor, you might want to rest where President Kennedy did on his last trip to Boston in 1963. The **Copley Plaza Hotel** on Copley Square is not officially Victorian (it's Edwardian), but it's the nicest way we can think of to end a day of Victoriana. Erected in 1912, the Copley offers much to admire. Relax over morning coffee or take high tea while sitting on a comfy sofa or chair arranged in the continental style of the grand hotels of Europe. The Plaza Dining Room has wood paneling that is not only mahogany, but faux bois, another decorative style popular with the Victorians, made brighter for modern taste with lighter upholstery and drapes. Even if you're not staying in one of the gracious guest rooms, drop by for a break on one of your tours and enjoy this elegant establishment's hospitality. In earlier days you could have arrived in your own private train car at the Copley Square station, only a short block away. That was how the famous dancer Nijinsky, who could "leap up like a jet of water or a flame," arrived for his stay at the Copley Plaza.

If you still haven't had your fill of teas, try some more at the **Park Plaza Hotel** in the Swan Lobby Lounge, which is an ideal place to people-watch. When you are finished, walk over to the Public Garden to enjoy the swans that the hotel has brought back after a twenty-year hiatus. Stroll over to the **Ritz-Carlton Hotel** to take a look at the painting of the Boston Tea Party by Percy Morgan and relax to gentle harp music in the comfortable wing chairs in the lounge, as you partake of a truly elegant afternoon tea.

Tour Sites

Ames-Webster House
306 Dartmouth St.
Boston, MA 02116

Baylies Mansion (Boston Center
for Adult Education)
5 Commonwealth Ave.
Boston, MA 02116
267-2465

Burrage Mansion (Boston Evening
Clinic)
314 Commonwealth Ave.
Boston, MA 02116
267-7171

Colonial Theater
106 Boylston St.
Boston, MA 02116
426-9366

Copley Plaza Hotel
Copley Square
Boston, MA 02116
267-5300

Four Seasons Hotel
200 Boylston Street
Boston, MA 02116
338-4400

Gibson House
137 Beacon St.
Boston, MA 02116
267-6338
Admission fee.

Goethe Institute
170 Beacon St.
Boston, MA 02116
262-6050

Hotel Vendome
160 Commonwealth Ave.
Boston, MA 02116
267-8657
Can be toured during business
  hours, with permission.

Isabella Stewart Gardner Museum
280 the Fenway
Boston, MA 02115
734-1359
Call for concert schedule.

One-Eighteen Beacon St.
  (Fisher College)
118 Beacon St.
Boston, MA 02116
262-3240

Park Plaza Hotel
64 Arlington Street at Park Plaza
Boston, MA 02117
426-2000

Ritz-Carlton Hotel
15 Arlington Street
Boston, MA 02116
536-5700

Two Sixty-Seven Commonwealth
267 Commonwealth Ave.
Boston, MA 02116
267-6776

Victorian Society in America
137 Beacon St.
Boston, MA 02116
282-9830
Lectures, special events, walking
  tours in spring and fall.

Wilbur Theater
246 Tremont St.
Boston, MA 02116

RESTAURANTS

Café de Paris
19 Arlington Street
Boston, MA 02118
247-7121

Pearson's
160 Commonwealth Ave.
Boston, MA 02116
536-3556

Hampshire House
Bull & Finch Pub
84 Beacon St.
Boston, MA 02108
227-9605

Boston Greenery

Bostonians love gardens. This passion may be due to our English heritage, or to the fact that living in an area like New England, with its long gray winters and searing summers, we simply appreciate the bright colors of flowers all the more. Whatever the reason, Boston is full of green open spaces, some formal and elegant, some quaint and surprising. No tour of Victorian Boston would be complete without an in-depth exploration of the city's horticultural past and present. Flowers were as important to the Victorians as their moral standards. Indeed, they stood for purity, artistic sensibility, and virtue. Great floral arrangements were considered works of art, and Victorian ladies devoted much time and a great deal of effort into seeing that their homes and public spaces were graced with beauty indoors and out, all year long. It was, after all, during Victorian times that collecting botany and building greenhouses became *de rigueur* for wealthy families.

However the Victorians did not invent the Boston garden by any means. We'll begin our tour at one of Boston's oldest sites — **Old North Church** (see page 7). Several peaceful gardens are clustered at the back of the church, affectionately known to North Enders as the Old North Gardens. The space is arranged in a series of four small plots, each with a historic dedication plaque. One is the Washington Memorial Garden, which was established by the Beacon Hill Garden Club. When President Gerald Ford came to Boston for the Bicentennial, he placed a plaque on the wall as well. And there's a lovely herb garden, all surrounded by a pretty ironwork fence.

Paul Revere's cousin Nathaniel Hichborn lived just down the street from Revere, in a 1711 brick house built by Moses Pierce. Behind the **Pierce/Hichborn House,** the Paul Revere House, and an intervening home is an accurate replica of a colonial herb garden that flourishes during the summer months. It contains herbs for cooking, medicinal plants, and flowers for a potpourri that was used to scent the house to cover cooking odors. Both houses are open to the public.

Now on to Beacon Hill, where the modern gardeners dwell. The **Beacon Hill Garden Club,** whose headquarters are at 55 Mt. Vernon Street, was founded in 1929 and is one of the oldest continually operating horticultural clubs in the country. Its leading light was Elizabeth Sawyer Welch, a Beacon Hill resident who saw that the spaces normally used for trash collections on the already tightly packed hill might serve a more aesthetic purpose if they were made into gardens.

It's not surprising that the outdoor gardens of Beacon Hill took so long to catch on. Despite the proliferation of indoor displays and public gardens, most Beacon Hill residents moved out of town for the warm months to Brookline or the North Shore where they had greenery aplenty. But by the end of the Second World War, the garden club members — fresh from their charitable efforts with the city's victory gardens — were urging Beacon Hillites to tear down the walls that separated their rear plots and create connecting gardens, which are hidden to the public except during the club's annual Hidden Gardens Tour. Held once a year (rain or shine), the spring tour provides a map of Beacon Hill and a stroll through a dozen of these little green gems tucked away behind the Hill's labyrinthine brick façades.

In season, within these spaces you'll find yourself in the midst of a profusion of impatiens, tulips, holly, ivy, rhododendron, and wisteria. Flagstones provide a path and wrought-iron tables and chairs places to sit. Each garden reflects the personality of its creator, but all are equally enchanting. The tour offers a unique insight into the way Boston must have looked in an earlier day, since the sights and sounds of modern Boston are virtually nonexistent back in these private arbors.

Another annual event sponsored by the club is the Beacon Hill Window Box Contest, which each year pits local horticulturists against one another to vie for the honor of having created the loveliest or most unusual window box. Everyone on the Hill benefits from the sight and scent of their effort. Check local newspapers for either of these events, or call the club for information. If you're here in the off-season, browse through the attractive four-color book entitled *Hidden Gardens of Beacon Hill*, available at the **Book Store** on Beacon Street. While there, you might also want to look for the book on the Public Garden recently published by the Friends of the Public Garden.

As long as you're on Beacon Hill, stop in at the **Victorian Bouquet** on Charles Street, one of the city's finest florists. Owner Susan Bates, an artist with flowers, specializes in Victorian-style arrangements. In addition to cut flowers and plants, there are dried and silk flowers to delight the eye. The imported flowers and flowering plants will delight your senses when you step into **Rouvalis Flowers** in the next block on the west side of the street.

Continue down Charles Street to the corner of Beacon Street, where you will see the Public Garden on your right. The **Boston Public Garden** (see page 12) is the epitome of high Victoriana with its lagoons and footbridge, fountains, monuments, and carefully planted flowerbeds. Unlike the much older Boston Common, the Garden is a nineteenth-century creation, built on land reclaimed from the marsh. As a matter of fact, this land marks the spot where, in April of 1775, the British launched their attack on Lexington and Concord — by boat. The Redcoats set off near the present Charles Street entrance to the Garden from what was then the only portion of "Round Marsh" not flooded at every high tide (see page 19).

There is an interesting story about the return of the swans to the Public Garden in 1989. After the two swans had acclimated themselves to the pond, they were brought to the Park Plaza Hotel, which had donated them, to be returned with pomp and circumstance to the lagoon on a luggage rack. A very large crowd gathered, but unfortunately not for the swans. These people thought that Presidents Bush and Mitterrand, who were speaking at the

Boston University Commencement, were coming out of the hotel. The two swans that emerged from the lobby were not what they were expecting!

When the land was set aside in 1838 for a horticultural park to be cultivated by a group of private citizens, the Garden became America's first botanical preserve. City government tried vainly to sell the property in the 1840s and again in the 1850s, but local residents strongly resisted development. In 1859, the Massachusetts legislature and the citizens of Boston ordained that the Garden would forever be preserved for public use, and that no buildings except those for horticultural purposes be built on it. It was then that the Garden was designed in pretty much the form we know it now, and by the late 1800s, it was a showcase for some 90,000 plants and 1500 trees.

In the twentieth century, however, neglect took its toll, and the Garden was reduced to a few overgrown paths and a crumbling bridge amid patches of dry grass. By the early 1970s a group of Bostonians, who called themselves the Friends of the Public Garden, decided to take matters from the city's inept hands. They lobbied for funds and support, and convinced the Boston Redevelopment Authority to step in. Eventually $8 million was allocated to restore the ailing trees, replant the dead flowers, and repave the pathways. Today, all the fountains and monuments have been restored and the plantings, maintained by a special Parks and Recreation Department staff of six, are replaced as soon as they wilt.

As you stroll, you'll notice that the paths are not laid out logically to expedite passage from one place to another by the shortest possible route. The Victorians valued their promenades far too highly for such pragmatism, and let their walkways meander with no apparent purpose beyond the beauty of the walk itself. Victorians weren't totally impractical, however. Even they tired of walking around the lagoon, and in 1869 construction was completed on the miniature suspension bridge that bisects it.

The Public Garden is a mini-arboretum with most of its trees labeled, and every season has its particular delights. Magnolia, crab apple, and dogwood bloom in the spring, along with an exuberant display of tulips. Summer brings the blossoming of the Garden's prized Japanese pagoda trees, roses, and subtropical plants. In the autumn, the Garden is an excellent place for foliage viewing; in the winter, the local bird population enlivens the otherwise barren branches.

Many of the Garden's monuments are also pure Victorian, including the equestrian statue of George Washington that stands guard at the Arlington Street entrance, and the Ether Monument (also facing Arlington Street) across from George. The superb wrought-iron fence that encloses the garden is a replica of the one installed in 1865. And of course there are the **Swan Boats,** which date back to 1877 and have been continuously operated by the Paget family. Today's two-ton boats are replicas of the originals, which cost five cents to ride in Victorian times. They're still a bargain at sixty cents for children (see page 200).

> *Robert Paget got the idea for the swan decoration on his boats from his favorite opera,* Lohengrin *(in which the hero glides to the rescue of his beloved on a boat pulled by a swan).*

Leaving the Garden via the Commonwealth Avenue gate and heading due west will take you farther along the Emerald Necklace, Frederick Law Olmsted's ribbon of greenery that stretches from the Common to Franklin Park in Jamaica Plain, and represents the longest green space through an urban center in the United States. The National Park Service has designated the Emerald Necklace a National Historic Landmark, and hardy walkers will be well rewarded by a trek down its five-mile course.

Olmsted, best known for creating Central Park in New York, idealized nature to an almost religious degree. He was a romanticist who believed that one could commune with God through His natural wonders, and Boston was one of the few cities where he was allowed free reign to implement his romantic concept. His plan of interconnected parks was designed for Boston in 1887, although he had been working on the idea for at least a decade

before that. The Necklace includes the Common and Garden; the Commonwealth Avenue Mall where you are now standing; the Esplanade running along the Charles River; the Riverway, or Fens; the Arnold Arboretum; and Franklin Park.

The Commonwealth Mall itself is modeled after French Victorian style, as is so much of Back Bay architecture. Adorning it is a magnificent stand of great American and English elms, one of the largest in the country. It was here, amidst the elms, statuary, and flowers, that Victorian Bostonians were wont to stroll after their meals, certain that they would see and be seen by everyone who was anyone in local society. Even today, when promenaders are likely to be overtaken by joggers, the Mall lends the avenue its undeniable air of stately elegance.

The Commonwealth Mall cross streets, as you move from east to west, are named alphabetically after English dukes and earls, reflecting Boston's ongoing intrigue with all things English and royal: Arlington, Berkeley, Clarendon, Dartmouth, Exeter, Fairfield, Gloucester, and Hereford.

The Winston family dominates the floral scene in the Back Bay. The grandfather began **Winston Flowers** at 131 Newbury Street over fifty years ago, supplying his neighbors with flower arrangements, cut flowers, and plants. His grandsons have expanded the operation to the **Greenhouse,** at 553 Boylston Street.

The flowers arrive by plane from Holland, the plants are from local Massachusetts greenhouses, and the street scene is enhanced with the beautiful plants and cut flowers displayed outside.

To your right is the Charles River Esplanade, which joins the Mall farther west. Take a detour over to the Charles River and stroll the meandering Esplanade paths for a while. The connecting link is at Arlington Street, at the beginning of the Mall, where the Arthur Fiedler Memorial Footbridge spans Storrow Drive. The Esplanade, although conceived by Olmsted, was not built until the early 1930s when banker James Storrow's widow provided the city with funds to landscape what was until then just a simple river walk. The addition of Storrow Drive, between 1949 and 1951, was a necessary travesty never envisioned by the Esplanade's benefactor.

Today, the Esplanade provides a dazzling variety of natural settings, from the bosky paths by the Hatch Shell (where outdoor music is performed all summer long) to the open spaces and duck-filled lagoons farther west. The Esplanade is wonderfully well used from Beacon Hill to Boston University by Boston residents and visitors, and on any sunny day you'll find it full of joggers, bikers, skaters, and picnickers. On a hot summer day, as you drive along Storrow Drive you can imagine that you're on a beachfront, for all the folks sunbathing in swim trunks and bikinis. (See page 235 for more on the sporting opportunities available on the Esplanade.)

The Fenway was designed by Olmsted between 1881 and 1885, when he personally oversaw the draining of the stagnant and malodorous Muddy River and Stony Brook to install the next link in his emerald chain. At one time, the Fens was the crown jewel of the Necklace. With Mrs. Jack as a pacesetter, it became the center of the cultural and residential neighborhood created when the wealthy Beacon Hill and Back Bay Brahmins fled to the "suburbs" west of Massachusetts Avenue.

One delightful area in the Fens is the Rose Garden. It is still maintained and is spectacular, especially in July, when it blooms with thousands of wild and cultivated varieties. Next to the Rose Garden is a Japanese Temple Bell, given by the mayor of Kyoto to Boston as a symbol of sisterhood, peace, and friendship. You can see it between the garden path and footbridge leading to the back door of the Museum of Fine Arts.

Another unusual aspect of the Fens are the Victory Gardens, the oldest in the United States. Because food prices were skyrocketing during World War Two, Mayor Maurice Tobin had the four-and-a-half-acre site cleared so people could grow vegetables. The garden was so successful that it spread all along the banks of the river from Jamaica Plain to Cambridge. After the war, the area was reduced, but the **Fenway Garden Society,** working in cooperation with the Parks and Recreation Department, still maintains about one hundred plots, used by individual members.

While various neighborhood organizations work for their immediate area, the **Boston Greenspace Alliance** speaks with one voice for all the civic group and public agencies that belong to the coalition. Their aim is to upgrade and maintain all the parks and open spaces in the city.

If you were to continue along the Jamaicaway by car you would pass Jamaica Pond, the largest body of water in the Emerald Necklace, where an Olmsted-designed boathouse provides the public with rowboats for a pastoral outing. Proceed to the **Arnold Arboretum,** the most impressive of Olmsted's projects. The Arboretum was designed in 1872 with the help of the first director, Charles Sprague Sargent. The land is today owned by the city of Boston, which has leased it for 999 years to Harvard University with the provision that they maintain the arboretum and keep it a living museum of trees, shrubs, and flowers, open to the public for both study and pleasure. Depending on the season of your visit, you will be rewarded with breathtaking vistas of lilacs, lilies, azaleas, and flowering trees of every variety. The lilacs, celebrated with their own special Sunday in May, are the greatest favorite because they herald the true end of winter; but at any time the free lecture tours at the arboretum are both illuminating and rewarding. (It is also a favorite site for outdoor weddings.)

The last stop in the chain is **Franklin Park,** the site of the Franklin Park Zoo (see page 203). Designed in 1885, Olmsted considered Franklin Park his magnum opus. It is the largest green space (520 acres) in the Necklace, and was named after Ben Franklin. Currently the Franklin Park Coalition works very hard to raise money for and awareness of the many programs that take place in the park. A newly expanded eighteen-hole golf course covers almost half the park, and the African Tropical Pavillion has been completed in the zoo. Frequent tours are given in the park, which is patrolled by Park Rangers.

During the winter the Emerald Necklace has little to recommend it to horticulture buffs. Fortunately, there is much to be seen indoors, or in semiprotected settings, so you needn't feel deprived of natural beauty should you be in Boston during the long, gray season. You might, for example, like to stop by the **Boston Public Library,** with its charming outdoor courtyard modeled after an arcade in the Palazzo della Cancelleria in Rome. The garden here was designed by the members of the Back Bay Garden Club, who contribute plantings, and it offers something to delight the eye even when snow is on the ground.

Also along Boylston Street, in between the Boston Public Library and Trinity Church, is **Copley Square Park.** The Park has a fountain that serves as a small amphitheater for concerts when it is dry. The London plane trees and sugar maples shade areas paved in patterns of brick, granite, slate, and concrete. Following the wishes of the surrounding neighborhoods, there is a large area of grass with flower beds at one end. The nearby food pavilion and farmer's market cater to one's hunger. The park is the result of cooperation between the city, the citizens, and the Copley Square Centennial Committee.

And of course, there's the garden court in the **Isabella Stewart Gardner Museum,** an atrium filled with beauty that is impervious to the weather. Mrs. Jack established an endowment for the collection and care of the indoor garden. Seasonal plantings, augmented by outrageous out-of-season blooms, fulfill her desire. The museum has its own greenhouse to supply the garden court with growing things, and you can ask for a tour of that in addition to a museum tour (see pages 42–44).

There's a lot of greenery too, at the nearby **Museum of Fine Arts,** where the "ladies committee" (volunteers) keeps the huge stone urns overflowing with flowers all year round. Aside from their color and profusion, these arrangements are artistically designed to enhance the art collections, and remind us that Victorian flower arranging was considered an art on a par with fine painting and sculpture. Early every May, the Museum sponsors Art in Bloom, a time when garden clubs throughout the state create lavish arrangements for public display in the galleries. Floral arrangements are placed near the artworks that inspired them, and the result is an exuberant celebration of spring's return.

On Massachusetts Avenue, near Huntington Avenue, is **Horticultural Hall,** home of the Massachusetts Horticultural Society, founded as a nonprofit organization in 1829 to "encourage and improve the science and practice of horticulture." Its continuing existence as the oldest and largest organization of its kind in the country proves once again that the Victorian love of growing things still exists in this city today. The society is best known for its New England Spring Garden and Flower Show, which has been held annually since 1871 (the show is now held at the Bayside Exposition Center). Horticultural Hall, constructed in 1900, is also home to the society's extensive research, educational, and informational programs, which offer free advice and assistance to anyone calling with a horticultural dilemma. They run an educational program for adults and children. Seeds, books, catalogues, and rare botanical prints are also sold in the gift shop.

If for some reason your thirst for nature is still not satiated, head over to Cambridge, where you can visit the astonishing glass flower exhibit at Harvard's **Botanical Museum.** The flowers, all made of glass, are so accurately created that they have been called "marvels of science in art and art in science." They are the work of Leopold and Rudolph Blaschka, father and son German glassblowers who built their collection in Dresden between 1887 and 1936. The remarkable collection was given to Harvard as a memorial to Charles Elliott Ware by his wife Elizabeth. The botanically perfect oversize flowers were made by a process that was lost with the deaths of their creators, so the glass flowers are even more rare than some of the specimens they depict. Their only natural enemy is sonic booms, which have caused some to shatter, never to be replaced.

If you're in Cambridge and the weather is good, you really shouldn't miss the **Mount Auburn Cemetery** about a mile away (see pages 110–111). It was the first garden cemetery in America, and has a spectacular land-spaced arboretum incorporated into its acreage. Horticultural maps of more than three thousand trees, of which eighty percent are labeled, are available in the office at the entrance. The Friends of Mount Auburn offer a wide variety of walks, lectures, and activities.

To finish up your tour of green spaces, come back to Boston and make your way to the waterfront for two more restful places. Although it is technically not a green space, the **Harborwalk** that stretches from the Northern Avenue Bridge along the waterfront to the North Washington Bridge to Charlestown affords the walker unparalleled views of the harbor and its blue and grey space. Along the way, stop in the **Christopher Columbus Waterfront Park** for a rest, and visit the **Rose Fitzgerald Kennedy Garden,** which is, appropriately enough, planted with roses.

Further inland in the heart of the Financial District is **Post Office Square.** The Friends of Post Office Square, Inc., built a park at street level over a 1400-space parking garage. Winter or summer, it will welcome the public with an indoor-outdoor café. The brick granite and wooden details add a much-needed public green place for downtown workers and shoppers. Make sure you look at the Angell Plaza Memorial at the apex of the triangle. The bronze creative fountain has a frog on a lily pad and ducks floating in the water.

The Victorians loved their many-roomed homes, their multi-colored gardens, and their multiple-course dinners. Eating was a ritual that consumed hours, serving as an excuse for inviting guests and providing a platform for discussion of the latest business schemes and gossip. It's hard to guess whether or not they would have approved of the culinary tours we offer next, but there's no doubt they would have appreciated the ready ease with which food is now available. Their own meals could take days to prepare!

Tour Sites

Arnold Arboretum
The Arborway
Jamaica Plain
Boston, MA 02130
524-1717

Beacon Hill Garden Club
55 Mt. Vernon St.
Boston, MA 02108
227-4392

Book Store, Inc.
76 Chestnut St.
Boston, MA 02108
742-4531

Boston Greenspace Alliance
44 Bromfield St.
Boston, MA 02108
426-7980

Boston Public Library
666 Boylston St.
Boston, MA 02116
536-5400

Botanical Museum
Harvard University
11 Divinity St.
Cambridge, MA 02138
495-2248
Admission fee.

Copley Square Park
Boylston St.
Boston, MA 02117

Fenway Garden Society
P. O. Box 493, Aster Station
Boston, MA 02123

Franklin Park
Blue Hill Ave.
Dorchester, MA 02121
442-2002

Franklin Park Coalition
170 Morton St.
Boston, MA 02130
524-9685

Gardner Museum
  See Isabella Stewart Gardner
  Museum

Greenhouse
553 Boylston St.
Boston, MA 02116
437-1050

Horticulture Hall
Massachusetts Horticultural
  Society
300 Massachusetts Ave.
Boston, MA 02115
536-9280

Isabella Stewart Gardner Museum
280 the Fenway
Boston, MA 02115
734-1359

Mount Auburn Cemetery
580 Mt. Auburn St.
Cambridge, MA 02138
547-7105

Museum of Fine Arts
465 Huntington Ave.
Boston, MA 02115
267-9300

Old North Church
193 Salem St.
Boston, MA 02113
523-6676

Victorian Bouquet
53 Charles St.
Boston, MA 02114
367-6648

Pierce/Hichborn House
29 North Square
Boston, MA 02113
523-1676

Winston Flowers
131 Newbury St.
Boston, MA 02116
536-6861

Rouvalis Flowers
70 Charles St.
Boston, MA 02114
266-2255

General Resources

GARDENING

Boston Urban Gardeners (B.U.G.)
33 Harrison Ave.
Boston, MA 02111
423-7497
A nonprofit urban organization
  dedicated to helping low-
  income families grow
  vegetables.

RECOMMENDED READING

Bunting, Bainbridge. *Houses of Boston's Back Bay: An Architectural History, 1840–1917.* Cambridge, Mass.: Belknap Press of Harvard University Press, 1967.

Drake, Samuel Adams. *Historic Mansions and Highways Around Boston.* Rutland, Vt.: Charles E. Tuttle Co., 1971.

Hidden Gardens of Beacon Hill. Boston: Beacon Hill Garden Club, 1987.

The Public Garden: Boston. Boston: Friends of the Public Garden and Common, Inc., 1988.

CHAPTER THREE

Beyond Baked Beans

The same dismissive air that pervades any discussion of British cuisine used to pertain to Boston cooking as well. Boston was known for its hearty, bland fare: broiled scrod, baked beans, Indian pudding, and of course, the ubiquitous New England "boiled dinner," in which the merest whiff of a spice among the cabbage, potatoes, and corned beef was enough to make a dyed-in-the-wool New Englander shout treason.

There's nothing wrong with traditional fare; certainly a plate of simply prepared, very fresh scrod is a tasty treat. But even Fanny Farmer would applaud the fact that today Boston has progressed far beyond such earnest food and has scaled the heights of culinary daring and variety.

As the city's population grew and diversified, so did the city's cuisine. In fact, you now have to look hard for restaurants that serve up only "traditional New England fare." It's much easier to find a place that serves terrific Thai food, or Cajun cooking, or even a restaurant that specializes only in dishes made with the delectable local calamari, or squid. There are markets offering the ingredients to make anything from sushi to sauerbraten, and enough cooking schools to make Mrs. Farmer gape in astonishment.

Our first tour will take you through some of Boston's most venerable pubs and taverns — places where history is served up in portions as generous as the food and drink. Then we'll go off on some of our personal favorite jaunts, exploring what this city has to offer in the way of seafood, ice cream, and chocolate.

Pubs and Taverns

When the Puritans first settled in the Boston area, they had their own strict vision of life. They were a stern, uncompromising bunch, and the laws prohibiting any form of entertainment — including the usual complement of wine, women, and song — were strictly enforced.

But the Puritans hadn't counted on the natural inclination of folks to gather together to discuss community affairs, politics, or neighbors' foibles. And, as the settlement began to expand, people had to travel to see friends and do business. Public travel meant public accommodations, and accommodations meant food and — inevitably — wine, women, and song.

So the birth of the New England tavern was one of necessity, and its evolution was as natural as the expansion of the city itself. We begin our tour in the courtyard of the **Bostonian Hotel** across from historic Faneuil Hall and Quincy Market. While we're here, note the granite fountain beside you. It is a re-creation of the Boston harborline and original street pattern as they existed in the early eighteenth century. (The little piece of black marble marks the Bostonian Hotel's original location.)

Inside the Bostonian Hotel, which was remodeled in 1982 from an old warehouse, is a friendly little place called the **Atrium Café,** where you can sit and look out at the food-oriented bustle of Quincy Market. And while you're at the Atrium, you can see the display of early artifacts gleaned during the hotel's construction. The entire block is known as the Blackstone Block, named after the outspoken Reverend William Blaxton, who gave the seventeenth-century Puritans so much trouble because he expounded on the pleasures of good books and Madeira wine. (For his other eccentricities, see pages 10–11.) The Puritans tried to curb Blackstone's ribaldry and then tried to convert him. But Blackstone got the last word, selling the city the Boston Common land for the then-exorbitant sum of $50, and choosing to move to the more permissive state of Rhode Island.

From the Bostonian, cut through Scott Alley, a narrow passageway on the north side of the building abutting the hotel. Although the brick structures were built between 1824 and 1980, you probably won't be able to tell which is original and which is new, since the builders of the hotel took such pains to maintain an authentic appearance. Scott Alley, by the way, was the site of the Green Dragon Tavern, where the Boston Tea Party plans were hatched.

There is a very old tavern still in operation nearby. The **Bell in Hand Tavern** is the oldest pub in the country. It got its name from the original proprietor, a man named Jim Wilson, who served as Boston's town crier until 1794, when he opened the pub, which currently stands on the site of Ben Franklin's childhood home. The Bell in Hand refers to the bell Wilson used to hold and ring as he traveled through the town reciting the day's news. Jim Wilson was a hospitable soul who loved his drink, and his legacy lives on in the Bell in Hand, where you can still sit and nurse an excellent ale. Today, in addition to a fine selection of beers, you can enjoy such modern snacks as nachos and chicken wings instead of the pickled eggs and pig's feet that graced the old oak bar in earlier times.

> *The Blackstone Block is the only remaining original seventeenth-century street in Boston. Your footsteps will fall on stones trod by Declaration of Independence signatory John Hancock, who built a house here in 1767 for his brother, Ebenezer.*

Outside the Bell in Hand you face Government Center, which was built on the site of old Scollay Square, once the rowdiest spot in all of Boston, which succumbed to urban renewal in the 1960s. (Newspaper Row used to be here before a fire caused it to relocate to the downtown area. See page 91.) Scollay Square was Boston's Times Square, filled with pubs, taverns, tattoo parlors, strip joints, and houses of ill repute. It was also the home to some more-or-less legal rapscallions, such as the notorious mayor James Michael Curley, who ruled the city three times between 1914 and 1949. You can see Mayor Curley, in two bronze reincarnations, sitting and standing near his old stomping grounds in Curley Park, across from the Bell in Hand. Sit down beside him on the bench or try his lap for size. Some say even now he will try to influence your vote if you stay long enough.

One of the few remaining eateries from that early boisterous era is the **Union Oyster House,** just down the street to your right. Built in 1714 as a house, it became a tavern in 1826 and has been serving New England–style food ever since. It is considered to be the oldest restaurant operating under the same name in the country, and you can still feel the rambunctious atmosphere that pervaded the old Scollay Square, especially if you try to crowd in there on a Saturday night. The raw bar has been a favorite seafood stop for generations, and Presidents Theodore Roosevelt and John F. Kennedy ate there in their youth. Louis-Philippe of France lived above the restaurant in 1797 and supported himself tutoring French, long before becoming king in 1830.

Another historic tavern is **Clarke's Turn of the Century Saloon,** located on Merchant's Row. Thomas Clarke was instrumental in the Irish Rebellion of 1916. His home was turned into a warehouse, and wasn't reclaimed until the present owners restored it and opened the tavern in 1975. Clarke's, a convivial pub with a full menu and an emphasis on sporty camaraderie, is partly owned by former New York Knicks basketball star Dave DeBusschere.

From Clarke's, head down State Street to number 160, the home of another of Boston's most venerable taverns. The **Black Rose** is a Boston institution as steeped in Irish tradition as the city itself. (The Black Rose, or Roisin Dubh, as it's called in Gaelic, is a symbol of the persecution of the Irish Catholics in Ireland.) Although the Black Rose has only been in existence for about a decade, it has a reputation for great Irish music and food and talk. Full meals are served along with Irish spirits, Irish music, and good Irish coffee.

Backtrack now to Quincy Market, where you can make one more stop at a tavern, this one traditionally English in atmosphere.

Lord Bunbury, in the North Market, is authentic down to the fixtures themselves, which were brought in piece by piece from England. The place was named for a seventeenth-century political cartoonist, whose work hangs on the walls.

Leaving Lord Bunbury, you'll find yourself next door to **Faneuil Hall Marketplace,** currently the food mecca of the city. The market was an eighteenth-century warehouse for butchers, produce merchants, and cheese makers, and was renovated by the Rouse company in 1976. More than one hundred thousand people come through here on a busy day, wandering from stall to stall (or being pushed along by the crowd), sampling everything from pickled mushrooms to gourmet peanut butter. Although most of the concessions are new, there are some tenants who can trace their rent receipts back to the original wholesale food center. **Berenson Prime Shoppe** meats, and **Doe Sullivan's Old Market** cheese are worth a visit, not only because they are historic tenants, but because they sell fine food as well.

You can eat in the central hall of Quincy Market, returning to the stalls until you've had your fill, or you can go back over to the North Market and sit down to a real meal. You might choose to sample the famous **Durgin-Park,** whose motto, inscribed on the façade, rightly claims it was "established before you were born." (It was founded in 1855.) The food is hearty and copious; we can promise you that the long communal tables will be crowded and the waitresses surly, though efficient. Long a favorite among tourists and Bostonians alike, the restaurant accepts no reservations and no checks or charges.

A large, upscale after-work crowd with a fun-loving attitude is also known to gather at **Chatterly's, Stocks and Bonds,** and **Lily's.**

High ceilings, a hardwood floor, copper tabletops, vents, and brew kettles, along with overlapping conversations and clanging beer glasses, combine to create the casual and relaxed atmosphere of the **Commonwealth Brewing Company.** Boston's first and only brew pub, this establishment is known for outstanding location-brewed beer. Besides sitting alongside the brew kettles, you can tour the downstairs brewery on Saturdays and Sundays. Some popular dishes include the Boston baked beans, the sauerkraut and knockwurst sandwich, and the carrot cake. You can even purchase memorabilia such as T-shirts and glasses at the register.

If the brewing atmosphere is for you, then head out to Jamaica Plain to the **Boston Beer Company** brewery, home of Samuel Adams Boston Lager, Boston Lightship, and Boston Ale. Your tour of the facilities includes the chance to view some historical items from Boston's old breweries as well as a brewer's description and demonstration of how beer and ale are made. As the grand finale, you'll even get to sample some beer!

Tour Sites

Atrium Café
Bostonian Hotel
North and Blackstone Sts.
Boston, MA 02109
523-3600

Bell in Hand Tavern
45 Union St.
Boston, MA 02108
227-2098

Berenson Prime Shoppe
104 Faneuil Hall Marketplace
Boston, MA 02109
523-1206

The Black Rose
160 State St.
Boston, MA 02109
742-2286

Boston Beer Company
30 Germania St.
Jamaica Plain, MA 02130
522-3400

Chatterly's
200 Atlantic Ave.
Boston, MA 02110
227-0828

Clarke's Turn of the Century
Saloon
21 Merchants Row
Boston, MA 02109
227-7800

The Commonwealth Brewing
Company
138 Portland St.
Boston, MA 02114
523-8383

Doe Sullivan's Old Market
200 Faneuil Hall Marketplace
Boston, MA 02109
227-9850

Durgin-Park
340 Faneuil Hall Marketplace
Boston, MA 02109
227-2038
Also located at Copley Place,
266-1964.

Faneuil Hall Marketplace
Boston, MA 02109
523-1300

Lily's
29 North Quincy Market
Boston, MA 02109
720-5580

Lord Bunbury
6 Faneuil Hall Marketplace \
Boston, MA 02109
227-7004

Stocks and Bonds Restaurant and
    Deli Night Club
One Exchange Place
Boston, MA 02909
723-8505

Union Oyster House
41 Union St.
Boston, MA 02108
227-2750

Chocowalk

Ah, chocolate! Is there anything else edible in this universe that arouses such passion, and provides such pure pleasure? Chocolate is an institution in Boston, but it wasn't always so. Early Bostonians, weaned on blancmange and boiled puddings, thought of the exotic chocolate bean as a sinful departure from Puritanism's stony path.

> *The word* choco *is Aztec for "foam," since the original concoction was a mixture of ground cacao beans, vanilla, and spices whipped to a froth.*

Fortunately for all of us, that changed. As Boston became a port of entry for exotica from all over the New World, word of the "choco" drink brought back by the traders from Mexico and Peru soon traveled through the colonies.

Once Boston adopted the new taste, there was no going back. Cocoa beans were first used as currency by Gloucester fishermen, and the first chocolate mill in the United States was founded in Dorchester by Walter Baker. Chocolate is no longer manufactured in the building, but as a condominium it houses many chocolate lovers. The city that once prided itself on its baked beans now prides itself on its chocolate creations, and you can indulge on a tour of the city's best without any guilt or remorse. After all, if Bostonians don't feel it's sinful anymore, why should you? One word of warning: pace yourself and try not to overindulge on your first stop.

We'll start our chocolate indulgence in Quincy Market at **Serendipity,** a branch of the New York emporium that was opened in Greenwich Village in 1954 by three out-of-work actors who were tired of slinging ice cream on salary. They decorated the original with some of their favorite personal possessions, all of which were for sale. That tradition continues today, and everything you see in the overstuffed and eclectic place can be purchased. But the thing not to miss is Serendipity's Frozen Hot Chocolate, so thick the straw stands up by itself, so big even a chocoholic might not finish it. Or try the original Blackout Cake, a dense, double-thick fudgy concoction that was allegedly born during the New York Blackout of 1974. If you have a child who has inherited your passion for chocolate, look into Serendipity as the site of your next birthday party. They have highchairs and booster seats and give balloons to the young at heart.

Cross Quincy Market to the North Market where you'll find **Sweet Stuff,** the kind of penny candy store that kids have always dreamed about but probably have never seen. Sweet Stuff has artfully arranged their vast selection of more than 150 varieties of sweets in tall, clear plastic bins so that everything from jelly beans to Hersey's Kisses is visible in vast sugary quantities.

Aside from the bulk displays, however, Sweet Stuff carries

the complete line of **Harbor Sweets,** a Massachusetts firm that started out as a one-man kitchen operation and has grown into a huge mail-order and retail business. Ben Strochecker opened his little shop in Marblehead in 1977, and fashioned his hand-dipped chocolates after the local harborside scenery. You can buy Sand Dollars, Sweet Sloops, Sweet Sea Shells, and their most popular item, Marblehead Mints, which have tiny sailboats embossed on a sea of bittersweet chocolate with a delicate touch of mint.

> *As you leave Quincy Market remember the not-so-sweet Great Molasses Flood in the nearby North End. On an unseasonably warm day in January of 1919, a four-story silo full of molasses exploded on Commercial Street near the harbor. The ensuing sticky tidal wave was fifty feet high and traveled at a speed of thirty-five miles per hour, crushing buildings, destroying bridges, and killing a dozen people. (Whoever said "slow as molasses"?) Some North End residents say that on a hot summer's day the smell of molasses still rises from the asphalt.*

If peanut butter comes second to your love of chocolate, head over to **Peanut Butter Fantasies,** where you will find chocolate and peanut butter sailboats, white chocolate almond dreams, and peanut butter truffles. For chocoholics, Tombley's Peanut Butter makes a chocolate and raspberry peanut butter — one taste and you'll feel you've died and gone to heaven.

If you still haven't had enough chocolate, continue through Faneuil Hall marketplace to **Boston Brownies** (there is also one in Copley Place). Here you'll find rich, dense, fudgy chocolate brownies that are definitely not cakey. Among the twenty varieties, you'll be able to sample Heavenly Hash and Boston's Best — white fudge nut on the bottom and blond chocolate chip on top. For those who wish they could be in Boston with you on the chocolate tour, you can send a Brownie Gram anywhere in the United States by next-day-air. Your last stop at Faneuil Hall will be at the **Chocolate Dipper,** noted for friendly personnel and chocolate-covered fruit, such as mangoes, strawberries, bananas, blue-berries, and pineapple.

Head up Congress Street to One Devonshire Place and you'll find **J. Bildner & Sons,** a grocery and specialty store that evokes the feeling of old-time general stores, with its black and white tiles and sumptuous food displays. The store sells a Grand Marnier Chocolate Cake and Dolci Torinesi, a devilish cross between a mousse and a cake, as well as David's chocolate chip cookies.

Another market worth a stop is **Rudi's,** at the corner of Washington and Milk Streets. Rudi's, a bakery, also produces handmade chocolate truffles that have been awarded a "best in the city" citation by a local magazine. On certain Saturdays they give truffle demonstrations, but on any day you can enjoy these meltaway delicacies along with their Sacher Torte, Black Forest Cake, and delectable chocolate croissants.

Farther down Washington Street is the **Lafayette Hotel,** one of Boston's newest grand hotels and the cornerstone of the Lafayette Place shopping plaza. Stop by at the registration desk in the lobby and feast your eyes on the hugest bowl of bite-sized chocolates you've ever seen. The hotel is owned by the Swiss-based Nestlé's corporation, which manufactures these Cailler chocolates in Switzerland. Try to guess how many there are while you sample their chocolate Cremant, Chocmel, or Frigor varieties.

Then stop in at **Aux Chocolats Ltd.,** on the first floor of the Lafayette Place mall. It's a little candy box of a place in which impeccably bow-tied salespeople sell delicious truffles. They carry Swiss chocolates and are adding their own line of handmade chocolates. Their most popular specialty line of truffles is not available anywhere else in the city.

Now it's time to change neighborhoods. Either walk or take the subway to Copley Place in the Back Bay. Your first visit should include a look-see at **Godiva Chocolatiers** — the chocolate crowned jewels in their well-recognized box are worth eating here or buying as gifts. If you like a more contemporary environment, head for **Sweet Temptations.** The colorful display with lucite and mirrors highlights every kind of candy and candy-related gift. Thirty to forty percent of the store is dedicated to chocolate. If you are the type of person who must do it all, seek out **Confetti,** with lots of ready-made gift packages to be shipped anywhere in the world.

If no distance is too far for your beloved chocolate, rent a car or take the "T" (Green Line C) to Brookline Village and seek out **I Love Chocolate** at 52 Boylston Street. Even their name is for chocolate lovers. Specialties include pumpkin pie fudge, chocolate lobster lollipops, and Belgian chocolate roses with silk leaves. They are also a representative for Champlain chocolates of Birmingham, Vermont. The owner, Sharon Holdner, loves to make up gift baskets through their mail-order business and carries such specialties as butter crunch made with Vermont maple syrup. The *pièces de résistance* are the New England hand-rolled creams.

As the triumphant grande finale to your chocolate tour, plan on spending a Saturday afternoon at the **Hotel Meridien.** One of the exclusive features at their Café Fleuri is the "Chocolate Buffet." Cookies, brownies, cake, chocolate drinks, and fresh fruit with chocolate syrup are among the thirty chocolate desserts they serve. You can go back as many times as you want and fulfill all your chocoholic desires! And now stop. We could go on, but we want you to save room for our next tour.

Tour Sites

Aux Chocolats Ltd.
1221 Avenue de Lafayette
Lafayette Place
Boston, MA 02111
542-1151

J. Bildner & Sons
One Devonshire Place
Boston, MA 02109
367-1350

Boston Brownies
Faneuil Hall Marketplace
Quincy Market
Boston, MA 02109
227-8803

The Chocolate Dipper
200 State St.
Boston, MA 02109
439-0190

Confetti
Copley Plaza
100 Huntington Ave.
Boston, MA 02116
247-2883

Godiva Chocolatiers
Copley Plaza
100 Huntington Ave.
Boston, MA 02116
437-8490

Harbor Sweets
85 Leavitt St.
Salem, MA 01970
508-745-7468

Hotel Meridien
250 Franklin St.
Boston, MA 02110
451-1900

I Love Chocolate
52 Boylston St.
Brookline, MA 02146
734-LOVE

Lafayette Hotel
One Avenue de Lafayette
Boston, MA 02111
451-2600

Peanut Butter Fantasies
1 Faneuil Hall Marketplace
Boston, MA 02109
742-0928

Rudi's Bakery
1 Milk St.
Boston, MA 02109
542-8660
Also located at 1336 Beacon St.,
    Brookline, (232-2532).

Serendipity
120 Faneuil Hall Marketplace
Boston, MA 02109
523-2339

Sweet Stuff
353 Faneuil Hall Marketplace
Boston, MA 02109
227-7560

Sweet Temptations
Copley Plaza
100 Huntington Ave.
Boston, MA 02116
424-0605

Ice Cream Dream

Bostonians are as serious about their ice cream as Californians are about their tacos, and as opinionated about their preferences as New Yorkers are about their pastrami. Boston and Cambridge residents consume more ice cream per capita than residents of any other city in the United States. The stormy winters, oddly, don't seem to make that much of a difference. There's even a separate guidebook on the subject, *The Boston Ice Cream Lover's Guide*, by Eugene and Lori Kaufman.

Bear in mind that Massachusetts, with its reputation for idiosyncracy, has its own ice cream terminology. A milk shake here is strictly milk and syrup. If you want the ice cream added, ask for a frappe (or a frosty, or a Fribble, depending on which shop you're in). Sprinkles are called jimmies, and if you order a chocolate ice cream soda you'll get vanilla ice cream with chocolate syrup. To get all chocolate, ask for a double chocolate, a black cow, or a chocolate ice cream soda with chocolate ice cream.

But the true addict won't eat just any ice cream; only the pure and unadulterated is acceptable to the Boston-bred connoisseur. It also has to come in unusual flavors, so we can argue the relative merits of Herrell's Chocolate Pudding ice cream over J. P. Licks' Negative Chocolate Chip, and Ben & Jerry's Dastardly Mash.

For those watching their fat or calorie intake, frozen yogurt has taken hold throughout the ice cream community of Boston. There are still subtle distinctions between types of frozen yogurt; the many establishments we show you here offer a full variety.

If you are in search of the perfect scoop among Boston's many worthy establishments, we suggest you travel in a group of at least four, and only order one cone per place. Almost every shop on this tour makes it a practice to hand out tiny taste spoons of whatever strikes your fancy, so you *can* taste the alternatives.

There's no better place to begin an ice cream tour than in Coolidge Corner, Brookline, the real heart of Jewish Boston. Nestled between Jewish bakers, bookstores, Kosher meat markets, and delis, you'll find some of Boston's most exciting ice creameries. It can be reached on the Green Line C trolley.

The first stop, **TCBY,** is one of the best places for frozen yogurt. Six flavors each day, homemade wafflecones, and tofu flavors make this chain special. Just around the corner at Harvard Street you'll find a **Steve's.** Ice cream, frozen yogurt, and sorbet are all served here. A special machine mixes frozen fruit into the yogurt, and a trivia board endlessly amuses guests. Across the street is **J. P. Licks,** where you should ask for Vince, the owner, founder, flavor creator, and bookkeeper. Unusual flavors such as oatmeal cookie, wild blueberry, and chocolate macadamia abound here.

Once you finish your cone at the nearby playground on Harvard Avenue, it is a short walk down Beals Street to the John F. Kennedy Birthplace, where you can hear the voice of his mother, Rose, reminiscing about family life in Brookline. Those childhood memories may make you ready for some more ice cream or frozen yogurt, so take Beacon Street or hop the Green Line to Kenmore Square.

If you are looking for a Northeast chain that offers old-fashioned ice cream, the **White Mountain Creamery,** at 627 Commonwealth Avenue, is perfect. You can watch them make ice cream in the window, and eat a sandwich with your old-fashioned soda fountain drink. Their most famous item is the lime rickey, a dish with fresh limes in a cup, syrup, and fizz. Further down Commonwealth Avenue at number 472, **Luscious Licks Frozen Yogurt** caters to the health-conscious and college students. Thirty-five toppings each day and plenty of tables and chairs make this place popular with the locals.

Walk down Commonwealth Avenue or take the "T" one stop to Auditorium to **Steve's,** on Massachusetts Avenue at Newbury Street. By now the orange and blue cone logo should be familiar to many visitors, since Steve's has been successfully franchised all over the country. But few people know about the intense ice cream war waged over the original Steve's in nearby Somerville's Davis Square. Steve Herrell started that shop in 1973 and soon became locally famous for his great ice cream and unusual "mix-ins" (candies, nuts, or cookies mashed into the ice cream to order). Long lines of devotees waited in line outside and wound through the store, past the old player piano and award plaques, to pick up their huge cups of Chocobanana with Heath Bars, or Coffee Oreo with Reese's Pieces.

But in 1977, Herrell sold out to neighbor Joey Crugnale, whose nearby emporium, Joey's, wasn't doing as well. Steve went off to Northampton, Massachusetts, and Joey parlayed that one store into a franchise he later sold for a reputed $5 million. But Steve missed the Boston area, and in 1982, after losing a court battle to reopen as "The Original Steve's," he opened **Herrell's Ice**

Cream in Harvard Square. Both Herrell's and Joey's are now doing fine, although some contend that the Steve's franchises aren't as great as the original in Davis Square.

Across the street from Steve's and a short walk down Newbury Street is **Emack and Bolio's,** located in the front parlor of a Victorian townhouse. Emack and Bolio's was started in 1976 by two lawyers who represented rock bands, and was named after their first two clients. (No one knows what became of Emack and Bolio, but their names have become synonymous with gourmet ice cream in impeccable flavors.) The proprietors claim that they invented the now-ubiquitous Oreo ice cream, and certainly theirs is one of the best in the city, but they also make a terrific Chocolate Moose (their mascot), Apple Brown Betty ice cream, and great ice cream cakes. Their latest invention is a crunchy hand-rolled cone dipped in chocolate and coconut that is destined to go down in ice cream history.

It's time to move on to Copley Place, home of the upscale elegant shopping mall in the heart of Back Bay's Copley Square. If you're having an ice cream fit while waiting in line for the movies

or need to take a break from your shopping, then head for **Frusen Glädjé** on the second floor. There are lot of tables and chairs to rest your weary feet, and the unique specialty here is Dole Whip — a frozen fruit dessert with no cholesterol. A "Flurry" machine even mixes various toppings in with the frozen yogurt! Now that you've had the international flavors, let's head for a bit of Vermont in Boston.

Ben and Jerry's ice cream is made in Burlington, Vermont, but their product isn't exactly country simple — it's some of the most sophisticated ice cream around. The flavors, from an elegant berry sherbert to the most complex (like Kahlua Amaretto and Chocolate Mystic Mint) are extremely dense and powerful, heightened by the use of pure ingredients and slow processing. Ben and Jerry have been so successful that Pillsbury, which markets another premium ice cream, Häagen-Dazs, got nervous about the young ex–New York upstarts and tried to squeeze them out of their burgeoning retail market. To mobilize support and inform the public about the activities of the larger corporation, Ben and Jerry added the mischievous question, "What's the Doughboy [Pillsbury] afraid of?" on their containers, with a toll-free number to call for the answer. The two companies reached an agreement regarding distribution in 1984, and the slogan no longer appears on Ben and Jerry's containers. **Ben and Jerry's Ice Cream** at 20 Park Plaza has fabulous flavors, such as New York Super Fudge Chunk, That's Life Apple Pie, Sambuca Chocolate Chip, and Reverse Chocolate Chunk. They also sell T-shirts portraying their famous cows.

Michael's Frozen Yogurt on Charles Street caters to the health-conscious with tasty lowfat and nonfat flavors. After spending 1979 to 1983 as a frontline player for the Bruins hockey team, owner Michael Fidler opened this shop, one of the first frozen yogurt places in the actual city of Boston. Nestled among a variety of Charles Street restaurants, this shop is patronized by shoppers, diners, and residents alike. In fact, Michael says that many of his Beacon Hill neighbors come in for conversation more than for yogurt!

Il Dolce Momento, a slick urban café at 30 Charles Street, happens to serve exquisite semisoft and smooth gelati. Gelati, in case you've never been fortunate enough to try it, is Italian ice cream with an egg base. At Il Dolce Momento ("the sweet moment") you'll find gelati of every description, from the dense creamy hazelnut to the light kiwi "semifreddo." The more adventurous can even try carrot-flavored gelati, but it is definitely an acquired taste. Gelati has a shelf life of only one day. It melts quickly too, so eat up! Tomorrow's batch may be as good as today's — but it won't be the same.

For those among you who feel up to another stop, travel across the river on the MBTA's Red Line and get off at Kendall Square, near the Massachusetts Institute of Technology. MIT was the alma mater of one of the world's most famous ice cream impresarios. This fellow, who majored not in chemistry but in engineering, later went on to create an ice cream empire. His name was Howard Johnson.

You can end your tour at **Toscanini's,** a few blocks down Massachusetts Avenue in Cambridge. Named after a great classical composer who had nothing to do with ice cream, Toscanini's has an impressive flavor list (Orange Chocolate Chip, Coffee Macadamia Nut, Mango). Their vanilla recently tied for first place in a national taste test, but take an old Cantabrigian's advice and pray that you visit on a day when they've made their Vienna Finger Cookie flavor. You'll think you've died and gone to heaven — which may well be the case if you've overindulged on this tour.

For tomorrow, you can follow another complete ice cream tour at Faneuil Hall. You'll find **Steve's, Colombo Frozen Yogurt, Swenson's,** and **Italian Ices** in the Quincy Marketplace.

Tour Sites

Ben and Jerry's Ice Cream
20 Park Plaza
Boston, MA 02116
426-0890

Colombo Frozen Yogurt
Faneuil Hall Marketplace
Boston, MA 02109
227-2926

Emack and Bolio's
290 Newbury St.
Boston, MA 02116
247-8772
Other locations in the Boston
   area.

Frusen Glädjé
Copley Place, 2nd Floor
100 Huntington Ave.
Boston, MA 02109
262-5559

Herrell's Ice Cream
15 Dunster St.
Cambridge, MA 02138
497-2179
Other locations in the Boston
   area.

Il Dolce Momento
30 Charles St.
Boston, MA 02114
720-0477

Italian Ices
Fanueil Hall Marketplace
Boston, MA 02109

J. P. Licks Homemade
  Ice Cream Co.
311-A Harvard St.
Brookline, MA 02146
738-8252
Other locations in the Boston
  area.

Luscious Licks, Inc.
472 Commonwealth Ave.
Boston, MA 02215
437-0404
Other locations in the Boston
  area.

Michael's Frozen Yogurt
60 Charles St.
Boston, MA 02114
523-0933

Steve's Homemade Ice Cream
191 Elm St.
Somerville, MA 02143
776-4990
Other locations in the Boston
  area.

Swenson's
Faneuil Hall Marketplace
Boston, MA 02109
723-3635

TCBY
1328 Beacon St.
Brookline, MA 02146
734-3232
Other locations in the Boston
  area.

Toscanini's
899 Main St.
Cambridge, MA 02142
491-5877

White Mountain Creamery
627 Commonwealth Ave.
Boston, MA 02115
236-0212
Other locations in the Boston
  area.

Catch of the Day

Boston is often referred to as "Home of the Bean and the Cod." While the evolution of Boston as "Beantown" may not be obvious to the casual observer (beans were a staple in the early American diet and a main element of trade), there is very clear and present evidence of the cod's supremacy in this seaport city. Boston started out as a fishing port and still has the tang of the sea running deep in its lifeblood.

As a matter of fact, there is a gilded wooden memorial to the Commonwealth's long association and dependence on fish, hanging in the State House. "The Sacred Cod" was first hung in the Old State House in 1784. In 1895, wrapped in an American flag, the four-foot effigy was paraded to its new home in the House of Representatives. As a symbol of the wealth of the state, it is no longer relevant (perhaps it should be replaced with a microchip), but it still serves to indicate the power of the fecund Atlantic over this harbor city. The cod casts its doleful gaze north when the Democrats have control of the House, and south when the Republicans are in favor.

> *On every menu and in every fish market you'll find Boston scrod listed prominently. Although the stories vary widely as to the origin of the word, the explanation is quite simple. Scrod (or schrod) is the fisherman's term for young cod, haddock, or pollock, the most frequently caught fish in this area. The mnemonic device goes this way: if it's spelled with an "h," it's young haddock, otherwise it's cod. Of course, that doesn't take the poor pollock into account, nor does it explain the other spelling variations such as "shrod" or "scod." Just assume that it's young, fresh, white-fleshed fish and enjoy it.*

Not only have Bostonians long made their living by the sea, but they have long been fish eaters as well. Decades before the Irish Catholic immigration, which made fish on Friday a tradition, the Beacon Hill Brahmins used to serve the cheap and plentiful protein to their servants, saving the more costly beef and mutton for themselves. Few Bostonians escaped childhood without tasting codfish cakes, creamed cod, or the smoked haddock dish, finnan haddie. To this day, no real Yankee Fourth of July is considered complete without a dinner of poached salmon, boiled new potatoes, and green peas.

A word to the wise about chowder: when you order a bowl, make sure you don't ask for it Manhattan style. Patriotic Bostonian restauranteurs have been known to eject patrons who expect to eat the tomato-based "red stuff" instead of the one "true," cream-based chowder.

Plan to rise early for your Catch of the Day tour. The best and busiest time to visit the **Boston Fish Pier,** across the Northern Avenue bridge in South Boston, is shortly after 6 A.M., when the boats are just beginning to pull back into the harbor. The ornately arcaded Pier was opened for business in 1914 when Boston still had a fishing fleet berthed there. Despite the fact that much of the fleet has gone to other ports, such as Gloucester or New Bedford, the Pier is still a hotbed of activity.

Fish are sold directly off the boats via auction, with the wholesalers and retailers bidding together for boatloads of the product. The men work as efficiently as possible to get the fish off the boats and onto the refrigerated trucks without losing a moment's freshness. You're welcome to try your hand at bidding for a smaller portion, but a word of caution to the buyer: before you buy, ask the fishermen how long the boat has been at sea. A fish that's been sitting in the hold for a week, even on ice, obviously won't be as fresh as one hooked that day.

After you've viewed the hawkers and the sellers, the fishermen in their hip-high boots and the scavenging seagulls overhead, you can head back toward town. You'll be passing through a veritable seafood Hall of Fame, although it's not likely that anything will be open if you're as early as you should be.

Cherrystones has many claims to fame. Located on Boston Harbor in the waterfront park at Commercial Wharf, this is one of the few fish restaurants that will take reservations. Whether you come for the picturesque view or for the baked lobster, you'll be pleased with this friendly service attitude.

Anthony's Pier Four restaurant was made nationally famous through the efforts of Albanian owner Anthony Athanas, who used to offer cab drivers free meals in exchange for a recommendation. The restaurant is known for the fresh popovers and the corn-on-the-cob delivered to your table by colonial-garbed waiters.

At **Jimmy's Harborside,** owned and operated by the son of its Greek founder, the fish is fresh and there is a good view of the harbor and airport. Established in 1924 as a nine-stool cafeteria, the

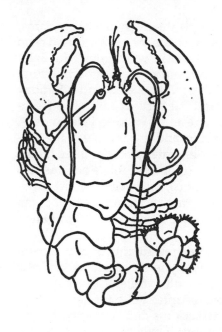

restaurant has evolved into a 550-seat gathering place for its loyal clientele and tourists alike. Note the lobster pool in the entrance hall, with its eight-pound inhabitants. For a family fish restaurant, **Jimbo's** is a good bet. Even the casual atmosphere is entertaining.

Another good choice is the **Daily Catch,** a tiny hole-in-the-wall North End restaurant that specializes in calamari, or squid, prepared in dozens of ways, all of them terrific. The Daily Catch even makes its own black squid-ink pasta, and their stuffed calamari is supreme. No reservations are taken, but you can enjoy chatting in line with other fish lovers. For a shorter wait, you might try their restaurant in Kendall Square.

Later in the day, walk along Atlantic Avenue until you come to the renowned **New England Aquarium.** The Aquarium is essentially a self-guided experience, so we'll leave you on your own here. But this is a perfect place from which to leave on a Whale Watch, an exciting trip out past Boston Harbor to see humpback and finback whales. The Aquarium sponsors two trips daily (between April and November only) leaving at 9 A.M. and 2 P.M., but other cruise lines offer whole and half-day trips as well. All the trips provide well-informed commentary on the vast whale lore of the North Atlantic, and most operators "practically guarantee" that you'll see at least two whales per trip. Some trips serve box lunches, but check beforehand. You may want to bring food along, as well as windbreakers and sunscreen.

If your appetite isn't sufficiently whetted after all this fish-gazing, head back under the elevated Southeast Expressway to Quincy Market. Your best bet here, if you want to go native, is to stop at the seafood bar and grille named the **Walrus and the Car-**

penter in the central market and sample their very fresh raw clams, oysters, and boiled shrimp, as well as steamers, mussels, and clam chowder. If there is a non–seafood lover in your group, the **Salty Dog,** a downstairs pub on the west end of that same building, offers the same fare, along with chargrilled steaks and a Sunday brunch. The **Seaside Restaurant and Bar** serves four to five fresh-caught items daily. The decor has a restored historical elegance. A lunch guest can order bountiful salads, and if you come in the evening, there is a full-service lounge with entertainment three nights a week. The **Fisherman's Net** is noted for fried foods such as fish and chips, fried shrimp, clams, scallops, and various fried sandwiches. This is a stand-up or take-away restaurant, but you can take your food and sit in the rotunda outside or walk and shop while you eat.

At **Durgin-Park,** you'll find three restaurants in one. Downstairs is the traditional raw bar where you sit on stools, and the first floor houses the seafood grille with excellent lunch specials where you can try Indian pudding or coffee Jell-o for dessert. Upstairs, you'll find red checkered tablecloths and bentwood chairs. This floor is refurbished each year, but inevitably stays the same. Originally, butchers and fishermen would bring their own food and the cooks at Durgin-Park would prepare it for them.

President John F. Kennedy was a regular patron of the **Union Oyster House,** and Louis-Philippe, future King of France, once lived upstairs and taught French. The longest continuously operating restaurant in the United States, the Union Oyster House has excellent clam chowder and a popular Oyster Bar.

From Faneuil Hall you can cross back over to Waterfront Park and then head down Commercial Street to the fifty-year-old **Bay State Lobster Company.** You can buy from the huge retail fish counter — forty feet of display area, one quarter of it for shellfish alone! The wholesale operation ships thousands of pounds of Maine lobster per week all over the world, making it the country's largest distributor.

No tour of Boston's seafood establishments would be complete without three fine hotel restaurants. In the Westin Hotel at Copley Place you'll find **Turner Fisheries,** which has won the Boston Chowderfest prize for best chowder since it first entered the annual contest in 1984. In 1986, Turner Fisheries was retired to the Chowderfest Hall of Fame so that other restaurants would have the opportunity to gain recognition for outstanding chowder. The menus are printed with new prices daily.

Then head for the Park Plaza Hotel, home of **Legal Sea Foods.** Owner George Berkowitz, whose original market-cum-restaurant first opened in Cambridge's Inman Square in 1950, says he got the name from his father's Harry's Legal Cash Market, which already had a neighborhood reputation for quality and fair dealing. Legal has become a local institution, now in several locations and much fancier than the original communal-style eatery. Try the steamed dishes. Vegetables are cooked with the fish (shrimp, clams, or scrod), and the mixed juices give a flavor that can't be duplicated. Legal has run a mail-order business for several years now, to satiate the cravings of Bostonians who have moved to other shores. They can ship lobsters or a live clambake virtually anywhere, and their famous fish chowder was served during President Reagan's inaugural week festivities. The Legal motto says it all: "If it isn't fresh, it isn't Legal." You'll find the same quality fare in a low-key environment at their Cambridge location.

A nautical ambiance and a nice quiet atmosphere await you at the **Massachusetts Bay Company** of the Sheraton Hotel. The all-wood interior is similar to the inside of a boat, and you can eat your chowder at the bar. Not only do they serve fish broiled and baked, they are known for their mesquite and pasta specials.

Another seafood restaurant in the Back Bay is **Skipjack's Seafood Emporium.** This attractive, upscale eatery is part of the beautiful New England Life complex, which houses Bonwit Teller, Talbots, Eddie Bauer, and other designer shops. Skipjack's is also known for a fabulous Sunday jazz brunch.

If you feel like experiencing a clambake afloat, try the *Spirit of Boston* Lobster Clambake Luncheons, which depart from Rowes Wharf and feature entertainment and food for up to six hundred guests.

Now that we've shown you where to see, buy, and eat fresh seafood in Boston, the only thing left for you to do is go catch your own. There are very strict rules about lobstering, so we don't recommend trying that. But the omnipresent anglers, fishing from the bridges and wharves for hours on end, imply that there is still a good free lunch available in Boston. And if the old adage that fish is good brain food is true, we couldn't have brought you to a more appropriate conclusion. Our next tour deals with some of the great literary minds whose presence is still felt in Beantown.

Tour Sites

Anthony's Pier Four
140 Northern Ave.
Boston, MA 02210
423-6363

Bay State Lobster Company
395 Commercial St.
Boston, MA 02109
523-4588

Cherrystones of Boston
100 Atlantic Ave.
Boston, MA 02110
367-0300

Daily Catch
323 Hanover St.
Boston, MA 02113
523-8567
Also located at 1 Kendall Square,
   Cambridge (225-2300).

Durgin-Park
340 Faneuil Hall Marketplace
Boston, MA 02109
227-2038
Also located at Copley Place
(266-1964).

Fisherman's Net
Quincy Market
Faneuil Hall Marketplace
Boston, MA 02109
742-2872

Jimbo's Fish Shanty
245 Northern Ave.
Boston, MA 02210
542-5600

Jimmy's Harborside Restaurant
248 Northern Ave.
Boston, MA 02210
423-1000

Legal Sea Foods
Statler Office Building
27 Columbus Ave.
Boston, MA 02116
426-5566
Other locations in the Boston
   area.

Massachusetts Bay Company
39 Dalton St.
Sheraton Hotel
Boston, MA 02199
236-8787

New England Aquarium
Central Wharf
Atlantic Ave.
Boston, MA 02110
742-8870

The Salty Dog
Faneuil Hall Marketplace
Boston, MA 02109
742-2094

Seaside Restaurant and Bar
South Market Building
Faneuil Hall Marketplace
Boston, MA 02109
742-8728

Skipjack's Seafood Emporium
500 Boylston St.
Boston, MA 02116
536-3500

Spirit of Boston
Rowes Wharf
Individuals: 569-4449
Groups: 569-6867

Turner Fisheries Restaurant
10 Huntington Ave.
Boston, MA 02116
424-7425

Union Oyster House
41 Union St.
Boston, MA 02108
227-2750

CHAPTER FOUR

Booklovers' Boston

Boston is a city of booklovers. If it's been printed, it's not only been read in Boston, but probably reviewed, critiqued, annotated — or banned.

The Boston area is filled with bookstores of all shapes and sizes; in fact, there are more bookstores per square mile in Cambridge than in any other city in America. Boston also has the greatest number of used-book stores, which bears witness as much to an enduring love for the printed word as to our famed Yankee frugality. Our many libraries, both public and private, as well as literary events of every description, are always well attended in the "Athens of America."

A lot of Boston's bibliophilia is due to its extraordinary concentration of colleges and universities. The annual student population is well over two hundred thousand for Boston and Cambridge alone, and sometimes it's hard to find a Bostonian who's not a student of one sort or another. But even the nonstudents hold their city's literary tradition in high esteem. It sometimes seems the entire population has either just read a book, is deeply engrossed in one, or is writing his or her own.

We've divided this chapter into three tours, each one covering a specific geographic area. The first tour covers Boston from the downtown area up Beacon Hill to Charles Street, and the second covers the city west of Charles Street. The third covers Cambridge, which, for this subject area, was impossible to omit. In each, we take a look at some of Boston's literary lions, past and present — where they lived, worked, and met to share ideas. We'll look at some of the venerable institutions that house their work, and some of the more interesting bookstores where that work can be purchased. We'll also look at some of the publishing houses that printed the efforts of those authors, sometimes amidst much public outcry and dismay, as well as glance at the newspaper industry whose history is so completely interwoven with the city itself.

Literary Lions

At the corner of Washington and School Streets, in the heart of old downtown Boston, is the **Globe Corner Bookstore.** This handsome brick building, with its uncommon gambrel roof, houses a wonderful selection of books about Boston and New England, for both adults and children, with a large travel section on the second floor. The building's history is at least as impressive as its inventory. The location was the original site of Anne Hutchinson's house in the 1630s, before she was banished for her heretical ways. The place first became known as the Old Corner Bookstore in 1829, when a man named Timothy Carter opened his shop there, but it was William Ticknor and James Fields who, some years later, brought it to prominence as a bookselling/publishing firm bearing their names.

Ticknor and Fields were the original publishers of the *Atlantic Monthly* and the first, it is said, to pay royalties to their authors. The company published such luminaries as Longfellow, Holmes, Whittier, Emerson, Harriet Beecher Stowe, Hawthorne, Thoreau, and Mark Twain. (The editors, however, failed to recognize the genius of Walt Whitman, whom they refused as "unpublishable.") Many of these writers frequented the store themselves and could be heard declaiming to one another (or anyone else who would listen) about their work.

In recent times, the store came perilously close to demolition until in 1960 a group of concerned citizens raised money to buy the 1711 building. After it was restored, the *Boston Globe* newspaper used it as office space and opened the Globe Corner Bookstore in 1982.

One block south on Washington Street, at the corner of Milk Street, in the basement of the historic Old South Meeting House of 1729, is **Goodspeed's Book Shop,** full of antiquarian treasures such as old maps, books, and prints. The store has a copy of a volume of poetry by Phyllis Wheatley, who was America's first published black woman poet. The church itself is a stop on the Freedom Trail (see page 16), so don't forget to go upstairs and see it.

Back out on Washington Street is something you can't actually see, but can easily imagine if you stand looking north. This area was once called "Newspaper Row," since all five of Boston's major papers had their homes here until the area buildings burned in the Great Fire of 1872. At the time, all five papers were fiercely competitive and used to vie with one another for the latest headlines, which were hung on strips of paper outside the office door. Young Bostonians used to run back and forth from the *Globe* to the *Post*, past the *Transcript* to the *Record American's* offices, and over to the *Herald*. The paper that was able to provide the latest score for the Red Sox game being played across town at Fenway Park got the most avid delivery boys to distribute its editions.

> *There has been a great debate as to whether Pi Alley should be spelled "Pi" or "Pie." One school holds that the alley was called "Pie" because of a well-known coffee shop there, Thompson's Spa, that advertised "coffee and . . .". The other, and more popular version, holds that the alley (and Thompson's) was frequented by printers from Newspaper Row. These fellows, who worked with small pieces of lead-mixed print known as "pi" (the Greek letter), always had tiny pieces of type left in their pockets, and these pieces were constantly falling to the ground as they made their way between Thompson's and their jobs on Newspaper Row — hence, Pi Alley.*

Between Washington and Tremont Street near Park Street is a tiny place known as Pi Alley, the original home of the Bell in Hand from the 1820s until Prohibition (see page 65).

If you continue down Tremont Street to West Street you'll find another Boston booklovers' institution — a stop that has become something of a pilgrimage for bibliophiles. The **Brattle Book Shop,** at 9 West Street, has roots that go back to 1825, and its long-time proprietor George Gloss could be counted on to tell fascinating literary stories and facts about every year. Sadly, Mr. Gloss died in 1985 after thirty-five years with the store, but his son Kenneth can recount much of his father's verbal history, including the seven relocations and two major fires that brought the Brattle to where it stands today. The firm, which specializes in used and rare books and autographs, currently occupies a three-story building. Weather permitting, they daily place over 2000 books outdoors for sale at $1 apiece, a bargain in anyone's book.

While you're on West Street, stop in at number 15 at **Cornucopia,** a restaurant with a literary history as varied as its cosmopolitan menu. The building was home to the Peabody family from 1840 to 1854, and daughter Elizabeth opened a bookstore in the front parlor, which was to become the first in the nation to offer works by foreign authors. With her good friend Ralph Waldo Emerson, Elizabeth Peabody also published *The Dial*, a quarterly periodical of transcendentalist poets, and her lecture series on Wednesday afternoons became landmarks in the history of American feminism.

Elizabeth wasn't the house's only literary connection. In the rear parlor of the building, her sister Sophia married Nathaniel Hawthorne in 1842, and her sister Mary married Horace Mann the following year. Kristine Fayerman-Piatt, the proprietor of Cornucopia, will be glad to relate the family history to you as you enjoy her novel cuisine.

Backtrack up Tremont Street to the **Omni Parker House Hotel,** "the oldest continuously operating hotel in America," on the corner of Tremont and School Streets. The hotel's dining room, now known as Parker's, is chock full of literary history. Among those who dined on Parker House rolls (named for this establishment) were a group of intellectuals and writers who called themselves "The Saturday Club" (because of their practice of meeting at the hotel on the last Saturday of every month). Members included Ralph Waldo Emerson, poets Henry Wadsworth Longfellow, Oliver Wendell Holmes, Sr., and John Greenleaf Whittier, and novelists Richard Henry Dana, Nathaniel Hawthorne, and Charles Francis Adams. The Saturday Club met in a private dining room of the restaurant, where they shared literary gossip, poetry readings, opinions of new books, and seven-course meals!

Another group with many of the same members, called "The Magazine," met at Parker's to plan the founding of a new literary magazine, *The Atlantic Monthly*. The first issue appeared in 1859, and the journal soon became the most prestigious of its kind. It has been published continuously in Boston ever since.

In 1867, the British novelist Charles Dickens stayed at the Parker House and gave readings from his work at the nearby Tremont Temple. Dickens's immense popularity at the time had endowed him with celebrity status — so much so that the hotel had to keep a guard outside his door to fend off curious fans and autograph hunters. Inside his sitting room at the hotel, in front of a large and ornate mirror, Dickens rehearsed his performance. The mirror and an accompanying plaque now hang at the end of a corridor on the mezzanine level. On the same floor, the marble mantelpiece from Dickens's suite graces a conference room named after the writer. In fact, all of the conference rooms are named after famous writers or politicians.

In more recent history, John F. Kennedy announced his 1960 presidential bid in the Parker House Press Room. Once President, he used the Parker House facilities for various functions. The Kennedys still frequent the Omni Parker House, and other well-known guests have been John Wilkes Booth, Hopalong Cassidy, and Joan Crawford. Malcolm X worked as a waiter at Parker's, and it is rumored that Ho Chi Minh worked in the kitchen.

The Omni Parker House has begun a public memorabilia campaign to collect memorabilia from past guests of the hotel. Such mementos have included a 1919 Christmas menu, a Parker House handblown vase dated from 1860 to 1880, books, pictures, postcards, and menu covers. The Omni Parker House plans to continue the program indefinitely.

Outside the Parker House hotel and across Tremont Street is the King's Chapel Burial Ground (see pages 17–18), the oldest in

America. Although no famous colonial authors can be found there, the cemetery is the site for a famous literary inspiration. Elizabeth Swain, said to have been the source for Nathaniel Hawthorne's Hester Prynne in *The Scarlet Letter*, lies buried here. In the nearby Old Granary Burial Ground (see page 18) another literary heroine, of quite another sort, lies interred. Etched into an old stone are the words: "Here lies Mary Goose, wife of Isaac Goose." Although scholars dispute Mary's title as author of those famous nursery rhymes, schoolchildren from all over the world seem to feel that the ground is especially hallowed because of her humble presence. The actual Mother Goose was named Elizabeth, who in 1715 married Isaac Vergoose, a widower with ten children. After producing ten more of her own, she had her hands full keeping them quiet. It is said her creative tales, later written down by her son-in-law Tichnor, did the trick.

From the Burial Ground you can see the rear of our next stop, the Boston Athenaeum. But as you go up Park Street, stop at number 1, the home of **Houghton Mifflin Company**'s editorial offices since 1880. Houghton Mifflin dates its origins back to 1852, when William Ticknor and James Fields began an association with Cambridge printer Henry Houghton. The two companies merged and became known as Houghton Mifflin and Company in 1880, adding Mifflin, another publisher, and absorbing Ticknor and Fields.

The house had (and still has) an educational department that produced paperbound American literature classics in the 1930s which, at 15 cents a copy, were the precursors of modern paperback publishing. Their literary division has published, among others, Willa Cather, Henry James, Kate Douglas Wiggins, who wrote *Rebecca of Sunnybrook Farm*, and H. A. Rey, of *Curious George* fame. Contemporary authors include Roger Tory Peterson, Margaret Atwood, Tracy Kidder, Louis Auchincloss, David MacAuley, Jane Goodall, John Kenneth Galbraith, and Pat Conroy.

At the top of Park Street, facing the golden dome of the State House, turn right and go to number 10½ Beacon Street, the main entrance to the **Boston Athenaeum.** The Athenaeum is a private library founded in 1807 that reflects the patrician elegance and eccentricity of the proper Bostonians it has served for generations. It is a place of oriental carpets and rare antiques, but smoking and dogs are permitted. It is a place to which, at first glance, membership seems most restricted. The actual ownership is divided into 1049 shares, the last of which was issued in the 1850s. All of the shares can be traced back to their original owners, some of them illustrious, all of them Brahmin. But owning a share is not the only way to gain access to this Beacon Hill institution. The Athenaeum welcomes visitors to the first and second floors of the 1840s building, and free guided tours are given on certain days of the week.

During the Athenaeum's early development, great emphasis was placed on art collecting. The library's early efforts in that direction, in fact, paved the way for the Museum of Fine Arts. An art gallery is still maintained on the second floor, and monthly exhibitions range from shows of nineteenth-century American glass to displays of contemporary silversmiths.

According to director Rodney Armstrong, the Athenaeum has a healthy attitude about its collection. Most of the library's books are on accessible shelves, and the art treasures are open to view and use. "If we have an antique chair, we'll sit on it," he says. "If we have an oriental rug, we'll walk on it." The library boasts a fine collection of history, biography, English, American, and gypsy literature, as well as the world's largest collection of Confederate imprints, and volumes from George Washington's private library. The genteel shabbiness of the Athenaeum is encouraged, deemed more conducive to constructive thought. Repairs made in 1962 to the brownstone façade were done so carefully that then-director Walter Muir Whitehill was asked why the façade had been screened for several months, then uncovered without anything having been done to the building!

As you return to Beacon Street, cross over to Bowdoin Street where, at number 22, you can see the house where John Fitzgerald Kennedy lived in 1947 while a member of the House of Representatives. An interesting literary legend has grown up around Kennedy. It is said that he read extensively, but had no library of his own. The knowledge in the books was precious, not the possession of them. He read paperbacks, and instead of marking his place with a marker, he simply tore out the pages he had already read!

Back on Beacon Street, head down the Hill (although the numbers will be going up). This street could well be Boston's most literary thoroughfare. It was home to Julia Ward Howe, Oliver Wendell Holmes, philosopher George Santayana, and transplanted midwesterner William Dean Howells, who once wrote to Henry James, "Sometimes I feel it an extraordinary thing that I should have been able to buy a house on Beacon Hill."

At number 22 is the Bellevue apartment building where Louisa May Alcott kept a city flat away from her Concord home. The gracious twin Greek revival bowfronts of numbers 39 and 40 housed, respectively, Fanny Appleton, who married Longfellow in her front parlor, and Daniel Parker of the Parker House. Number 40 is now the headquarters for the **Women's City Club.** Founded in 1913, the City Club today draws booklovers to its well-known Boston Literary Hour series, sponsored by the Globe Corner Bookstore. The events begin with cocktails, followed by an author lecture and informal autographing. Past guests have included Roger Tory Peterson, Joan Didion, Paul Theroux, Rosalyn Carter, and, more recently, Maxine Hong Kingston, Sara Lawrence Lightfoot, and Tracy Kidder.

The 1825 mansion at number 34 is the headquarters of **Little, Brown and Company,** established in 1837. At first, copublishers Charles C. Little and James Brown focused on British imports, but as the business grew, so did their interest in American authors. By the latter half of the nineteenth century, the firm was publishing American western historian Francis Parkman (who lived on Beacon Hill himself), John Bartlett's *Familiar Quotations*, and Fanny Farmer's blockbuster, *The Boston Cooking School Cookbook*. The purchase of a list from another publisher brought in authors like Emily Dickinson, Edward Everett Hale, and Louisa May Alcott. The company moved to its current address in 1909 from Washington Street and kept a retail bookstore here until the early 1920s. In this century, Little, Brown's list reads like the Who's Who of American and European letters: Erich Maria Remarque, Samuel Eliot Morison, J. D. Salinger, Ogden Nash, Evelyn Waugh, A. J. Cronin, and Peter De Vries, many of them published under the joint Little, Brown/ Atlantic Monthly imprint, which was established in 1925.

Number 55 was the home of William Prescott, the famed historian who wrote of the early Mexican and Peruvian civilizations in the middle of the nineteenth century. Blinded from an accident while a student at Harvard, Prescott developed a system for reading and writing that preceded Braille, and went on to live a full and illuminating life. The house is also known as the Colonial

Dames House, because it is owned by a club of that same name, whose members can trace their ancestry back to the American Revolution.

By now you might be ready for a good read, so head for **Barnes and Noble** discount bookstore at Downtown Crossing. There you will find two floors of discount books, including best-sellers and current fiction, children's books, and a generous selection of fiction and nonfiction.

In its new location in the Architects Building at 50 Broad Street, the **Architectural Book Shop** carries a broad range of books on the architecture of Boston and New England, books to help you with your next building project or decorating scheme, along with architecturally inspired gifts. Take the *AIA Guide to Boston* in hand to do a complete architectural tour of Boston. Another special collection, a must for gardeners, is a little-known bookstore where you'll find the best selection of horticulture books in the city. The **Massachusetts Horticultural Society Bookstore,** at 300 Massachusetts Avenue, is an ideal place to browse and dream about the springtime during the dead cold of winter.

Tour Sites

The Architectural Book Shop
50 Broad St.
Boston, MA 02109
262-2727

Brattle Book Shop
9 West St.
Boston, MA 02111
542-0210

Barnes and Noble Discount
  Bookstore
Downtown Crossing
Boston, MA 02116
426-5502

Globe Corner Bookstore
3 School St.
Boston, MA 02108
523-6658

Boston Athenaeum
10½ Beacon St.
Boston, MA 02108
227-0270

Goodspeed's Book Shop
7 Beacon St.
Boston, MA 02108
523-5970

Houghton Mifflin Company
1 Beacon St.
Boston, MA 02108
725-5000

Little, Brown and Company
34 Beacon St.
Boston, MA 02108
227-0730

Massachusetts Horticultural
 Society Bookstore
300 Massachusetts Ave.
Boston, MA 02115
536-9280

Women's City Club
40 Beacon St.
Boston, MA 02108
227-3550

RESTAURANTS

Cornucopia
15 West St.
Boston, MA 02111
338-4600

Omni Parker House Hotel
60 School St.
Boston, MA 02108
227-8600

Book Routes

Charles Street is our imaginary (and arbitrary) dividing line between tours. Not only is it a haven for booklovers, you can also satisfy your culinary taste here. For example, look no further than **Paramount Restaurant,** an institution on the hill if you want good food at a reasonable price. There is a variety of Greek, mideastern, and American food at any time of day in this self-service restaurant. You may rub elbows with a politician from any level of government or a professor from one of the local colleges, and most Beacon Hill residents have eaten there at one time or another.

Once you have stopped at the windows of **Rebecca's** to watch a meal being made, you will find it difficult to resist going inside to eat in this fern-filled, brick-walled restaurant. The food is French-influenced continental style, with a menu that ranges from appetizers to ligher fare and entrées. You can also stop at **DeLuca's Market** for carry-out, and picnic on the Boston Common. If you have children with you, a copy of *As I Was Walking on Boston Com-*

mon by Norma Farber or *Make Way for Ducklings* by Robert Mc-
Closkey (see below) make for relevant reading while you lunch in
this oldest American public park.

Once you get to the corner of Beacon and Charles Streets,
head north on Charles. This is another literary neighborhood. Both
publishers Ticknor and Fields lived here; Fields's mother hosted
renowned literary soirées. Contemporary literary lights of the
neighborhood include James Carroll and Robin Cook, who lives in
nearby Louisburg Square.

Opposite to where Fields once lived, a Thai chef uses the
freshest ingredients to prepare Thai food at **The King and I** restaurant. At 42 Charles Street you will find an improvisational approach to Italian cooking at the **Bel Canto Restaurant.** Use your
own imagination to design a thick pan pizza from a variety of fresh
ingredients or try a calzone, which consists of dough wrapped
around a filling and slow-baked. Although the restaurant is rather
small, the menu is large and varied. Once you have almost had
your fill of food at these neighborhood restaurants, stop for a rest
and treat yourself to some delicious gelati (Italian ice cream), a cup
of cappuccino, or a homemade pastry at **Il Dolce Momento.** Linger
a while for a soup, salad, or sandwich and taste the flavor of Italy
on a corner of Beacon Hill.

Having followed the trail of famous authors who lived on
"the Hill," pop into the **Book Store** at 76 Chestnut Street to find
out what present-day residents are reading. Be sure to duck your
head as you enter through the narrow alleyway to the shop that is
presumptuous enough to call itself by such a straightforward
name. Inside, the shop is cozy and has an excellent children's
section.

Filling the back of the shop that he shares with Sher-Morr
Antiques at 82 Charles Street, Ernie Morrell has collected used
books on the performing arts, with a special emphasis on dance,
in a space most fittingly called **ChoreoGraphica.** Fortunately, the
store is open seven days a week, and you can browse to your
heart's content among these books and those on many other subjects. If you want to extend your travels in New England or improve your garden, **Lauriat's,** right down the street at number 20,
is the place to find just the right book. Current fiction and nonfiction also fill this bright and spacious store.

Across Charles Street from the Common is the lovely Public

Garden, a romantic and elegant counterpoint to the Common's populist spread. It was also the home of Mr. and Mrs. Mallard and their eight little ducklings, made famous by Robert McCloskey's immortal *Make Way for Ducklings*. Cross the Garden diagonally, making a stop if you like to ride the Swan Boats on the Lagoon (see pages 200–201).

Number 20 Boylston Street, which borders the Garden on the west side, is the home of several notable monthly magazines. *The Writer* magazine, established in 1887, calls itself "the pioneer magazine for literary workers," and its articles focus on practical techniques for authors. *Plays*, published by the same company, is a drama magazine for young people.

The illustrious *Atlantic Monthly*, at 745 Boylston Street, is the renowned literary and public affairs periodical founded in 1857 by that splinter group of the Saturday Club, which met at the Parker House. Ever since, the magazine has tried to adhere to its original purpose of "concentrating the efforts of the best writers upon literature and politics under the light of the highest morals." The magazine's first editor was poet James Russell Lowell. Succeeding him were William Dean Howells and Thomas Bailey Aldrich. Over the years, the magazine, considered a citadel in the literary barrenness of the New World, has published the works of such luminaries as Emily Dickinson, Nathaniel Hawthorne, and Harriet Beecher Stowe. Other writers on their roster include Ernest Hemmingway, Susan Sontag, John Sayles, and James Fowler.

The **Arlington Street Church,** on the corner of Boylston Street, is worth a look not only because of its architecture but because it was home base for the Reverend William E. Channing, who espoused early abolitionist causes and invited Harriet Beecher Stowe and William Lloyd Garrison to read their antislavery treatises to his congregation. One block north on Arlington Street, on the corner of Newbury Street, is the

grande dame of Boston hotels, the **Ritz-Carlton.** Authors too numerous to mention have stayed here while on literary tours. E. B. White was inspired to write a marvelous children's book called *The Trumpet of the Swan*, in which the swan actually spends a night in a Ritz bathtub.

Continuing down Newbury Street, you'll find the **New England Historic Genealogical Society** at number 99. Founded in 1845, the NEHGS is the nation's oldest and largest nonprofit organization devoted to the preservation of family and community records and the promotion of genealogical research. With a library of two hundred thousand family and town histories, city directories, and other documents, the NEHGS is *the* place for sleuthing into the mysteries of New England family histories. Access to the archives is free to members: visitors can use them for a fee. For a rare treat, turn off Newbury Street to 234 Clarendon and go up to the second floor shop of **David L. O'Neal–Antiquarian Booksellers, Inc.** In addition to the manuscripts from the thirteenth century and modern first editions, there are fine leather bindings and sets and original historical and decorative European and American prints.

Now we arrive at the great **Boston Public Library,** which can be reached either by the Green Line subway from Arlington to Copley, or by walking down Boylston Street to the block between Dartmouth and Exeter Streets. The BPL identifies itself as "the first free public city library in America." It was established in 1848 and moved to its present location in Copley Square in 1895. The Central Library houses more than 5.4 million books and 17 million items in other formats; it comprises the Research Library and the General Library.

The Research Library building, a National Historic Landmark, is a treasure-house of neoclassical art and decoration with murals, sculpture, paintings, and a beautiful courtyard. Artists such as John Singer Sargent, Louis and Augustus Saint-Gaudens, Puvis de Chavannes, and Edwin Austin Abbey collaborated with architect Charles Follen McKim to fashion this building into a place of exceptional beauty. The General Library building, opened in 1972, was designed by nationally renowned architect Philip Johnson. In addition to the General Library, the building houses the Community Library Services Office, which oversees the activities of the BPL's twenty-five neighborhood libraries.

A good place to start your tour is at the Research Library's entrance on Dartmouth Street. Note that the mosaic ceiling inside the Dartmouth Street entrance is decorated with a vine-covered trellis and inscribed with the names of illustrious New Englanders, including Adams, Emerson, Franklin, Hawthorne, Longfellow, and Pierce.

Puvis de Chavannes's murals of the cycle of Arcadian allegories adorn the walls of the Grand Staircase's upper flight and the second corridor. Adjoining the Chavannes vestibule, you will find the book delivery room. American artist Edwin Austin Abbey's Arthurian cycle of murals entitled the *Quest of the Holy Grail* graces the eight-foot frieze. Abbey (1852–1911) designed this room as a setting for the colorful medieval romance.

In the main reading room, Bates Hall, there are white marble busts representing great authors and eminent Bostonians. A long corridor on the third floor of the library houses the religious murals of John Singer Sargent, who devoted thirty years to the inspired panels on Judaism and Christianity. Sargent (1856–1925) looked upon his mural decorations as the supreme achievement of his career. On the third floor, you can also visit the Print Department's Wiggin Gallery and the Rare Books and Manuscripts Department, both of which offer ongoing exhibits.

From the third floor you can take the elevator in the Music Department to the first floor of the General Library building, where a visit to the current exhibitions in the Great Hall and the Boston Room will be worthwhile. The Rabb Lecture Hall, located in the General Library building, has frequent film and lecture programs; check the schedule for the latest.

Flyers provide interpretations of the works of art within its walls, and the library's 1977 publication, *A Handbook to the Art and Architecture of the Boston Public Library*, is an excellent guide. Before leaving, don't miss the opportunity to stop for a rest in the courtyard, which is modeled after an arcade in the Palazzo della Cancellaria in Rome.

If you didn't bring a bag lunch to eat in the library's courtyard, go around the corner to Newbury Street and stop at the **Harvard Bookstore Café.** This combination bookstore and restaurant is a favorite of local writers such as James Carroll and John Updike, when he is in town. In warm weather, the outdoor tables are especially nice for lunches, and the Café, in collaboration with the

BPL, sponsors literary soirées that celebrate the publication of new titles by local writers and others such as Susan Sontag, Margaret Atwood, Arthur Miller, and Bobbie Ann Mason. The store even puts out a monthly newsletter, *The Envoy,* which reports on literary activities in the area.

After a meal, and before heading farther west, you might want to stroll down Commonwealth Avenue Mall, that eminently Victorian promenade that runs from Arlington Street to Massachusetts Avenue one block north of Newbury Street (see page 53). At number 199 is the St. Botolph Club, a private literary and arts club for "men of letters." John Updike is a member, as were Robert Frost and naval historian Samuel Eliot Morison, whose book *One Boy's Boston* is a charming account of what it was like to grow up in the city at the turn of the century. Morison's statue, erected in 1982, stands outside the club on the promenade. He is wearing a raincoat and sitting on a rock in a casual contemporary pose that contrasts sharply with the elegant formality of the Victorian statuary that graces the rest of the Mall.

Buddenbrooks Back Bay Booksmith, opposite the Prudential Center at 753 Boylston Street, stocks a wide selection of new books. It is unique in also carrying rare and antique books and first editions. They will search for out-of-print books and complete special orders. Right down the street at 607 Boylston is another **Barnes and Noble** discount bookstore where you can find best-sellers, current fiction, and nonfiction.

The place to find a Spenser book is at **Spenser's Mystery Bookshop,** at 314 Newbury Street. The large selection of mystery books is supplemented by some science fiction and general literature. In this high-ceilinged basement space are paperbacks from the 1940s that have become collectibles, with their garish and colorful cover art. You can browse in the **Avenue Victor Hugo Bookshop,** at 339 Newbury Street, a booklover's dream, but the challenge comes when you try to leave without buying a book from the tempting array of science fiction, mystery books, and popular fiction. At the very least, a back issue of *Life* or a postcard of a writer or jazz musician may tempt you. At the far end of Newbury Street, at 338, is the **Trident Booksellers and Café,** where you may browse through the large selection of paperback books on Eastern religions, New Age topics, and other philosophies. They also carry alternative fiction from the small presses. When your energy flags, refresh yourself with a selection from their eclectic sandwich menu or indulge in a freshly baked dessert.

Continuing west, you can wander at will through the Back Bay's orderly array of streets and stop at some of the area's many bookstores (see listing on page 106). Then you can take the Green Line from Auditorium Station (at Massachusetts Avenue and Boylston Street) to Kenmore Square, home of the **Boston University Bookstore,** New England's largest bookstore. The BU Bookstore carries an extensive collection of books in print and will be able to help you find that hard-to-locate book you've been wanting to get your hands on. The Bookstore carries clothing, stationery, housewares, souvenirs, as well as books, and also has a lovely little café on the premises, which serves a variety of coffees, light selections, and homemade desserts.

> *Spenser, the tough-talking detective hero of Robert B. Parker's books, frequents the Harvard Bookstore Café in the novel* Ceremony.

Farther down Commonwealth Avenue, at number 771, is the **Mugar Library** of Boston University. The Mugar has a massive special collection, most of which is open to the public. BU was one of the first academic institutions to systematically collect the papers of contemporary public figures, and its twentieth-century archives contain the papers and memorabilia of more than a thousand interesting people, both well known and of lesser renown. The library holds many works by and about Theodore Roosevelt, Martin Luther King, Jr., Abraham Lincoln, Franz Liszt, and Bette Davis. There is also an exhaustive collection of Robert Frost memorabilia, in a special room, and poetry lovers will find the changing public display of his material fascinating to browse through.

Tour Sites

Arlington Street Church
351 Boylston St.
Boston, MA 02116
536-7050

Boston Public Library
666 Boylston St.
Boston, MA 02116
536-5400

Boston University Bookstore
660 Beacon St.
Boston, MA 02215
267-8484

Mugar Memorial Library
Boston University
771 Commonwealth Ave.
Boston, MA 02215
353-3708

New England Historic
  Genealogical Society
101 Newbury St.
Boston, MA 02116
536-5740

RESTAURANTS

Bel Canto Restaurant
42 Charles St.
Boston, MA 02114
523-5577

DeLuca's
11 Charles St.
Boston, MA 02114
523-4343
Also located at 239 Newbury St.
  (262-5990).

Harvard Bookstore Café
190 Newbury St.
Boston, MA 02116
536-0095

Il Dolce Momento
30 Charles St.
Boston, MA 02114
720-0477

The King and I Restaurant
145 Charles St.
Boston, MA 02114
227-3320

Paramount Restaurant
44 Charles St.
Boston, MA 02114
523-8832

Rebecca's
21 Charles St.
Boston, MA 02114
742-9747

Ritz-Carlton Hotel
15 Arlington St.
Boston, MA 02116
536-5700

Additional Resources

BOOKSTORES

Architectural Book Shop
10 Broad St.
Boston, MA 02109
262-2727
One of the largest selections of
   architecture/design books in the
   country.

Avenue Victor Hugo Bookshop
339 Newbury St.
Boston, MA 02115
266-7746
New and used popular books and
   magazines.

Book Store
76 Chestnut St.
Boston, MA 02108
742-4531

Boston University Bookstore
660 Beacon St.
Boston, MA 02115
267-8484

Bromer Booksellers
607 Boylston St.
Boston, MA 02116
247-2818
The only seller of miniature
   books in New England.

Brown & Connolly, Inc.
1315 Boylston St.
Boston, MA 02115
262-5162
Medical books.

Buddenbrooks Back Bay
   Booksmith
753 Boylston St.
Boston, MA
536-4433

Bumblebee Book Shop
6 Hemenway St.
Boston, MA 02115
437-1927
Jazz specialists.

ChoreoGraphica
82 Charles St.
Boston, MA 02114
227-4780

David L. O'Neal–Antiquarian
  Booksellers, Inc.
234 Clarendon St.
Boston, MA 02116
266-5790

Lauriat's
20 Charles St.
Boston, MA 02114
523-0188

Rizzoli Bookstore — Records &
  Gallery
Copley Place
Boston, MA 02116
437-0700
Hard-to-find books and records.

Spenser's Mystery Bookshop
314 Newbury St.
Boston, MA 02115
262-0880

Trident Booksellers and Café
338 Newbury St.
Boston, MA 02115
267-8688

Under the Spreading
Chestnut Tree

We're breaking our rule about limiting tours to Boston because no literary look at Boston would be complete without a stop
in Cambridge, whose very name implies a rich literary heritage.
Even crossing the river on the MBTA's Red Line has a literary connection: the bridge you ride over is named for the poet Henry
Wadsworth Longfellow, whose Cambridge home is open to the
public. (The span is also known as the "Salt and Pepper Bridge"
because the shapes of the stone towers in the middle resemble salt
shakers.)

If you're coming in to Harvard Square from very far away,
even from another country, you can first stop at **Out of Town
Newspapers** in the ornate kiosk that stands just outside the Harvard Square "T" Station. The newsstand carries newspapers from
every major American city, as well as from many large cities
around the world. During recent reconstruction of the subway system, the 1921 kiosk (which has been designated a National Historic
Landmark) was lifted away from the site, then returned to its (ap-

proximately) original location. The selection here is well worth a quick examination.

Harvard Yard (if you don't want to be identified as a tourist, call it "the Yard") itself deserves a stroll, being the epicenter of America's oldest university, founded in 1636. The **Widener Library,** the mammoth gray building with twelve giant columns and a grand staircase at the rear of the Yard, is the largest privately owned library in the world. In this country only the Library of Congress and the New York Public Library have more than the Widener's three million volumes, and this number does not count the holdings of Harvard's ninety or so departmental libraries elsewhere on campus. Widener's stacks are not open to the public unless you have a Harvard affiliation or special permission, but you can visit some of the reading areas and displays. In the Widener Memorial Room is a case holding a Gutenberg Bible, one of only fifty remaining, and a First Folio of Shakespeare's plays, the first collected edition, dated 1623. The university's rare-book collection is housed in the **Houghton Library,** a short walk away, where there is one room open to the public that always offers a fascinating display.

From Harvard, proceed at your leisure to some of the area's twenty-five-plus bookstores (one reason why the Harvard Square area is called the "book mecca of the world"). The intellectual climate of this neighborhood is so intense that you will find highly specialized wares, as well as superbly stocked general collections. **Schoenhof's,** for example, carries foreign-language books, while **Grolier's** carries only poetry. There are shops for rare-book collectors, science fiction and mystery buffs, and lawyers, as well as a good number of secondhand bookstores for bargain hunters. One good way to get a bargain book or a record is from sidewalk vendors who display their "private collections" on weekends on the

corner of Church Street and Massachusetts Avenue. And, as the motto of the **Cambridge Booksmith** store in the square avows, the shops in this area are "dedicated to the fine art of browsing." Feel free to take your time and page through their offerings (see end of chapter for a list of shops).

While you're in the neighborhood of the **Pangloss** and **Starr Bookshops** be sure to look at the **Harvard Lampoon Castle,** at the corner of Mt. Auburn and Bow Streets. The eccentric architectural details of this wedge-shaped building are almost as amusing as *The Harvard Lampoon*, the undergraduate satire magazine that spawned but is not connected to the *National Lampoon*. "Poonies" have long been associated with audacious humor. In 1933, they even went so far as to kidnap the Sacred Cod (see page 81) from the State House.

The Harvard Cooperative Society, at 1400 Massachusetts Avenue, sells everything from books to toothpaste to lingerie with the Harvard seal. Known to generations of students and Cantabrigians as "the Coop" (as in chicken), the book, record, and poster departments, now located in an annex across the rear alley, is a rich storehouse of fiction, nonfiction, and textbooks, as well as out-of-print books and records.

From Harvard Square walk north down historic Brattle Street, known as Tory Row because it housed wealthy British sympathizers before the Revolution. On the way, make a point to stop at **Words Worth Bookstore** to browse through the wide range of general books at discount prices. As their motto says, they have "books of the uncommon *interest*," such as British titles that are not published in this country. During the academic year they sponsor a reading series once a month at the Brattle Theatre, featuring such authors as Alice Walker, Calvin Trilling, and Ann Beattie. The owner, Hillel Stravis, has assembled a staff that is friendly, knowledgeable, and ever ready to help. The computer program they have developed to keep track of their inventory is used in over two hundred bookstores in this country and abroad.

At number 56 stands an old yellow house called the **Blacksmith House Bakery and Café,** operated by the **Cambridge Center for Adult Education.** The house was owned by blacksmith Dexter Pratt, about whom Longfellow wrote the immortal poem "The Village Blacksmith." Although the spreading chestnut tree Longfellow referred to succumbed to blight years ago, a plaque on the corner of Brattle and Story Streets preserves its memory.

The **Longfellow House,** at 105 Brattle Street, is where the poet lived and wrote for forty-five years. The house, a Georgian mansion erected in 1759, was originally the home of an affluent Tory, Major John Vassall. The major and the rest of the Tories high-tailed it out of town just before the Revolution began, and ironi-cally, his home served as the local headquarters for General George Washington during the British seige of Boston.

Longfellow himself initially lived here as a lodger, until his wealthy father-in-law bought the place in 1843 as a wedding gift for the poet and his second bride, Fanny Appleton (see page 96). Today, the mansion is open to view, operated as a National His-toric Site by the National Park Service. On alternate Sunday after-noons in the summer there are free classical music concerts on the east lawn, and it is a favorite meeting spot for students and per-manent residents alike.

Much of the interior of the house is preserved in circa 1870 splendor. It was in his study here that Longfellow wrote the ma-jority of his poetry, including "Evangeline," "The Children's Hour," and "Hiawatha." Also in the study is what remains of that spreading chestnut tree: a carved armchair hewn from the tree's wood. The chair was a birthday gift to the seventy-two-year-old poet in 1879 from the schoolchildren of Cambridge.

Longfellow died at his home in 1882, and was buried farther out Brattle Street in the **Mount Auburn Cemetery,** a place he had called "the city of the dead." In this beautiful garden cemetery, the first of its kind in America, are the graves of many luminaries — literary and otherwise — of nineteenth-century Boston. In the world of letters alone, one can see the graves of Longfellow, James Russell Lowell, Oliver Wendell Holmes, Amy Lowell, Charles Eliot Norton, Julia Ward Howe, and Messrs. Little and Brown (of the publishing company that bears their names), who are buried side by side.

It was not just coincidence that Mount Auburn became the final resting place of so many eminent people, from abolitionists to zoologists. For the Proper Bostonian, after all, there was a cor-rect way to die as well as to live. As the editor L. H. Butterfield put it in an article for *The American Archivist* (April 1961), "For Bos-tonians the suitable place for depositing one's earthly remains has for a long time been Mount Auburn Cemetery; for one's books, either Harvard or the Athenaeum; for one's family papers, the Massachusetts Historical Society."

The cemetery is located at 580 Mount Auburn Street, on the Cambridge-Watertown line. The easiest way to get there is by the number 71 or 73 bus from Harvard Square, or by car or taxi. At the office, you can obtain maps of notable graves and interesting trees. (For more information on the cemetery as arboretum, see page 57.)

Cambridge deserves much more time and attention than we have been able to give it in this brief tour. Harvard alone, which celebrated its 350th anniversary in 1986, could keep you busy for days. We strongly recommend that you return. The information booth in the square will tell you all about tours and special exhibits. And while you're in the square, take time to visit some of the area specialty boutiques. It's a good way to work yourself into the mood for our next series of tours, which take you on some terrific shopping expeditions.

Tour Sites

Blacksmith House Bakery and Café
56 Brattle St.
Cambridge, MA
354-3036

Houghton Library
Harvard University
Harvard Yard
Cambridge, MA 02138
495-2441

Harvard Cooperative Society ("The Coop")
1400 Massachusetts Ave.
Cambridge, MA 02138
492-1000

The Longfellow House
150 Brattle St.
Cambridge, MA 02138
876-4491

Harvard Lampoon Castle
57 Mt. Auburn St.
Cambridge, MA 02138
495-7801

Mt. Auburn Cemetery
580 Mt. Auburn St.
Cambridge, MA 02138
547-7105

Out of Town Newspapers
Zero Harvard Square
Cambridge, MA 02138
354-7777

Widener Library
Harvard University
Harvard Yard
Cambridge, MA 02138
495-4166

Additional Resources

BOOKSTORES

Ahab Rare Books
5 JFK St.
Cambridge, MA 02138
547-5602

Cambridge Booksmith
25 Brattle St.
Cambridge, MA 02138
864-2321
General.

Asian Books
12 Arrow St.
Cambridge, MA 02138
354-0005

Grolier Book Shop
6 Plympton St.
Cambridge, MA 02138
547-4648
Poetry.

Barillari Books
1 Mifflin Pl.
Cambridge, MA 02138
General.

Harvard Book Store
1256 Massachusetts Ave.
Cambridge, MA 02138
661-1515
General.

Robin Bledsoe Books
1640 Massachusetts Ave.
Cambridge, MA 02138
576-3634
Out-of-print, art history,
   archeology, and architecture.
   New, used, and imported horse
   books.

Harvard University Press Display
   Room
Holyoke Center
1350 Massachusetts Ave.
Cambridge, MA 02138
495-2625

Kate's Mystery Books
2211 Massachusetts Ave.
Cambridge, MA 02138
491-2660

Mandrake
8 Story St.
Cambridge, MA 02138
864-3088
Therapy, philosophy, art,
    architecture, design.

McIntyre & Moore Booksellers
8 Mt. Auburn St.
Cambridge, MA 02138
491-0662
Rare and out-of-print books.

H. L. Mendelsohn
1640 Massachusetts Ave.
Cambridge, MA 02138
576-3634
Out-of-print history of
    architecture, city planning,
    gardens, design.

Pangloss Bookshop
65 Mt. Auburn St.
Cambridge, MA 02138
354-4003
Rare and out-of-print books,
    secondhand books.

Reading International
47 Brattle St.
Cambridge, MA 02138
864-0705 or 864-0706

Schoenhof's Foreign Books, Inc.
76a Mt. Auburn St.
Cambridge, MA 02138
547-8855

Seven Stars Booksellers
58 JFK St.
Cambridge, MA 02138
547-1317
New age, occultism, Eastern and
    Western esoteric tradition,
    astrology.

Sky Light Books
111 Mt. Auburn St.
Cambridge, MA 02138
491-8788
Holistic, spirituality.

Starr Bookshop, Inc.
Harvard Lampoon Building
29 Plympton St.
Cambridge, MA 02138
547-6864
General used books.

Words Worth Bookstore
30 Brattle St.
Cambridge, MA 02138
354-5201

General Resources

SPECIAL LIBRARIES

Bostonian Society
15 State St.
Boston, MA 02109
720-1713
Boston business, architecture,
    sports, religion, history,
    politics, and some fiction. City
    directories, neighborhood
    information, a large map, and
    photography collection from the
    1850s onward.

John F. Kennedy Presidential
    Library
Columbia Point
Boston, MA 02125
929-4500
John F. Kennedy and Robert F.
    Kennedy papers and
    memorabilia, as well as the
    papers of Ernest Hemingway.

Massachusetts Historical Society
1154 Boylston St.
Boston, MA 02215
536-1608
Early American history, including
    Boston and New England.

Massachusetts Horticultural
    Society Library
300 Massachusetts Ave.
Boston, MA 02115
536-9280
Country's largest collection of
    horticultural books, including
    landscaping, architecture, old
    seed catalogs, and out-of-print
    and antiquarian books.

Society for the Preservation of
    New England Antiquities
    (SPNEA)
SPNEA Library
141 Cambridge St.
Boston, MA 02134
227-3956
Architectural drawings, photos,
    English and American
    architecture books.
By appointment only.

State Library of Massachusetts
State House, Rm. 341
Beacon St.
Boston, MA 02133
727-2590
Law, local and town history,
    genealogy.

RECOMMENDED READING

Levine, Miriam. *A Guide to Writers' Homes in New England.* Cambridge,
Mass.: Apple-wood Books, Inc., 1984.

CHAPTER FIVE

Spendiferous Boston

There are four distinct areas in Boston that are shoppers' paradise, each one extensive enough to occupy an inveterate shopper for hours and hours. Temptation comes in many forms, and each section has its own extent and character. In their wisdom the town fathers declared that there would be no sales tax levied on clothing in Massachusetts, making great savings possible for people who purchase high-ticket items.

We've divided our shopping tours into two categories — Boston by Design and Amiable Antiques — but most of your footwork will be done in the same four areas of the city: Faneuil Hall Marketplace, Downtown Crossing, Charles Street, and Newbury and Boylston Streets. (A note to shoppers from out of town — loosening of the Massachusetts "blue laws," which forbid establishments to open on Sundays, is relatively new. Many retail stores are now open from noon to 5 P.M. on Sundays. Quincy Market is always active, but many other shops take a Sunday break. Call first to be certain.) Most of these areas have free guides to the entertainment, shopping, and dining in their vicinity. Just ask for one at a shop in each area.

Boston by Design

FANEUIL HALL MARKETPLACE

This is the jewel in the crown of the city's waterfront restoration project and one of the most successful retail developments in the country. The Marketplace is actually four separate buildings. Quincy Market, the central market with its Greek Revival entrances, houses the food emporiums, as does the first floor of Faneuil Hall itself, but it is the North and South Markets we're interested in as shoppers.

Part of the pleasure of shopping at Faneuil Hall Marketplace is the combination of old and new, highbrow and relaxed, costly and nearly free. You can spend hundreds of dollars on an article of clothing, original objets d'art, or home furnishings, and then stop off for a slice of pizza or a bagel while you watch the street performers strut their stuff on the piazza between the buildings. The Marketplace was designed to provide more than a place to shop. It offers sustenance, entertainment, and human contact as well as worldly goods.

Both the North and South Markets contain boutiques and shops in which you can find unusual and original items. New ones are being added all the time; so go to the Rotunda in the center of Quincy Market and you'll find an information booth that offers a complete list of tenants, as well as excellent floor plans.

While in Quincy Market, don't forget to stroll past the push-carts known collectively as "the Bull Market," where you can find originally designed trinkets and accessories, as well as regional souvenirs at reasonable prices.

Some of the more charming or outstanding shops in the Marketplace are:

Allen Lawrence: Distinctive clothing for distinctive men. Custom-made shirts, shoes, blazers, and accessories.

Boston Pewter: Pewter flatware, plates, goblets, candlesticks, jewelry, pins, and fantasy pewter figurines.

Boston Scrimshanders: The place to find beautiful scrimshaw jewelry and ivory collectibles, a New England specialty. Here, you can watch owner/artist Don Kiracofe carry on the old New England art of engraving whaling scenes on man-made ivory. Also for sale are the owner's version of the famous Nantucket Lightship baskets.

Cat Country: Cat collectibles for the finicky. Perfect cat gifts, most of them are handcrafted.

Concord Hand Designs: Local and East-coast handcrafts make this shop both interesting and unique. It offers a variety of handpainted, handstenciled, and handmade items.

Geoclassics: Finally, there is a shop in Faneuil Hall that specializes in gems!

Have a Heart: Everything for the "young at heart." The colorful accessories range from barrettes to notebooks to canvas bags to mugs. Stock up here now for Valentine's Day.

Hog Wild: Another "subject speciality" boutique, this charming little store is filled with pigs, hogs, and piglets; children will particularly enjoy browsing here.

Lefty: If you're left-handed, this will be your mecca. This shop features unique items, such as scissors, oven mitts, and other practical tools, for anyone who's left-handed.

Pavo Real: At Marketplace center, Sergio Bustamante's brightly-colored papier-mâché animal sculptures offer an exciting visual addition to your home decor. The shop also has a beautiful collection of Mexican wedding dresses.

CHARLES STREET

This, our second major shopping area, is one of the preeminent antique centers in the country. (Antiques are covered in the next tour in this chapter.) Charles Street is a uniquely Boston experience, combining the best of the past and the present. Colonial brick sidewalks and the gas lantern atmosphere of Beacon Hill blend perfectly with the up-to-date élan of a fashionable city neighborhood. Remnants of the 1960s, when the street was full of used-clothing stores and leather shops à la Haight Ashbury, cohabit peacefully with the antique shops and chic cafés. And the people-watching is some of the best in the city!

Try to allow time to peek into every intriguing nook and cranny on both sides of the curving avenue, which runs between Beacon and Cambridge Streets. Again, there are too many shops to mention *all* our favorites, but to give you a sense of the area, we'll list a few to get you started.

Kennedy Studios, number 31: Framed and unframed prints and limited editions of Boston and Cape Cod by Bob and Michelle Kennedy and other local artists. They also have some antique prints of the city of Boston.

Eric's of Boston, Ltd., number 38: Step into a mini-museum that carries a wide variety of imported cards and gift wrap, handloomed ribbons, dollhouse miniatures, and unique Christmas ornaments.

Communications, number 40: It's pretty hard to pass the window of this store without going in. They've been known to have live bunnies and chickens in their display. The store is best known for its clever toys and outrageous card collection, but it also shows the clothing of several up-and-coming young Boston designers.

Blackstone's, number 46A: The gold pineapple outside the door signifies hospitality, and Blackstone's carries an exhaustive and unique array of household items and gifts, such as glassware and desk paraphernalia, including exclusive English enamel and Limoges boxes.

Linens on the Hill, number 52: Has bed, bath, and table linens, along with nightgowns and robes for women. Most of the goods are white, although there are some lovely gifts in pastels.

Grey's Fine Jewlery, number 69: The owners design and make their own jewelry. They do repairs on the same day, restore pearls, and repair old clocks and watches.

The Grand Trousseau, number 88: Carries romantic vintage clothing from the Victorian era through the 1940s, with formal and dressy wear from the 1920s. The small shop also has a limited selection of antique jewelry and accessories.

Carrollton Fine Yarns and Handknits, number 96: This is the only boutique in the United States that carries the full line of Filatura D. Crosa yarns with patterns by Missoni and Valentino. The shop is filled with one-of-a-kind handknits that serve as examples of these sophisticated designs.

Charles Street Woodshop, number 102: This shop has something for all ages in a variety of woods. The toys and cabinets of maple are from their mill in Maine, the kitchen and serving utensils are from Haiti, and the vases and jewelry are from Argentina.

The Designers – Leather Clothiers, number 103: Custom-designs and manufactures leather clothing by hand for men and women. There is a wide selection of colors in deerskin and English lambskin and suede, along with a variety of accessories.

Beacon Hill Sports, number 107: Caters to the tennis player and runner with shoes, equipment, and clothing for these and other sports that can be played indoors and outdoors year-round.

Helen's Leather Shop, number 110: Walk through the door and just smell the odor of fresh leather. Inside, you'll find New

England's largest selection of handmade western boots featuring such makers as Lucchese, Tony Iama, Justin Dan Post, Larry Mahan, Rios, and Frye. In addition to the boots, you can also browse through a beautiful collection of leather jackets, bags, backpacks, and Birkenstock sandals.

Period Furniture Hardware Company, number 123: You just might find the antique doorknob, reproduction, lighting, hardware, and fireplace equipment you've been looking for for years in this busy little hole-in-the-wall.

COPLEY PLACE AND BOYLSTON STREET

From Charles Street you *can* walk to our third area of indulgence. **Copley Place** is the first indoor mall to be erected within Boston city limits. With its shiny brasswork, marble floors, and opulent flowing fountains, Copley Place shouts "expensive," and when it first opened in 1984, Bostonians were sure it would never survive. Too upscale, they said, too suburban. Too *Texas*. But Copley Place has done more than survive. Today it is the center of the universe for shoppers who want the best of everything. Aside from the big-name shops like **Neiman-Marcus, Tiffany, Williams-Sonoma,** and **Sara Fredericks,** there are a number of small boutiques that carry exciting, though pricey, items.

Brookstone: Nirvana for the up-scale hardware store junkie.

The Artful Hand Gallery feels like a museum because you'll want to browse about and not miss anything. There are contemporary crafts of hundreds of American artists, and many media, such as glass, ceramics, metals, and woods are included.

Georgette: This shop carries exquisite, one-of-a-kind evening clothes, as well as dresses and gowns for the entire bridal party. A young debutante just coming out can even have a custom-made dress by Georgette herself. Traditional bridal gowns are the popular item here, mostly designed in white or cream.

Tissages: The place for special clothing made of handloomed fabrics, much of it made to order by owner Joanne Leef.

Ports International: Classic business clothes for the classy working woman.

Jaegar: Exclusive English women's sport shop. Classic, comfortable, and durable. Superior wools, cottons, and silks.

For you inveterate **Ralph Lauren** fans, here at Copley Place you'll find your traditional polo store for the sporty, country look. They also sell new and antique jewelry accessories.

From Copley Place, it's a short walk to the corner of Boylston Street, where you can stop in at the **Eddie Bauer** outdoor clothing store, started in Seattle as a store for naval flyers and noted for their goose-down parkas. Next door is **Bonwit Teller,** in the elegant, breathtaking New England Life building, with a fountain and crystal chandeliers, designed by Phillip Johnson. The mix of classic and contemporary outside only begins to prepare you for the elegance inside.

Across the street at the corner of Berkeley you'll find an imposing brick and brownstone building, which is now the home of **Louis.** Built in 1863, the French Academic style building originally housed the Boston Museum of Natural History. Architect William Gibbons Preston began designing the museum before the Civil War, but construction was delayed during the war, and the building was completed in 1865. In 1987, Louis embarked on an eighteen-month complete restoration of the building. The color and fixtures were even created to replicate the originals. Period moldings and hardwood floors were installed to achieve the nineteenth-century look of Boston's stylish yet conservative men's clothing store. Louis' fine, European imported line is expensive, elegant, and understated. Louis likes to think of itself as a point of view more than a haberdasher, and they have added an undeniable element of panache to the usual Brooks Brothers image of the properly dressed Bostonian. They also have a women's department, noted for casual, tailored elegance. After absorbing all of the architecture, decoration, and fine clothing, you can relax and view the landscaped lawn while sitting at the **Café at Louis.** The ceramic tiled restaurant with etched-glass doors is on the first floor and serves a light continental menu for breakfast and lunch.

Just down the block is one of Boston's best shops for children's clothing, greeting cards, and tasteful household gift items, the **Women's Educational & Industrial Union.** Above the doorway of this venerable institution floats the gilded swan that is its symbol, and just inside, on the left-hand wall, is a lovely stained-glass panel that came from the 1893 Women's Pavilion at the Chicago Exposition, at which the Union was represented.

Most of the items in the store are handmade, and all reveal the Union's genteel inclinations, which have their roots in a long tradition of service. The Union was founded in 1877 by forty Boston women (including Julia Ward Howe), who were interested in helping the city's disadvantaged women. The swan logo was decided upon because 1877 was the same year in which the Swan Boats were launched on the Public Garden Lagoon. The Union's oldest social service department is its career services program, through which Amelia Earhart once found a job (although not as a pilot).

Nearby, on Boylston Street, you'll find **Shreve, Crump & Low,** practically a Boston institution, established in 1899. This store houses a traditional selection of gifts and is known for its Bridal Registry. (By the way, they have a large selection of Nantucket Lightship baskets.) For antique lovers, be sure to find your way to the second floor for furniture, prints, and collectibles. Also in this second floor space is a handsome collection of Steuben glass, quality stationery, and baby gifts.

Across from the Public Garden and next to the Four Seasons Hotel, you'll find the **Heritage on the Garden** at Arlington and Boylston. This elegant brick condominium complex houses some of Boston's most elegant restaurants and shops and a spa. The shops include **Berk,** "the first cashmere store in Boston," established by an English family, which carries mostly Ballantyne. They do have a few of their own label, though, and will send from their own shop in London for delivery within twenty-four hours. One customer service is that they are able to speak every language. You'll recognize the names of designer shops in the Heritage, such as **Hermes,** known for his silk clothing and particularly loved for his signature print scarves. Many people collect these as works of art. For example, Hermes's Bastille Day scarf was purchased by the Museum de Paris. Hermes started with handstitched harnesses and saddles and now retails some of the most distinctive handstitched purses in the world.

While you're in this city block, you might want to stop in at **Sonia Rykiel, Escada,** and **Yves Saint-Laurent.** If looking at all these upscale places has whetted your appetite, you can go for some quality food at one of the accessible restaurants. **Biba,** made famous by Boston chef Lydia Shire, is located in the Heritage as well. The menu features cuisine from all over the world, and the decor is a mix of warm Mediterranean colors with an art deco influence. Turkish kilin rugs cover the banquette area, and the floor is made of intriguing exotic woods handcrafted in Boston. Biba's unique design is truly an aesthetic statement for Boston.

NEWBURY STREET

Now on to the most diverse of the city's shopping areas. Newbury Street, with its authentic nineteenth-century charm, has been home to the city's finest merchants and art dealers for over a century. When Beacon Hill residents moved into this area after its creation in the mid-1800s, the shops that were serving Beacon Hill residents moved here along with them. Everything from imported rugs to groceries was sold here, and the street today displays the same broad selection of goods.

As you browse along, don't forget to look up at the eccentric rooftops and the bay and bowfront windows, and down at the tiny patios with their surprising little gardens and occasional sculpture. No space is wasted on this street. You'll notice that many shops occupy either the second story or basement levels, and that the buildings have been put to both commercial and residential use.

We've listed some of our personal favorites here, along with a few not-to-be-missed entries. They're divided into four categories: jewelry, furs, home furnishings, and clothing.

Jewelry

Firestone and Parsons, Ritz-Carlton Hotel, 15 Arlington Street: Filled with diamond and gold estate pieces and silver candlesticks that have been "in the family" for years, this is the quintessential old-guard jeweller. Legend has it that several Beacon Hill matrons who were forced by declining circumstances to part with some of their family heirlooms still stop in daily to visit their treasures. Antique tea services are a specialty.

Dorfman Jewelers, number 24 Newbury St.: In this husband-and-wife operation you'll be greeted graciously by Barbara or Sumner Dorfman and shown 18-karat gold European classics as well as high fashion designs. Known for their elegant diamonds and sapphires, this shop is truly exclusive.

John Lewis, number 97: Lewis and his wife, Louise, design silver, gold, and precious stones in freeform styles that are reminiscent of the 1960s. The couple live on a boat in Boston's Waterfront Harbor, and indulged their nurturing tendencies by planting a tree in front of their shop instead of their backyard.

Body Sculpture, number 127: Here you'll find unusual contemporary jewelry. They are generally one-of-a-kind pieces, in colorful styles, and made of gold, brass and polyester resin. The shop sells work by local as well as internationally known designers.

Furs

Roberts-Neustadter, number 69: This store carries trendy styles, like Fendi furs and Juliana Teso. Closed the month of July.

Kakas, number 93: Over a century old, this shop is the backbone of old-line Boston. The bear in the reception area has been there since the beginning. Now in its third incarnation, the six-foot polar bear was originally made from the largest skin the Hudson Bay Company could acquire. The furs are traditionally styled, opulent, and well made.

And don't forget Filene's Basement, with the highest fur turnover on the East Coast (see pages 129–131).

Home Furnishings

Most home furnishings can be found within a one-block stretch of Newbury Street, between Dartmouth and Exeter Streets. You'll find branches of popular midpriced stores, which carry a wide range of necessities from European and American lines, as well as some unique Boston stores you'll want to visit.

Bath and Closet Shop, number 139A: Owner Billie Brenner will design a special bathroom for you from her stock of accessories, from sinks to soap dishes.

Placewares, number 160: Original, complete furniture systems. They specialize in organizing closet space.

Kitchen Arts, number 161: Kitchen tools for the serious cook. Cutlery is their specialty, and they carry a wide variety of gadgets.

Scandia Down Shop, number 166: Down comforters, pillows, and bed linens from West Germany, Italy, and France are the specialty here.

London Lace, number 167: This gem of a second-floor shop is the brainchild of Diane Jones, who regularly travels to England, Scotland, and Ireland to collect the finest in antique linens and lace, with an emphasis on Scottish lace.

Decor International Rugs, number 171: Handmade decorative rugs and wallhangings from around the world, and ethnic jewelry and pottery.

Monhegan, number 173: Specializes in fine wool blankets, all-cotton sheets, American and European linens. The offerings are often handloomed, in delicious soft colors, and locally produced.

La Ruche, number 174: A "thing" store owned by Maria Church and Apple Bartlett, daughter of noted New York decorator Sister Parrish, which carries tableware, silk flowers, and lots of elegant knickknacks and small furnishings. Don't miss the hand-painted trompe l'oeil furniture, created by several excellent local artisans.

Conran's, 26 Exeter Street: Once a church, then a movie theater, this building is now a store selling quick-assembly home furnishings, bath, linens, kitchenware, and china. You can buy everything to furnish an apartment or home on a low budget.

Clothing

Newbury Street has been a mecca for shoppers for over a century. At the helm of the street is **Burberry's,** a store of traditional men's and women's quality clothing direct from London, most widely noted for their famous plaid. Two shops on Newbury Street that have outfitted generations of Boston women are **Stuart's,** at number 10, and **Darée,** at number 11. They know their customers well and present classic to high-style clothing.

Charles Sumner, number 16: This was the first Boston store to carry designer clothing. The founding Goldman family recently sold the thriving business to three Boston women who are carrying on the tradition of Valentinos, Sonia Rykiels, and Delman Shoes. Very tasteful merchandise and accessories, such as scarves and artistic jewelry.

The sophisticated Parisian flair of Newbury Street is represented by **Guy Laroche,** at number 32, and **Rodier Paris,** at number 144, noted for its classic design Chanel influence, knit fabrics, and washable wool blends that don't stretch or pull.

Alan Bilzerian, number 34: If you could pick one place to shop in Boston for the most avant-garde men's and women's clothing, it would have to be Bilzerian's. Alan got his start in Worcester, selling colorful clothing to college kids in the 1960s, and made a name for himself by selling to rock stars, such as James Taylor and Carly Simon. When he moved to Boston, he changed his image from casual to *au courant,* and now carries clothing that is notable for its cutting-edge elegance and high price. His wife, Bê, sister-in-law of noted French designer Emmanuel Kahn, is a talented designer in her own right, and you'll find her pieces along with a good selection of Japanese and Italian lines. The atmosphere for all this is as decisive and sleek as the clothing itself. If you've only come to browse, keep in mind that Bilzerian's has regular customers who spend $10,000 in a season!

At number 35, Suzanne of **Suzanne's** will show you what Newbury Street service is all about. She has some wonderful party clothes and will be happy to personally pick out something for that special occasion.

Martini Carl, number 77: This shop specializes in European apparel for men and women that only a handful of stores in the world carry. The shop itself is notable because it was the original home of Sara Fredericks's fashion salon. (Fredericks's career began almost half a century ago. She was a pioneer in raising Boston women's fashion consciousness. The elegant interior of this shop, which she designed, bears testament to her exquisite taste. Her sense of style is alive and well in the shop that bears her name in Copley Place.)

The Newbury Street outfitter for sports enthusiasts is **Feron's,** at number 103. This is the specialist store in tennis and racquet sports as well as swimwear and lots of athletic footwear.

Cuoio, number 115: Come here for ladies' Italian shoewear in a wide range of colors and textures such as leather and suede. From casual to high fashion, you are bound to find the perfect shoes at Cuoio. They also carry hosiery.

Junior League Bargain Box, number 117: For those of you

who like vintage clothing, you can find some really elegant clothes recently worn by the residents of Boston and Beacon Hill. There are some really good buys to be had!

Botnes, number 118: Women can buy or rent elegant eveningwear ranging from semiformal to very formal at this specialty shop. They also offer accessories such as jewelry, purses, and hats.

Goods, number 123: The unique Boston shop for fine cotton and silk lingerie. This elegant shop is a treasure-trove of femininity. The Swiss "Hanro" label is particularly noteworthy. Their unusual store next door houses all sorts of toys and gimmicks.

Priscilla's, number 129: Newbury Street has become a sort of mini-capital of the bridal industry in Boston, and Priscilla's is at the epicenter of the resurgence in wedding wear. Priscilla Kidder has been a bridal consultant since 1946, and she has orchestrated the nuptials of well-dressed brides from the Back Bay to the White House. (The Nixon girls were outfitted with Priscilla's designs.) If you aren't in a hurry to find your special gown, Priscilla has a favorite charity to which she donates dresses she finds unsaleable. A discreet phone call might gain you information about the whereabouts of these gowns.

The international fashion beat of Newbury Street continues at two exclusive Italian women's clothing stores. **Italia 2000,** at number 125, and **Serenella,** at number 134, are Boston's exclusive Italian woman's clothing representatives. Italia 2000 only has one item per size, so you don't need to fear someone looking exactly like you in that fashionable purchase!

The European flair is also evident at 167 Newbury Street, where **Rae Brewer** sells English and Scottish updated traditional women's sportswear. This store is the exclusive outlet for Paul Costello, Irish designer of suits and sportswear.

From down under at 140 Newbury Street, we find **Country Road,** an Australian company that features comfortable clothing in well-made fabrics from Australia, but which are tailored in Hong Kong.

Alfred Fiandaca, also at 140 Newbury Street, has dressed First Ladies and Boston Brahmins, and is one of the few ateliers on Newbury Street open to the public. He is surely the preeminent name in Boston couture. He decided against a New York career years ago and settled comfortably on Newbury Street, where his custom design house has been turning out better dresses, suits, and gowns without ever stooping to the trendy or flashy. He dresses the woman who wants a special look, and customers swear by his perfect fit and detailing.

Javian, 156 Newbury Street: This shop carries clothing designed by the students at the nearby Fashion Institute, as well as the shop's own line, designed by V. G. DiGeronimo. It is an excellent place to find an exciting article of clothing at a decent price, as well as to spot the new trends from the designers of tomorrow. DiGeronimo works well in natural fabrics to create contemporary women's classics.

DOWNTOWN CROSSING

The Downtown Crossing is the inner city's answer to the suburban mall. The bricked pedestrian paths (no cars allowed), cart vendors and benches, along with a lively collection of street musicians, hawkers, gawkers, and lookers-on, has made the Crossing a great place to shop and hang out, as the daily crowds testify.

This area used to be Boston's main shopping area. It still has many stores worth a look, but undoubtedly the most famous, in fact the ultimate Boston shopping experience is **Filene's Basement.** The most well known and well stocked discount outlet in New England, perhaps in the country, the Basement is certainly as famous as London's Harrods Department Store. But its reputation is far less reserved and polished than that esteemed institution. Although there are now other Filene's Basement stores located in suburban malls in New York, New Jersey, and even Maine, none compares to what you'll find in the original, subterranean paradise.

William Filene opened his first retail store in 1851. The Basement was opened in 1908 by his son Edward, who started the first
credit union, devised the Better Business Bureau, and created the
markdown system. Filene's has reigned supreme among serious
shoppers ever since. You can find unbelievable markdowns on
quality clothing from high-priced shops like Neiman-Marcus or
Saks, as well as bargain-basement-quality brands. The merchandise is often the season's hottest item, and it is rarely out-of-date
and almost always in good condition.

The Basement is actually four underground levels, although
levels three and four are not open to the public and are used entirely for receiving, storing, and marking the merchandise, which
comes in at a rate of four to five trailers a day. The first public level
stocks an impressive array of lingerie, gifts, shoes, and menswear.
The second level carries women's clothing: coats, suits, and furs,
and some children's clothing and "domestics."

Shopping at Filene's Basement requires skill, perseverance,
and endurance. The vast array of merchandise may begin the day
neatly enough on racks or in piles. But within thirty minutes of
opening, the most popular items are likely to be strewn chaotically
across the room, as frantic shoppers vie for choice goods. It takes
patience, too, to sort through the mountains of merchandise; the
Basement is able to price its wares so successfully by buying in
bulk, displaying it all, and creating a quick turnover. The dressing
rooms were added only recently, and long-time customers rou-
tinely try on apparel over or under their clothing and in varying
states of undress.

The price tags may read like a secret code, but are really simple to understand. All merchandise is dated when it's put on regular display — starting out as much as 40 to 60 percent off the
original retail price established elsewhere. After fourteen shopping
days, the price is reduced by 25 percent. After twenty-one days, it
drops another 25 percent, and after twenty-eight days, the price is
75 percent off the original Basement price. Any item not sold after
thirty-five days is donated to charity, or if you're lucky, you can
have it by making out a check for the final price to one of the char-
ities on Filene's approved list (tax deductible, of course).

There are lots of regulars who enjoy the gamble involved in
waiting for the next markdown on a big-ticket item. They'll make

special trips to the store in hopes of "hitting the date," although there's always the risk that some other lucky browser will have come across the prized item and bought it first.

Occasionally, the Basement has a special single-day sale, when the doors open at 8 A.M. Most popular are the $70 suit sale, and the $14 dress sale, when twenty thousand dresses can be sold in a single day. All special sales are advertised one day in advance in the local newspapers, but be forewarned: those early crowds can be large and wild. No trip to Boston, however, is complete without at least a brief swing through "the Basement."

Tour Sites

FANEUIL HALL MARKETPLACE

Allen Lawrence
South Market, Faneuil Hall
  Marketplace
Boston, MA 02109
227-1144

Concord Hand Designs
South Market, Faneuil Hall
  Marketplace
Boston, MA 02109
227-2270

Boston Pewter
South Market, Faneuil Hall
  Marketplace
Boston, MA 02109
523-1776

Geoclassics
4 North Market, Faneuil Hall
  Marketplace
Boston, MA 02109
523-6112

Boston Scrimshanders
175 G Faneuil Hall Marketplace
Boston, MA 02109
367-1552

Have a Heart
Faneuil Hall Marketplace
Boston, MA 02109
523-4503

Cat Country
North Market, Faneuil Hall
  Marketplace
Boston, MA 02109
523-9393

Hog Wild
Faneuil Hall Marketplace
Boston, MA 02109
523-7447

Lefty
Faneuil Hall Marketplace
Boston, MA 02109
523-2050

Siam Malee
South Market, Faneuil Hall
   Marketplace
Boston, MA 02109
227-7027

Pavo Real
200 State Street
Marketplace Center
Boston, MA 02109
523-2715

CHARLES STREET

Beacon Hill Sports
107 Charles St.
Boston, MA 02146
742-5850

Communications
40 Charles St.
Boston, MA 02114
523-0884

Blackstone's of Beacon Hill
46A Charles St.
Boston, MA 02114
227-4646

The Designers – Leather Clothiers
103 Charles St.
Boston, MA 02114
720-3967

Carrollton Fine Yarns
   and Handknits
96 Charles St.
Boston, MA 02114
720-4454

Eric's of Boston, Ltd.
38 Charles St.
Boston, MA 02114
227-6567

The Grand Trousseau
88 Charles St.
Boston, MA 02114
367-3163

Charles Street Woodshop
102 Charles St.
Boston, MA 02114
523-0797

Grey's Fine Jewelry
69 Charles St.
Boston, MA 02114
523-0760

Helen's Leather Shop
110 Charles St.
Boston, MA 02114
742-2077

Linens on the Hill
52 Charles St.
Boston, MA 02114
227-1255

Kennedy Studios
31 Charles St.
Boston, MA 02114
523-9868

Period Furniture
  Hardware Company
123 Charles St.
Boston, MA 02114
227-0758

COPLEY PLACE AND BOYLSTON STREET

The Artful Hand Gallery
Copley Place
100 Huntington Ave.
Boston, MA 02116
262-9601

Le Chapeau
Copley Place
100 Huntington Ave.
Boston, MA 02116
236-0232

Berk
314 Boylston St.
Boston, MA 02116
426-5586

Eddie Bauer
500 Boylston St.
Boston, MA 02116
262-6700

Bonwit Teller
200 Boylston St.
Boston, MA 02116
267-1200

Escada
308 Boylston St.
Boston, MA 02116
437-1200

Brookstone
Copley Place
100 Huntington Ave.
Boston, MA 02116
267-4308

Georgette
Copley Place
Boston, MA 02116
267-3270

Hermes
22 Arlington St.
Boston, MA 02116
482-8707

Jaegar
Copley Place
Boston, MA 02116
437-1163

Lord and Taylor
760 Boylston St.
Boston, MA 02116
262-6000

Louis
234 Berkeley St.
Boston, MA 02116
965-6100

Neiman-Marcus
Copley Place
Boston, MA 02116
536-3660

Polo Ralph Lauren
Copley Place
Boston, MA 02116
266-4121

Ports International
Copley Place
Boston, MA 02116
266-3442

Saks Fifth Avenue
Prudential Plaza
Boston, MA 02199
262-8500

Sara Fredericks
Copley Place
Boston, MA 02116
536-8766

Shreve, Crump & Low
330 Boylston St.
Boston, MA 02116
267-9100

Sonia Rykiel
280 Boylston St.
Boston, MA 02116
426-2033

Talbots
458 Boylston St.
Boston, MA 02116
262-2981

Tiffany & Co.
Copley Place
Boston, MA 02116
353-0222

Tissages
Copley Place
Boston, MA 02116
267-3903

Williams-Sonoma
Copley Place
Boston, MA 02116
262-3080

Yves St. Laurent Rive Gauche
304 Boylston St.
Boston, MA 02116
482-6661

Women's Educational &
   Industrial Union
356 Boylston St.
Boston, MA 02116
536-5651

NEWBURY STREET

Bath and Closet Shop
139A Newbury St.
Boston, MA 02116
267-6564

Brooks Brothers
46 Newbury St.
Boston, MA 02116
267-2600

Alan Bilzerian
34 Newbury St.
Boston, MA 02116
536-1001

Charles Sumner
16 Newbury St.
Boston, MA 02116
536-6225

Body Sculpture
127 Newbury St.
Boston, MA 02116
262-2200

Conran's
26 Exeter St.
Boston, MA 02116
266-2836

Botnes
118 Newbury St.
Boston, MA 02116
247-1957

Country Road
140 Newbury St.
Boston, MA 02115
262-3820

Rae Brewer
167 Newbury St.
Boston, MA 02116
267-5084

Cuoio
115 Newbury St.
Boston, MA 02116
859-0636

Darée
11 Newbury St.
Boston, MA 02116
266-2504

Decor International Rugs
171 Newbury St.
Boston, MA 02116
262-1529

Domain, Inc.
7 Newbury St.
Boston, MA 02116
266-5252

Dorfman Jewelers
24 Newbury St.
Boston, MA 02116
536-2022

Feron's
103 Newbury St.
Boston, MA 02116
266-3525

Alfred Fiandaca
140 Newbury St.
Boston, MA 02116
262-6580 or 262-4255

Firestone and Parsons
Ritz-Carlton Hotel
15 Arlington St.
Boston, MA 02116
266-1858 or 266-5962

Goods
123 Newbury St.
Boston, MA 02116
354-6440

Guy Laroche
32 Newbury St.
Boston, MA 02116
262-0610

Italia 2000
125 Newbury St.
Boston, MA 02116
266-2984

Javian
156 Newbury St.
Boston, MA 02116
536-7516

Junior League Bargain Box
117 Newbury St.
Boston, MA 02116
536-8580

Kakas Furs
93 Newbury St.
Boston, MA 02116
536-1858

Kitchen Arts
161 Newbury St.
Boston, MA 02116
266-8701

La Ruche
174 Newbury St.
Boston, MA 02116
536-6366

John Lewis
97 Newbury St.
Boston, MA 02116
266-6665

London Lace
167 Newbury St.
Boston, MA 02116
267-3506

Martini Carl
77 Newbury St.
Boston, MA 02116
247-0441

Monhegan
173 Newbury St.
Boston, MA 02116
247-0666

Placewares
160 Newbury St.
Boston, MA 02116
267-5460

Priscilla's
129 Newbury St.
Boston, MA 02116
267-9070

Roberts-Neustadter
69 Newbury St.
Boston, MA 02116
267-2063

Rodier Paris
144 Newbury St.
Boston, MA 02116
247-2410

Scandia Down Shop
166 Newbury St.
Boston, MA 02116
536-7990

Stuart's
10 Newbury St.
Boston, MA 02116
267-6900

Suzanne's
35 Newbury St.
Boston, MA 02116
266-4146

RESTAURANTS

Biba
272 Boylston St.
Boston, MA 02116
426-7878

Le Grand Café
651 Boylston St.
Boston, MA 02116
437-6400

Mr. Leung
545 Boylston St.
Boston, MA 02116
236-4040

Yamasushi
132 Newbury St.
Boston, MA 02116
424-8400

DOWNTOWN CROSSING

Filene's Basement
426 Washington St.
Boston, MA 02116
357-2100

Jordan Marsh
450 Washington St.
Boston, MA 02116
357-3000

Amiable Antiques

Occasionally New Englanders clean out their attics, and when they do, a lot of good stuff gravitates to Boston's antique stores. Whether you are an avid collector of antiques, would like to pick up a piece that was once treasured by another, or just want to browse, there are neighborhoods to head for in Boston proper.

The two major concentrations are in the Back Bay on Newbury Street and on Charles Street on Beacon Hill. Shops on Newbury Street are housed in Victorian buildings, while Charles Street on Beacon Hill is the original "antiques row" of Federal Boston. The items range from fine antiques to small, less-expensive items, and it is possible to make some real discoveries in both areas.

As you enter Charles Street from the end closest to the Public Garden, walk along the left-hand side of the street where most of the shops are located. Anglophiles can revel (in a decorous way) at **James Billings II Antiques,** 70 Charles Street. The shop embodies fine English traditions, and Billings himself is a member of the British Antique Dealers Association. An orderly and exquisitely appointed showroom, it displays quality seventeenth- and eighteenth-century English, French, and Danish furniture and paintings — but has little to offer if that period does not appeal to your taste.

Turn right into the first block on "the flat" of Chestnut Street and enter number 86 (on the left-hand side) to **Hilary House.** In

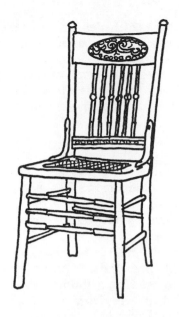

days past, you would have found the carriage houses and accommodations for the drivers and footmen employed "up the hill." Now in an area of elegant condominiums and homes, this particular house-cum-shop is owned and operated by interior designer Ann Sullivan. Combining vocation and avocation, she has a fine selection of English, American, and French antiques and reproductions. One of her specialties is fireplace accessories, a particular treat for people who don't want their bumpers, fenders, and screens too unabashedly new looking.

Tucked between the main thoroughfares of Beacon Hill at 40 River Street is a small shop that carries reasonably priced, small furniture and decorative accessories. This cozy shop, **Howard Chadwick Antiques,** was founded in the 1930s. After looking around, head back to Charles Street and take time for a cup of coffee at either **Rebecca's** or **Il Dolce Momento** while you contemplate the beautiful things you have seen and dreamed of owning.

For something affordable, there's no better way to remember your day of browsing than with a fine print of Boston from **Eugene Galleries,** at 76 Charles Street. The shop is full of antique prints, paintings, maps, and manuscripts from the thirteenth to the nineteenth century. A scene from the past, a botanical print, or a Barlett or Currier and Ives engraving could soon grace the wall of your home.

It would be worth your while to visit the small shop at 82 Charles Street that Jack Sherman shares with used-book store **ChoreoGraphica** for an interesting decorative print or a small antique curio to commemorate your trip. The owner of **Sher-Morr Antiques** is very willing to share his knowledge of the objects in his shop and his love of Charles Street. As an added benefit, the store is open seven days a week.

George Gravert Antiques is located at 122 Charles Street. The quiet grace of this honest and knowledgeable gentleman pervades his serenely uncluttered shop. Gravert specializes in eighteenth- and nineteenth-century continental antiques, and displays them with unusual country elegance. Here you can concentrate on one piece at a time and imagine how it would look in your own home.

Many of the Oriental antiques at 126 Charles Street are of museum quality. The porcelains, furniture, paintings, and small sculptures in **Alberts-Langdon, Inc.,** are mostly from China. The design of these pieces, which date from as long ago as 3000 B.C., are simple enough to enhance any decor. Mr. Alberts is a charming gentleman who will make you feel welcome even if you are not in the market for his wares.

A venerable Boston institution on this street is **Marika's,** at 130 Charles Street. Current proprietor Matthew Raisz is proud of his ability to show high-quality vases, candlesticks, paintings, jewelry, tapestries, and furniture from almost every corner of the globe. Founded by Raisz's grandmother, Marika's has a reputation for jewelry in particular (pocket watches, rings, jade, and strands of beads) that has brought the shop a faithful local following. Many of the clientele are on a first-name basis with the owner, another indication that this is an "insiders" store.

In contrast to the eclectic selection we have just left, down the street at number 138 you will find a real specialist. James Kilroy's shop, **Danish Country,** is limited by geography, though not by time. Denmark is the theme, and the scrubbed pine interior is reminiscent of Scandinavia's best. His wares include rugs, candles, and folk art, as well as antique pine armoires, chests, tables, and desks that range from 1750 through the 1900s. (The armoires are particularly useful to Beacon Hill residents. Because a tax was once imposed on the construction of closets, many homes on the hill lack them. That was all well and good when a family had a few outfits and wore them day after day, but it is a major hardship for modern residents.)

Much of the stock in the small shop at 125 Charles Street comes from people who live on Beacon Hill or in the vicinity. Here, in the aptly named **Reruns Antiques,** is your chance to bring home a momento of Boston from the selection of jewelry, bric-a-brac, and small pieces of furniture.

Next, walk up a few steps into the bright open space of **C. A. Ruppert** antiques, at 121 Charles Street, to view the fine continental and English furniture and decorative accessories from the eighteenth to the twentieth century.

At number 119 is the **Boston Antique Co-op I & II.** Since it is a cooperative with five different owners, it's like having five different shops under one roof. The diversity is reflected by the owner's specializations, and the two floors display a full range of American, European, and Oriental antiques, including some furniture and decorative objects. This place is a browser's delight.

Looking at the window display, it is not immediately apparent that **Kiku Sui Gallery, Inc.,** at number 101 is the largest Japanese print gallery in New England. Although not all of the prints are antiques, there is an ever-changing display from the eighteenth to the twentieth century in a variety of techniques such as woodblock, etchings, silk screen, and lithography. The knowledgeable owner, David Welker, enjoys his prints so much that you may have difficulty in convincing him to part with one.

The same original **Weiner's Antiques** that was once well known atop Beacon Hill can be found in Cambridge on Broadway in a more consolidated and manageable space for owner Paul Weiner. Paul Weiner is friendly and very knowledgeable about the Boston antiques scene. The Weiners have been in business for three generations, and the shop has a real grandfather's attic atmosphere. This is one of the few places where you can buy local goods. The merchandise is all purchased from estates within a fifty-mile radius of Boston. Some of the specialties include candlesticks, ginger jars, and dinnerware.

Now make your way back along Charles Street to the Public Garden, cross it, and start out afresh at the head of Newbury. The antique shops in the Back Bay extend from Arlington to Gloucester along both sides of Newbury Street, with a worthwhile detour near the end of Boylston Street.

At the corner of Newbury and Arlington Streets, above Burberry's, is **Skinner, Inc.** Skinner is known locally as one of the foremost auction houses. The element of chance and timing, of discovering a totally unexpected treasure in the bottom of the old trunk you bid on, make frequenting auctions a potentially addictive pastime. (Check the Sunday paper for who is auctioning what off where.)

The most formal French and English furniture and decorative accessories on Newbury Street can be found at number 29. **Slenska Antiques and Interior Design** carries items from the late 1700s and the early to mid-1800s.

In this first, prestigious block of Newbury Street, at number 115, look up to the second-floor window belonging to **Isabelle Collins of London.** This shop opened in 1981 as the American counterpart to its sister shop in London. The managers carry a wonderful range of pine English country furniture. They also specialize in blue and white majolica and linens and embroideries, as well as continental decorative furniture and arts.

Down the street at 125 Newbury Street is **Autre Fois,** a shop whose name means "formerly" in French. Charles Duncan Rowe and wife Maria have been in business for forty years, but in Boston only since 1985. Their shop is self-described as "piled to the ceiling." Although their main emphasis is on French country furniture, both plain and fancy, they also stock English and Italian furniture, antique French chandeliers and light fixtures, and lots of carved and Oriental accessories. Wade through; it's a fire fighter's nightmare and a tactician's delight.

Continuing down the street, but crossing to the other side again, stop at number 170 behind the perfumery to find **The March Hare, Ltd.** Owner Ruth Kennedy stocks a beautiful selection of eighteenth- and nineteenth-century furniture from England and France that is definitely *not* "country." The mahogany, walnut, and fruitwood pieces, with attending marquetry and parquet tables, are complemented by porcelain and other accessories. The owner has excellent taste, and shares it with her patrons graciously.

Marcoz, the "insiders" antique shop, is at 177 Newbury Street. Owner Marcoz has a style all his own — grand and alluring — and entering his shop is like taking a quick trip to England and France for eighteenth- and nineteenth-century furniture and decorative antiques. The eminent charming and charismatic man stocks many wonderful small pieces, such as engravings, vintage men's watches, and decorative desk objects. Downstairs, you can find English country furniture and equestrian prints. Marcoz was part of the Newbury Street scene long before it was fashionable.

Next, you should visit **Belgravia,** at 222 Newbury Street. This shop is the epitome of style and sophistication. Carolyn Schofield travels abroad six or seven times a year, and returns with eighteenth- and nineteenth-century furniture and decorative pieces of exceptional quality. The dining room tables with Chinese export porcelain look as if they were set up for guests, and indeed the owner has been known to serve dinner in her shop!

Wenham Cross Antiques, at 232 Newbury Street, is the only bailiwick of mother-and-daughter team Irma and Emily Lampert. Their warm and charming shop sells country and primitive furniture and decorative accessories, while the cupboards full of majolica and quimper beckon cheerfully. Mother Irma's knowledge extends far beyond the shop. She is an admired lecturer on art and antiques at the Museum of Fine Arts, and very much an expert.

A delightful mix of antiques awaits you at **The Barn at Hampton Falls,** at 249 Newbury Street. The changing displays of English, continental, and American antiques are replenished from the larger stock in New Hampshire. The furniture and furnishings are interspersed with reproductions in tasteful groupings.

Walk down several steps through the garden courtyard into **Newbury Street Jewelry and Antiques.** The small shop at 255 Newbury Street carries jewelry and antiques, just as the name implies, with an array of Rose Medallion and Rose Mandarin porcelain, silver tea and coffee services, and a variety of antique accessories.

The place to find a Victorian art object is at 811 Boylston Street, **Brodney Gallery of Fine Arts,** opposite the Hynes Auditorium. Owner Richard Brodney carries on the tradition begun over fifty years ago of buying from estates and private individuals to replenish the constantly rotating stock of antiques, jewelry, and small decorative pieces. Don't forget to check the basement, which is full of paintings and a few pieces of furniture.

Unfortunately, space simply doesn't permit our mentioning all the other excellent shops in Boston and the surrounding area. We've highlighted the truly special shops, due to style, personnel, stock, or quality, within the confines of the geographic area. Go home now, soak your tired feet, and try to remember where you put your cloths and polishes so that you can clean up that trinket you couldn't bring yourself to pass up today.

Tour Sites

CHARLES STREET AREA

Alberts-Langdon, Inc.,
   Oriental Art
126 Charles St.
Boston, MA 02114
523-5954

Boston Antique Co-op I & II
119 Charles St.
Boston, MA 02114
227-9810

C. A. Rupport
121 Charles St.
Boston, MA 02114
523-5033

ChoreoGraphica
82 Charles St.
Boston, MA 02114
227-4780

Danish Country
138 Charles St.
Boston, MA 02114
227-1804

Eugene Galleries
76 Charles St.
Boston, MA 02114
227-3062

George Gravert Antiques
122 Charles St.
Boston, MA 02114
227-1593

Hilary House
86 Chestnut St.
Boston, MA 02108
523-7118

Howard Chadwick Antiques
40 River St.
Boston, MA 02108
227-9261

James Billings II Antiques
70 Charles St.
Boston, MA 02108
367-9533

Kiku Sui Gallery, Inc.
101 Charles St.
Boston, MA 02114
227-4288

Marika's
130 Charles St.
Boston, MA 02114
523-4520

Reruns Antiques
125 Charles St.
Boston, MA 02114

Sher-Morr Antiques
82 Charles St.
Boston, MA 02114
227-4780

NEWBURY STREET AREA

Autre Fois
125 Newbury St
Boston, MA 02116
424-8823

Marcoz
177 Newbury St.
Boston, MA 02116
262-0780

The Barn at Hampton Falls
249 Newbury St.
Boston, MA 02116
859-0488

Newbury Street Jewelry
  and Antiques
255 Newbury St.
Boston, MA 02116
236-0038

Belgravia
222 Newbury St.
Boston, MA 02116
267-1915

Skinner, Inc.
  Auctioneers & Appraisers
2 Newbury St.
Boston, MA 02116
236-1700

Brodney Gallery of Fine Arts
811 Boylston St.
Boston, MA 02116
536-0500

Slenska Antiques and
  Interior Design
29 Newbury St.
Boston, MA 02116
437-0822

Isabelle Collins of London
115 Newbury St.
Boston, MA 02116
266-8699

Weiner's Antique Shop
356 Broadway St.
Cambridge, MA 02138
227-2894

The March Hare, Ltd.
170 Newbury St.
Boston, MA 02114
720-4687

Wenham Cross Antiques
232 Newbury St.
Boston, MA 02116
236-0409

RESTAURANTS

Back Bay Bistro
565 Boylston St.
Boston, MA 02116
536-4477

Rebecca's Restaurant
21 Charles St.
Boston, MA 02114
742-9747

II Dolce Momento
30 Charles St.
Boston, MA 02114
720-0477

Additional Resources

RECOMMENDED READING

New England Antiques Journal
Turley Publications
4 Church St.
Ware, MA 01082
413-967-3505

The Maine Antique Digest
Box 645
Waldoborough, ME 04572
207-832-7534

Sloan, Susan. *Sloan's Green Guide to Antique Dealers and Antiques Related Services.*
Boston: The Antique Press, 1989
105 Charles St., Boston, MA 02114
1-800-552-5632

CHAPTER SIX

The Art of Boston

In the past, Boston was not on top of the list of major United States art centers. Although the city had splendid museums, it did not have a large population of working artists. With the notable exception of some famous portraitists and landscape painters, artists did not find this a congenial city in which to live and work.

But all that has changed in the past few decades, and Boston now attracts art and artists alike. The city boasts some of the best schools, museums, and collections in the country in which preclassical and avant-garde material are treated with equal respect. Art enthusiasts won't find a scarcity of things to see. The main problem is where to begin and how to fit it all into a limited time schedule.

Your own interests will determine the sequence, but in the following three tours we'll usher you through the well-known and lesser-known highlights. We'll also show you where Boston's love of art has spilled over into the streets, onto the sidewalks, and even into the air.

Artists' Hideaways and Hangouts

In Paris during the 1920s and 1930s, the Left Bank was the place to be if you were an artist, whether you were a recognized or struggling one. The Left Bank was then somewhat physically isolated from the rest of the city, and the young iconoclasts who gathered there were proud of their separation from the mainstream culture across the Seine.

In Boston, that same kind of physical distance separates the new art community from the rest of the city. This first tour will take you into areas that may not, at first, look promising or even artsy. But persevere and you'll be rewarded with some exciting new talent. We've also included stops at some of the area's cafés, pubs, and restaurants, because that's where creative people gather, and where ideas and conversation flow as generously as the espresso. Before you start your tour, you will find it helpful to pick up a copy of the "Gallery Guide," available at most Boston Galleries.

Our tour starts in South Boston at Fort Point Channel, east of the city. Once a thriving area filled with busy import/export and wool processing companies, Fort Point was mostly abandoned by the 1950s. A decade ago it was discovered by a group of enterprising young artists, on their never-ending quest for affordable workspace with enough room and good light. Today, Fort Point Channel is home to the largest concentration of artists in the city; at least three hundred in twenty separate buildings that are in various states of renovation (or disrepair, depending on how you look at it). The neighborhood has often been compared to New York's SoHo, and as soon as you walk over the Summer Street Bridge from South Station, you'll see the similarities.

At number 249 A Street is the centerpiece for this district, the **Fort Point Arts Community, Inc.** (FPAC). The FPAC was formed in 1980 by a group of artists who pooled their resources and bought a former printing plant. The huge, high ceilings, large freight elevators, industrial floors, and excellent light made this building the perfect site for artists' lofts. Continuity is ensured by the cooperative's rule that when they move, artists must resell their spaces to other artists, and cannot make more than a ten percent profit on the deal. Turnover is small, though, because the building is so wonderful to work in.

In addition to acting as landlord for the artists-in-residence, FPAC is the central clearinghouse for a wide range of artists' concerns, from finding housing to finding gallery space, from fundraising to raising the city's awareness about the special needs of artists. The Fort Point Channel studios are open to the public one day a year or by special appointment or tour.

Alchemie, 286 Congress Street: Lawyer/photographer Ted Landsmark started this small nonprofit gallery, whose name implies the magical transformation of one substance into another. It specializes in photography and prints. Once you've feasted your eyes on this art, you can feast your appetite on burgers, sandwiches, or steaks at **Three Cheers** restaurant on the ground floor next to the gallery. For a special visual treat, just walk down to **Mobius,** located at 354 Congress Street and known for unusual displays. The gallery is not always open, so call before you go by.

Fort Point isn't only a place for visual artists. Dancers, writers, actors, and framers, live and work in the neighborhood too. Check out some of their watering holes if you'd like to mingle. **Sal's Lunch,** at 309 A Street, is known for its fabulous overstuffed and underpriced sandwiches. Sal's may appear closed because of the security grid covering the door and window, but look for a small "open" sign; the greasy spoon interior has something intimate and personal about it in spite of its unprepossessing exterior. It's also one of the few places in town open at 5 A.M., when you're as likely to see an artist with the late-night-can't-work blues as you are to see a trucker fueling himself for his morning haul.

Another local hangout is the **Hav-A-Bite,** at 324 A Street, where a similar ambiance prevails. The bagels and cream cheese are surprisingly good here, and, as with everything else on the menu, the price is modest.

Across the channel and back in Boston again, you can pay a visit to the Federal Reserve Building, or "the stainless-steel washboard" as the locals call it, designed by Hugh Stebbins and Associates. Once inside the bank, head toward the beautiful **Federal Reserve Gallery,** where exhibits change every six weeks. From the Federal Reserve Building you can see the newly restored South Station. In the past few years a new area of artists' hideaways has emerged in this neighborhood. Some galleries have even relocated from their high-rent, high-profile spaces on Newbury Street.

Bromfield Gallery, 90 South Street: Displays local, national, and international artists' contemporary work. Formed in the mid-1970s, this is the oldest cooperative art organization in Boston. Its fifteen members show their paintings, prints, and photographs in the nonprofit gallery. Every October, they sponsor a fund-raising event known as the "Black and White Ball," to which celebrants come dressed in outlandish black-and-white costumes.

Howard Yezerski Gallery, 186 South Street: Truly an exhibit hideaway for new and emerging Boston artists.

Robert Klein Gallery, 207 South Street: Known for its quality prints, this gallery exhibits, appraises, and purchases nineteenth- and twentieth-century collectible photography.

Thomas Segal Gallery, 207 South Street: Tommy made the decision to move his venerable Newbury Street Gallery to this large open space several years ago. Among the items he exhibits are paintings, sculpture, and lithographs by well-known contemporary artists.

Harcus Gallery, 210 South Street: Another Newbury transplant, Portia Harcus has developed a hugh space entered through a stunning marble office building lobby. Portia shows contemporary art from all over the world. She has always had a commitment to Boston artists, both emerging and established.

On South Street, the old leather district, next to many of the galleries we've mentioned, you may want to rest your feet at the **Blue Diner.** This forty-year-old landmark is an authentic American diner serving eggs, hamburgers, and grilled specialties. Even the jukebox plays authentic 1950s tunes.

At 129 Kingston Street (near Chinatown) is another off-the-beaten-path gallery, the **Kingston Gallery,** open Wednesday through Sunday from 12 P.M. to 6 P.M. This cooperative venture was established by Boston artists to present a variety of media, although paintings tend to predominate. The artists take turns running the space, so the works you see may have been done by the person in charge. The gallery prides itself on its "underground" affiliations, unlike the fancier Newbury Street shops, and browsers are encouraged. Another gallery in the neighborhood is the **Akin Gallery,** at 476 Columbus Avenue. Owner Allison Akin Righter shows some of New England's best emerging artists to an art-oriented clientele.

At first glance it may seem that South Boston and the South End have a lot in common. Both are fringe areas of Boston proper, and both have attracted many artists. But the South End is a neighborhood with a distinct flavor of its own, and very different from South Boston.

The South End section of Boston was created by filling in marshy land, starting in 1834. It preceded the filling of Back Bay, but unlike the Back Bay, with its focus on a broad avenue, it lacked a visual cohesiveness, and its wealthier residents deserted it for the more stylish Commonwealth Avenue addresses. The South

End homes, originally middle class, became multifamily residences of the vast and growing immigrant population that poured into Boston in the late 1800s.

The area is currently undergoing a "regentrification" due to Boston's rising housing costs, but the process is far from complete. South of Tremont Street, the South End is still dowdy; the buildings, once used for light industry and housing, have fallen into disrepair. Rooming houses and empty lofts abound, making it an ideal spawning ground for another of Boston's arts communities. The South End artists' community is an even newer phenomenon than that in South Boston's Fort Point, yet it already bears the imprint of a lively influx of energy and talent that is quickly transforming the moribound neighborhood (and raising the rents).

Unlike Fort Point, there has not been a concerted effort among the artists to maintain control of the South End. Architecturally and geographically, it is more desirable than South Boston since the Victorian buildings have survived pretty much intact, but redevelopment is threatening to squeeze out the artists as well as the other low-rent residents who preceded them.

The only focal point for the community is the **Boston Center for the Arts,** at 539 Tremont Street. The BCA's structure represents

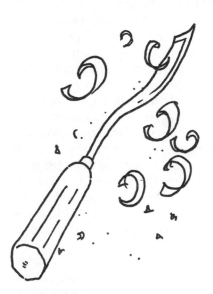

one of the most extensive and astonishing uses of found space in the city, and comprises several old converted buildings. Formerly a gas station, parking garage, warehouse, vaudeville theater, an apartment house, and a glass-domed exhibition hall, it is now an arts complex on a three-acre triangle between Warren Avenue and Union Park.

The large exhibition hall, known as the Cyclorama, is the centerpiece of the complex. It is a National Landmark building constructed in 1884 to house a four-hundred-foot-long circular painting of the Battle of Gettysburg by Philippoteaux, who was one of the world's premier painters of cycloramas at the time. But the Cyclorama's artistic origins were soon forgotten. It became a bicycle riding academy, then a wholesale flower market, and finally a garage space where Alfred Champion invented spark plugs.

Today the Cyclorama houses offices as well as the remarkable circular exhibition space. Since it opened, it has hosted student shows for the Museum of Fine Arts Museum School, the annual Ellis Memorial Antique Show, and exhibitions by BCA resident artists. It also houses the **Mills Gallery,** which represents the visual artists in the complex with a constantly rotating exhibition of their work. There is a low-key, friendly atmosphere to this nonprofit gallery, and it is very easy to get to meet the artists if you wish.

If you see anything you'd like to purchase at an exhibition, the Center will arrange for you to meet the artist in his/her studio, many of which are in the Tremont Estates Building next door. Once a factory, Tremont Estates has been divided into use as offices, studios for about fifty visual artists (all of whom are eligible to exhibit in the Cyclorama), and rehearsal space for performing artists. In keeping with the original mandate that all the arts be included in the BCA, Tremont Estates is the rehearsal home for the Boston Philharmonic Orchestra, the MJT Dance Theater, the Artists' Opera Company, City Stage, and Stage One, among others.

For some theatrical entertainment, try the **New Ehrlich Theatre,** next to the BCA, a small theater with 150 seats and a strong emphasis on new works and Sam Shepard plays. Around the corner is the Rennock Building, constructed in 1916 as a garage and now home to the School of the **Boston Ballet.** Although rehearsals and classes are usually off-limits to casual visitors, you might stroll through and catch a glimpse of earnest young students sweating out an adagio in the center of the huge, well-lit rooms, or even spot members of the company working on a pas de deux for their next performance. The company is currently housed in Newton, and it performs at the Wang Center. In a few years, however, the entire Boston Ballet will move into a modern brick building designed by Graham Gund. This will be the largest center for dance in New England.

For an elaborate, innovative meal, visit **Icarus,** at 3 Appleton Street. Icarus was opened several years ago by two novice restaurateurs from Provincetown whose cuisine quickly became a major league contender. A seasonal menu of food as artistic as the local residents awaits you in an elegant atmosphere. It's a bit more expensive than the average painter or dancer can afford on a regular basis, but a treat nonetheless. The aqua blue light at the rim of the ceiling is the subject of much debate, while the intricate mahogany woodwork interior, crafted by owner Tom Hall, gives the room a feeling of comfort and stateliness. You'll even find owner John Belliott serving customers at the bar two days a week.

Back on Tremont Street at 436, directly across from the BCA, is **Emilio's Pizza.** Open from 7 A.M. to 10 P.M., they offer Greek pizza and salads, and subs, all at moderate prices.

Club Café, at 209 Columbus Avenue (and Berkeley Street), is a restaurant that requires reservations. Although it is pricey, artists and art lovers meet and dine here, partly because of the fine continental food and partly because of the art displayed on the walls, which changes every few months and is available for purchase. The Club is known for its contemporary American cuisine, and each night features a pianist or vocalist. It shares space with **Club Cabaret,** a nightclub featuring local, regional, and occasionally nationally known jazz performers.

The South End seems to be a vest pocket for fine dining. Two more restaurants worth noting are **St. Cloud** and **Hammersley's.** St. Cloud, started by Rebecca's, is a hip, popular eatery and bar with windows around two sides. St. Cloud attracts a sizable afterwork crowd, for hors d'oeuvres and cocktails, and serves a fabulous Sunday brunch. Aside from traditional brunch dishes, you can order smoked codfish cakes with eggs, omelettes, pasta, and fish. For spicy French country dining, enjoy some chicken, fish, or meat at Hammersley's Bistro. The classical food here is known throughout the city. Two popular dishes are roast chicken with lemon, garlic, and parsley and the grilled garlic and mushroom sandwich.

The other anchor to the South End arts neighborhood is the Piano Factory at 791 Tremont Street. This is the former Chickering Piano Factory, and was converted in 1974 to artists' spaces. Officially known as the **Piano Craft Guild,** it contains a little bit of everything: a gallery, theater, and housing where artists of all kinds live and work. The shows in the gallery change approximately every three weeks and range from mixed media and sculpture to painting, photography, and dance.

If you want to see what's up-and-coming on the Boston art scene, visit the area's art schools: the **Museum of Fine Arts Museum School, Massachusetts College of Art,** and **Boston University's School of Fine Arts.** School exhibitions are always in progress at these institutions, and you are welcome to wander the halls to soak up both the visual and visceral feeling of the creative process.

Tour Sites

African Influence Gallery
150 Lincoln St.
Boston, MA 02111
426-3366

Akin Gallery
476 Columbus Ave.
Boston, MA 02118
266-3535

Alchemie
286 Congress St.
Boston, MA 02210

Boston Center for the Arts
539 Tremont St.
Boston, MA 02116
426-5000

Boston Ballet School
19 Clarendon St.
Boston, MA 02116
542-1406

Boston University Art Gallery
855 Commonwealth Ave.
Boston, MA 02215
353-3329

Bromfield Gallery
90 South St.
Boston, MA 02111
451-3605

Federal Reserve Gallery
600 Atlantic Avenue
Boston, MA
973-3464

Fort Point Arts Community, Inc.
Fort Point Artists' Community
    Gallery
249 A St.
Boston, MA 02210
423-4299

Harcus Gallery
210 South St.
Boston, MA 02111
262-4445

Howard Yezerski Gallery
186 South St.
Boston, MA 02111
426-8085

Kingston Gallery
129 Kingston St.
Boston, MA 02111
423-4113

Laughlin/Winkler Gallery
205 A St., 7th Floor
Boston, MA 02210
269-1782

Massachusetts College of Art
364 Brookline Ave.
Boston, MA 02215
731-2040

Mills Gallery
549 Tremont St.
Boston, MA 02116
426-5000

Mobius
354 Congress St.
Boston, MA 02210
542-7416

Museum of Fine Arts Museum
    School & Gallery
230 The Fenway
Boston, MA 02115
267-9300

New Ehrlich Theatre
551 Tremont St.
Boston, MA 02116
482-6316

Piano Craft Guild
791 Tremont St.
Boston, MA 02118
536-2622

Robert Klein Gallery
207 South St.
Boston, MA 02111
482-8188

Thomas Segal Gallery
207 South St.
Boston, MA 02111
292-0789

RESTAURANTS

The Blue Diner
178 Kneeland St.
Boston, MA 02111
338-4639

Club Café
209 Columbus Ave.
Boston, MA 02116
536-0966

Emilio's Pizza
436 Tremont St.
Boston, MA 02118
423-4083

St. Cloud
557 Tremont St.
Boston, MA 02108
353-0202

Hammersley's Bistro
578 Tremont St.
Boston, MA 02108
267-6068

Sal's Lunch
309 A St.
Boston, MA 02210
338-9009

Hav-A-Bite
324 A St.
Boston, MA 02210
338-7571

Three Cheers
290 Congress St.
Boston, MA 02210
423-4352

Icarus
3 Appleton St.
Boston, MA 02108
426-1790

Timeless Treasures

Bostonians have always been fascinated with old things, perhaps because their own history is so long and illustrious. If it's historical, venerable, aged, ancient, well worn, or just dusty, you can be sure it will be treated with respect by some Bostonian, even though a dozen appraisers may tell him or her to do otherwise. Bostonians have also had the wisdom to preserve the past in public institutions for present and future generations. This tour will take you through the high points of the city's art collection, but remember that private residences, businesses, and even city streets are also likely treasure repositories. Always keep your eyes open!

The place to start, of course, is the **Museum of Fine Arts,** the city's oldest and most revered cultural institution. It is also one of the preeminent museums in the country, ranked by some as second only to the Metropolitan in New York.

The MFA was incorporated in 1870 when the Boston Athenaeum, having run out of gallery space for its painting collection, loaned its influential support to the establishment of an independent art museum. When the Back Bay was filled in, space had been allotted by the city for public institutions, so the MFA commandeered some and opened its doors to the public in Copley Square (then called Art Square) in 1876.

The museum was already outgrowing its Copley Square headquarters by 1898, and in 1909, the collection was moved to the Fenway — then virtually a rural outpost of the city — by means of two horse-drawn carriages making several trips. Considering the degree of security involved in transporting artworks today, it's amazing to realize that no guards were considered necessary, and that nothing of value was broken or damaged in the move.

Today, the "new" museum building is the oldest, having been expanded in 1915, 1928, and again in 1981, with the addition of the sleek new West Wing, designed by I. M. Pei to hold the MFA's modern art collections.

In our search for timeless treasures, it is appropriate that we enter through the classic portals of the main approach on Huntington Avenue. The MFA offers far more than can be reasonably seen and appreciated in a lifetime of visits, let alone in one day. Fortunately, the museum has an excellent system of signs and plenty of staff around to direct and assist you, so you can feel free to let your own enthusiasm be your guide. There are also several guidebooks and specialized tours available at the front desk. Below is a brief listing of the curatorial departments and some of their highlights, in case you'd like to prepare before your visit.

Department of Asiatic Art: The twenty-six galleries of the beautifully restored Asian wing house art from China, Japan, and other Asiatic nations. Some of the most ancient pieces date from the third millennium B.C. and were unearthed by the MFA's own excavations in the Indus Valley.

Department of Egyptian and Near Eastern Art: The display of Egyptian antiquities represents a complete cross section of that ancient civilization but is strongest in its collection of Old Kingdom sculpture, an assemblage unsurpassed outside of the Cairo Museum.

Department of Classical Art: The ancient Roman, Greek, and

Etruscan collection is outstanding for its high artistic qualities as well as its representation of the everyday life of these long-ago societies. The museum publishes a handbook that especially highlights the masterpieces of this department.

In the early 1960s, a fourth-century B.C. *Greek earring disappeared from the MFA collection. The piece, a tiny gold rendering of Nike riding a chariot, had been missing for six months when the museum received a telephone tip about where it might be found. Volunteers were organized into a search party, which combed the banks of the adjacent Muddy River and finally found the treasure, lodged in a rusty tomato soup can. Apparently the thief had stolen the earring in order to impress his girlfriend, who was a student at the MFA's Museum School. The girl was not impressed, and the thief was caught.*

Department of Paintings: All the great painting traditions are well represented at the MFA, but the museum's collection of nineteenth-century French paintings is especially exciting. Much of it comes from wealthy Boston collectors of that era, who acquired works of Delacroix, Corot, Millet, and Courbet even before those artists came to be recognized in their native land. The French impressionists and postimpressionists were also a target of the Boston collectors, and the result is a dazzling assemblage of works by Renoir, Picasso, Monet, Manet, Van Gogh, Gauguin, and Cézanne.

Jean François Millet, who is represented at the museum by an astounding 150 works, has a special Boston connection. Millet, who eschewed the popular academic subjects such as religion and history to depict simple peasant people engaged in everyday activities, attracted several Boston patrons and painters, some of whom went to France to study with him. In particular, the interest of then–MFA president Martin Brimmer helped to create a Millet boom among wealthy Bostonians, which is why the MFA today owns the bulk of his work, much to the chagrin of the French.

Another more modern Boston benefactor was Russian-born Max Karolik, who amassed huge collections in American decorative arts, American paintings, and nineteenth-century American watercolors. All were intended for the MFA from the start and were carefully collected with an eye toward that end by Karolik himself. Today the Karolik Collection of American Painting is one of the finest in the country, and was largely responsible for reawakening interest in American primitive, rustic, and folk art.

Department of American Decorative Arts: This exhibition of furniture, silver, glass, pewter, and sculpture, places a particular emphasis on early New England works. It includes Paul Revere's famous silver Liberty Bowl. The collection's period rooms reconstruct several eighteenth- and nineteenth-century parlors, ranging from the rustic to the opulent, and there is an impressive display of old ship models that will appeal to maritime history buffs.

Department of European Decorative Arts: The strength of this department lies in its collections of Medieval works, Chinese export porcelain, English silver, and French furniture. The MFA's Musical Instruments Collection, which is part of this department, includes early clavichords, lutes, recorders, harps, and zithers. (There is a charming turn-of-the century violin carved in Maine from a wooden egg crate; the carved figure of a man holds the instrument's bridge, while the peghead is in the shape of a horse's noggin.)

Department of Textiles and Costumes: Colonial New England embroideries, Turkish velvets, European tapestries, and Indonesian batiks are all on display here. The MFA was the first museum in the country to grant textiles art status, and because the Boston area was the capital of the textile industry in the 1870s, the museum has always emphasized this collection.

Department of Twentieth-Century Art: It wasn't until the 1970s that the MFA established a department devoted exclusively to the study of twentieth-century art. Primary emphasis is placed on abstract paintings and sculpture, and artists such as Jackson Pollock, Georgia O'Keeffe, Robert Motherwell, and Larry Poons are well represented. The department's collection of twelve gigantic Morris Louis canvases is part of the largest single assemblage of that artist's work in the country. However, only a few of his works are on display.

The museum also has a growing department of prints, drawings, and photographs — but you shouldn't limit yourself to the exhibitions. Cast your eyes about the public spaces, and look for the murals by John Singer Sargent. Locate the three goddesses pouring water from urns — models for whom were borrowed from the Ziegfeld Follies!

When you're ready for a lunch break, head into the exciting new West Wing, and the Galleria Café on the first floor. This informal eatery offers an elegant selection of light meals, cheese, wine, and lavish desserts. Upstairs, the more formal restaurant offers a more substantial menu. For a truly quick stop (especially if you have children with you), you can eat in the basement cafeteria.

As soon as you're able to tear yourself away from the MFA, head back into Boston to Newbury Street, where the city's largest collection of galleries is located. (You may wish to spend the entire day in the Museum and save Newbury Street for another spree.) The selection of fine galleries on this busy thoroughfare, each with its perspective and specialization, is far too long to detail here. For a comprehensive listing pick up a "Gallery Guide," available at almost every stop. We'll highlight the more traditional galleries and save the contemporary ones for the next tour.

At 238 Newbury Street, the **Vose Gallery,** which has been run continuously by five generations of Voses, is certainly a leader among the city's traditionally oriented art emporiums. Specialties here are eighteenth-, nineteenth-, and twentieth-century American paintings. The cheerful blue front door of this bowfront brick townhouse welcomes you into an impressive array of art books and magazines, as well as the Vose's current exhibit.

Robert Vose, for years head of this art-dealing lineage, has retired, but his twin sons Robert C. Vose III and Abbot William Vose ably direct the family business. They may share a story with you about their great-grandfather, who often journeyed to France at the turn of the century, and once returned with the portrait of a male nude painted by Géricault. The client who purchased it thought it only proper, given the mores of the day, that the canvas be cut in half and the offending portion be discarded. It wasn't until the Voses were cleaning out their basement a few years ago that they came across the discarded portion of the canvas and donated it to the MFA to be reunited with its upper part, which had been previously contributed.

Another gallery that devotes itself to quality traditional work is the **Childs Gallery,** at 169 Newbury Street. The gallery, established in 1937, is devoted to American and European paintings, prints, drawings, and watercolors. Charles Childs, the original proprietor who retired in 1970, developed and established the gallery's reputation for excellence in taste and service. Childs publishes a newspaper-format bulletin which, aside from providing an extensive listing of their exhibitions and articles on printmaking, carries many excellent photos of their collection. Over the years, the Childs Gallery has become more involved with figurative sculpture.

158 Newbury Street is the home of the **Copley Society,** founded in 1879, the oldest art association in America. Soon after the MFA opened in Copley Square, a student of its art school named Alice Spenser Tinkham promoted among her peers the idea of establishing a separate group to further the study and appreciation of art. Tinkham and her friends started the Boston Art Student's Association, and immediately began organizing exhibitions of their work and the work of other artists of the day.

The name was changed in 1901 to the Copley Society as an appropriate expression of its aims. By that time, the Society had established a firm reputation for presenting art of national and international importance. John Singer Sargent showed his work there, and served as an honorary member and student advisor for

many years. The Society hosted an exhibition in 1904, and the next year, Claude Monet's first American exhibition of his impressionist works created quite a stir there. (It was underwritten by the St. Botolph Club, the gentlemen's arts and letters group that had rejected Sargent's "racy" portrait of Isabella Stewart Gardner. See page 43.)

The Society had its biggest coup in 1913, when Marcel Duchamp's controversial "Nude Descending a Staircase" nearly caused a riot among the guests, and brought the European Modern Movement to Boston for the first time. Today, the Copley Society still pursues its educational goals. Although it is dedicated to furthering appreciation of visual artworks over one hundred years old, artist members are encouraged to exhibit their work. The Society now has two floors of galleries and also sponsors shows elsewhere in the city.

Above the Copley Society, at number 158, is the **Alfred J. Walker Fine Arts Gallery.** Walk up the stairs and you'll feel as if you've stepped back into the nineteenth century. Alfred Walker presides over this Victorian treat of a gallery with soft-spoken graciousness. His collection, artfully displayed on easels, specializes in paintings, drawings, and etchings of the late nineteenth and early twentieth century, and concentrates on works by artists from the Boston School, such as Ripley, Lavalle, Goodwin, Paxton, Hale, and Woodbury. His greeting card business, called Boston Townhouse Press, reproduces nineteenth- and twentieth-century paintings as cards that can be purchased at **Shreve, Crump & Low** and other fine stores.

Haley and Steele, at number 91 Newbury Street, have been framers to Boston artists since 1899. Today, the firm specializes in painting conservation and nineteenth-century framing styles. In addition they have an impressive print collection, with themes ranging from floral and still-life motifs to traditional horse and hunting tableaux. They also have a large inventory of prints with New England maritime and natural history motifs.

Located at 162 Newbury Street, the **Guild of Boston Artists** is a nonprofit organization founded in 1918. The seventy members, from all over New England, are elected by consensus as an opening occurs, and must abide by the standing rule: that there be a painting by each artist on the wall in the upper gallery at any given time. The Guild also promotes one-person exhibitions and hosts different shows every three weeks.

An appropriate place to wind up our timeless treasures tour is the head of Newbury Street at the **Ritz-Carlton Hotel** on Arlington Street. A timeless treasure, the Ritz has been offering tea and hospitality to Boston society since 1927. Stop in for a drink at the newly remodeled bar, or head upstairs for high tea in the Tea Lounge. Settle back in one of the comfortable wing chairs and you will be served delicate sandwiches on crustless bread, scones with strawberry preserves, and excellent English Breakfast or Earl Grey tea. If you're unsure of the proper protocol for tucking into this repast, take a discreet look around you at the stately women who appear to have been born lifting their teacups and conversing with exactly the right degree of poise and pedigree. You are sitting among some of Boston's living timeless treasures.

Tour Sites

Alfred J. Walker Fine Arts Gallery
158 Newbury St.
Boston, MA 02116
247-1319

Haley and Steele
91 Newbury St.
Boston, MA 02116
536-6339

Childs Gallery
169 Newbury St.
Boston, MA 02116
266-1108

Museum of Fine Arts
465 Huntington Ave.
Boston, MA 02115
267-9377
Admission fee.

Copley Society of Boston
158 Newbury St.
Boston, MA 02116
536-5049

Ritz-Carlton Hotel
15 Arlington St.
Boston, MA 02116
536-5700

Fenway Art Center
50 Gloucester St.
Boston, MA 02115
536-0127

Shreve, Crump & Low
330 Boylston St.
Boston, MA 02116
267-9100

Guild of Boston Artists
162 Newbury St.
Boston, MA 02116
536-7660

Vose Gallery
238 Newbury St.
Boston, MA 02116
536-6176

Contemporary Currents

Boston is one of the best and easiest cities in the world to walk in — it's manageable, beautiful, and everchanging. Art is so pervasive in this city that you needn't limit yourself just to galleries and museums. There's art in the streets, in the buildings, and even on the people who stroll past you. So be alert, put on your walking shoes, and step out.

Once again, we direct you to begin your tour on Newbury Street. If it seems to you that *everything* seems to start on Newbury Street, from fashion and shopping to traditional and contemporary art, you're right. But remember that Boston is not a big city, so it's not surprising that all the good things are neatly wrapped up in one long skinny package on this crowded thoroughfare.

There is so much art on Newbury Street that twice a year — once in September and again in May — the galleries open their doors and invite the public inside. The street closes to vehicular traffic, while jazz and classical music is performed outside. This festive event, known as Art Newbury Street, has become a cultural tradition in Boston.

Start your contemporary gallery-hop at the corner of Newbury and Arlington Streets, site of the original St. Botolph Club. Since this end of the street is also the oldest, we'll find ourselves taking a chronological tour of the city's contemporary art scene; the more established galleries are on the east end of the street. Pick up a copy of the "Gallery Guide" and let your own tastes direct you, but we don't think you should miss the following.

Francesca Anderson Gallery, number 8: Specializing in contemporary realism, this gallery is also one of the largest portraiture galleries in New England.

Krakow Gallery, number 10: Represents several Boston-area artists, as well as a roster of artists from around the world. The focus here is on contemporary prints. The former fixture on the sidewalk in front of the building, Louise Nevelson's 1976 sculpture *Sky Landscape II*, has been sent back to her estate. In its place will be a bench by the provocative artist Jenny Holzer.

Levinson/Kane Gallery, number 16: Opened by two private art consultants, June Levinson and Barabara Kane, this gallery is focused on offering personalized service to clients. A variety of contemporary art forms from local, national, and international artists is displayed here.

Gallery Naga, number 67: Adventurous Boston-area art distinguishes this gallery, housed in the Church of the Covenant. The name is an acronym for the Newbury Associated Guild of Artists, since this gallery was established as a cooperative and remains one today.

Alpha Gallery, number 121: A long-standing, well-respected gallery. This is a must-stop for contemporary art.

Judi Rotenberg Gallery, number 130: The owner and her husband, Harold, have some of their own paintings on display, along with the work of Joe Solman, Douglas Yarborough, and Richard Crighton. Mostly Northeast American artists.

Randall Beck Gallery, number 168: Original contemporary prints and limited editions by contemporary American artists are the specialty here, as well as original works by emerging Boston artists.

Pucker/Safrai, number 171: This gallery features an unusual combination of contemporary artists from New England, Northeast Europe, and Israel. Owner Bernie Pucker, who is very active in the Newbury Street League, carries ceramic, sculpture, and photography as well as works of twentieth-century masters, notably Chagall, Picasso, and Braque. For a real treat, ask to see the work of Paul Nagamo. If you sign the guest book, you can receive Pucker/Safrai's semiannual newsletter, a well-illustrated catalogue of works for sale.

Society of Arts and Crafts, number 175: The oldest nonprofit crafts organization in the country runs a retail gallery of contemporary American crafts in all media, including jewelry, ceramics, glass, and studio furniture. You can also stop by the satellite location at 101 Arch Street.

Nielsen Gallery, number 179: Nina Nielsen has keen artistic instincts, and her stable of young talent includes many rising young stars. Her twenty artists represent Boston, New York, Mexico, and Europe. In addition to carrying sculpture, she has a fine collection of primitive antiquities from Africa, New Guinea, and China. Nielsen also mounts historical exhibitions, some with an emphasis on German expressionism.

Zoe Gallery, number 207: This gallery, named after the owner's dog, specializes in young, contemporary Massachusetts artists. Painting, sculpture, and photography are shown here, and occasional group shows mix locally and nationally known artists.

As you walk down Newbury Street, if the weather is good, you might see an elaborate chalk mural spread beneath your feet on the sidewalk. If you do, it's probably the work of Boston's redoubtable street artist, Sidewalk Sam. Sam Guillemin is a local artist who has created more than one thousand perishable oeuvres on Boston's streets in the past decade. He has painted Arthur Fiedler at the Downtown Crossing, Florence Nightingale by the Massachusetts General Hospital, and Nathaniel Hawthorne in front of the Old Corner Bookstore. Sam also executes amazing reproductions of famous masterpieces, usually at the behest of local corporate sponsors. You might encounter several of his pastels on your walk, and you might even come across Sam himself.

Take a break at the **Back Bay Bistro** for a bite to eat. The owners hang some wonderful contemporary artists' work on the walls, and you will have a great view of Copley Square as you sample a dish from their French country-style menu.

If you are on your way toward artists' hideaways, try lunch at **Rocco's,** a little hideaway in itself, situated in the brick transportation building around the corner from the Four Seasons Hotel. Your senses will be tantalized by the lively contemporary environment and eclectic sampling of art. Colorful and whimsical, the works represent many contemporary artists, and everything is for sale, from the folk art at the tables to the bronze pigs at the grill.

You will never forget this rich experience. Here is one place in Boston where the good is as creative as the art, with lunch- and dinner-sized portions.

Up Boylston Street past Hereford Street, you'll find the converted police station that houses the **Institute for Contemporary Art** (ICA). The ICA has a heavy, stone, Romanesque exterior, but its interior, redesigned by architect Graham Gund in 1976, is as up-to-date as the art it displays. The buildings, which date from 1885 and 1886, were originally designed to serve as a fire station, police station, and stable. The adjacent building, by the way, is still used as a fire station, and the entrance to the police station now houses an up-beat and extremely popular bar and restaurant, called **Division Sixteen,** after the previous tenant (see page 188).

The multilevel space inside lends itself to the often-changing displays of the visual arts, and the theater is the scene for the performing arts, both of which the ICA promotes in every medium and discipline. They have no permanent collection, but draw heavily on loans and local talent.

Around the block from the ICA, on Newbury Street, is the **Boston Architectural Center,** which sports a marvelous mural on its western wall. The trompe-l'oeil painting by Richard Haas, which contrasts whimsically with the 1960s building it adorns, is a depiction of a cross-sectional view of a Renaissance palace. The BAC itself is a school for architecture and interior design, and has a public gallery that displays architecturally related work.

At the other end of the block is another public artwork, painted by Morgan Bulkeley in 1981 and entitled **Tramount Mural.** The bright colors and bold, angular people create a welcome distraction in the cityscape. The old Wurlitzer building, renovated by architect Frank Gehry, now houses Tower Records, the largest music store in the world.

If you are an art lover and a food lover as well, you'll never have to leave Newbury Street. Every block has its share of coffee shops and cafés where you can catch a quick bite and linger over the paper. If you are into more serious dining, you can find restaurants as well. See the list at the back of this chapter.

Newbury Street is not the only place you can find art inside and out. There are over a dozen locations in the city where outdoor art has become an integral part of the visual surroundings. Sculptures, murals, and mixed-media installations are giving the entire city a face-lift as well as an infusion of first-rate talent, both local and national. We're including some of the most exciting examples, so that, while you're wandering on your own, you won't walk on by and miss these sometimes hidden treasures:

The Bedford Building Clock, between 89 and 105 Bedford Street: This clock is made entirely of stained glass, the work of Lynn Hovey, a contemporary Cambridge artisan. Located in a refurbished Victorian Gothic building, the best view of it is at night, from the Church Green Square, where Summer, Lincoln, High, and Bedford Streets meet.

New England Aquarium Outdoor Plaza, Central Wharf: An interesting piece of moving sculpture, "Echo of the Waves," is located here at the Aquarium. Its translucent wings interact with the wind, rising and falling with its power, and when illuminated at night, they form intriguing patterns on the ground.

Old John Hancock Building, Berkeley Street: Forty-eight light panels, each with thirteen neon tubes, light up the night high above Boston. Installed in 1949, the familiar red and blue lights are still used today to notify Bostonians about the weather. Steady blue: clear weather. Flashing blue: cloudy. Steady red: rain. Flashing red: snow. (And flashing red in the summer means a canceled Red Sox game!)

Perhaps the most unusual of the city's street art is behind **Haymarket.** This open-air produce market, which has operated at this site for over two hundred years, is particularly exciting on Thursdays through Saturdays when the crowded stalls full of vendors hawking their fresh produce create a living artwork of their own.

If you look down as you cross Blackstone Street following the Freedom Trail markings, you'll see some rather remarkable bronze reliefs laid into the pavement. This is Mags Harries's *Asaraton*, created in 1976 for the Bicentennial Commission. The Greek name *Asaraton* is taken from a second-century B.C. Roman mosaic depicting the leftovers of a banquet — the word means "unswept floor." Harries's *Asaraton* depicts bits and pieces of produce and other detritus that so liberally litter Blackstone Street after a long and successful market day. The bronze inlays, polished to a high sheen by the millions of feet and tires crossing them, seem ordinary and extraordinary at the same time. Egg crates, tomatoes, and crushed paper cups are among the discards immortalized in metal.

The idea that our everyday environment can be commented upon and enhanced by art is also found in another unusual setting — Boston's subway system, which is the oldest in the country. The MBTA's **Arts on the Line** project has been commissioning local artists to fill subway stations with evocative and sometimes controversial artworks, adding an exciting element to an otherwise drab and dreary environment. The Red Line is particularly prominent in these efforts, since it has recently been extended with four completely new stations. When you have time, we recommend a visit to any of the stops along the line, from Harvard to Alewife.

We have satisfied most of your senses by this point, from the taste of fudge sauce to the touch of fabric, the scent of the sea breeze to the sight of the skyline. But we have saved one sensory experience, because it deserves its own special treatment. Noise is omnipresent in any urban environment, but sound in the form of music is a legacy left to Boston from her earliest settlers. So continue with us into the next chapter, for a tour of the sounds of the city.

Tour Sites

Alpha Gallery
121 Newbury St.
Boston, MA 02116
536-4465

Boston Architectural Center
320 Newbury St.
Boston, MA 02116
536-3170

Arts on the Line
57 Inman St.
Cambridge, MA 02139
864-5150

Gallery in the Square
665 Boylston St.
Boston, MA 02116
426-6616

Randall Beck Gallery
168 Newbury St.
Boston, MA 02116
266-2475

Gallery Naga
67 Newbury St.
Boston, MA 02116
267-9060

Haymarket
Behind Faneuil Hall, adjacent to
the Southeast Expressway and
the entrance to the Callahan
Tunnel. Mags Harries's
Asaraton is located in the road
where pedestrians can cross
under the Expressway on the
Freedom Trail.

Institute for Contemporary Art/
Friends of Boston Art
955 Boylston St.
Boston, MA 02115
266-5151
Admission fee.

Krakow Gallery
10 Newbury, 5th Floor
Boston, MA 02116
262-4490

Levinson/Kane Gallery
16 Newbury St.
Boston, MA 02116
247-0545

Neilsen Gallery
179 Newbury St.
Boston, MA 02116
266-4835

New England Aquarium Outdoor
Plaza
Central Wharf
Boston, MA 02110
742-8870

Old John Hancock Building
Berkeley and St. James Sts.
Boston, MA 02116

Pucker-Safrai
171 Newbury St.
Boston, MA 02116
267-9473

Judi Rotenburg Gallery
130 Newbury St.
Boston, MA 02116
437-1518

Society of Arts and Crafts
175 Newbury St.
Boston, MA 02116
266-1810

Zoe Gallery
207 Newbury St.
Boston, MA 02116
536-6800

RESTAURANTS

Back Bay Bistro
565 Boylston St.
Boston, MA 02116
536-4477

Ciao Bella
240A Newbury St.
Boston, MA 02116
536-2626
Marilyn Monroe memorabilia
  adorns this Southern Italian
  restaurant, known for veal
  Parmesan, a huge veal chop,
  and outstanding pastas.

Davio's
269 Newbury St.
Boston, MA 02116
262-4810
Casual café upstairs for pizza,
  antipasto, calzones, pasta,
  salads, or cappuccino.
  Downstairs serves elegant
  Northern Italian cuisine.

Division Sixteen
955 Boylston St.
Boston, MA 02115
353-0870

Echo
279A Newbury St.
Boston, MA 02116
236-4488
Beautiful corner Victorian
  townhouse with lots of
  windows. Outdoor café serves
  brunch, lunch, dinner, and
  drinks.

Joe's American Bar and Grill
279 Dartmouth St. at Newbury St.
Boston, MA 02116
536-4200
Informal but refined American
  dining with a downstairs bar
  and outside tables.

Rocco's
5 S. Charles St.
Boston, MA 02116
723-6800

29 Newbury Street
29 Newbury St.
Boston, MA 02116
536-0290
Creative contemporary cooking
  with class. Eat while you enjoy
  the art on the walls. Serves
  lunch and dinner, cuisine from
  sandwiches to full-cooked
  meals, with a bar that is usually
  packed in the evenings.

CHAPTER SEVEN

The Sounds of the City

The air of Boston is full of music. Handheld "boom boxes" on Huntington Avenue blare over the ecstatic strains of Mozart issuing from nearby Symphony Hall. A band of street-musicians whip up a frothy reggae beat in Copley Square, while a Renaissance brass quintet echoes through the halls of the New Old South Church across the street.

When night falls on this city, the curtain rises on Boston's exciting and eclectic music scene. Boston offers musical opportunities to the classical and the avante-garde, the high-brow and the popular, the famous performer and the unknown jazz student. The city boasts the country's first music society, the Stoughton Musical Society, established by Stephen Billings in 1774, and arguably the country's greatest symphony orchestra, the Boston Symphony Orchestra. But it is also home to Berklee College of Music, which trains jazz and rock performers, as well as a host of new wave musical groups of every persuasion. For every headlining act at a local concert hall or club, there are a dozen aspiring young talents willing to "play for the door" at some little club or out on the street.

In Boston, we take our music wherever we can get it, from the lowliest subterranean subway station to the loftiest church gallery. Boston audiences are serious, well informed, and loyally partisan to their particular favorite musician or night spot, whether it's Jordan Hall or the Rat.

Unfortunately, it's difficult to organize tours around musical experiences. For one thing, musical events may be seasonal. The

BSO's season is in the autumn, winter, and spring, the Pops' in the summer, and everything else is subject to change. Both the concert halls and the clubs rotate their music calendars, so it would be impossible for us to predict whose music you'll hear on a given day, or even what kind of music it might be.

The first tour covers most of the classic institutions in the city and offers a look at the music in our churches. The second provides an overview of Boston's extensive night life, dividing the city by neighborhoods and giving you an idea about where to go in each. Don't be dismayed by the abundance of choices — you can always come back for more!

Monuments to Melody

In 1881, a local philanthropist and amateur musician named Henry Lee Higginson decided that Boston needed its own symphony orchestra. The city had already been home to a number of world-class musical productions, most notably the American premieres of Beethoven's First and Fifth Symphonies by the Boston Academy of Music, but Higginson felt there was a need for the city to develop its own musical identity.

The Boston Symphony Orchestra was born from his idea, and quickly established itself as a leader in both traditional and innovative music-making. Less than twenty years later the orchestra moved to its current home on the corner of Massachusetts and Huntington Avenues, and it is here, in Symphony Hall, that we begin our tour.

Symphony Hall deserves its reputation as one of the more acoustically superior listening and performing halls in the world, because its perfect bell shape transmits sound with the least amount of distortion. Acoustical engineers from all over the country have come to study the elements that make for this pure sound, and have used their state-of-the-industry knowledge to try to duplicate it elsewhere. To no avail. Even Stravinsky used to say that there was no finer symphony hall in the world.

The decor is serious, with just enough distractions to keep young concertgoers from wriggling on their hard, wooden seats. There is no carpeting, nothing flashy. The brilliance is provided by the music itself. One of the few concessions to "theatrics," no longer adhered to, was in the painting of the orchestra panel walls — green for the Pops and pink for the Symphony.

Symphony Hall is the home base for the famous **Boston Symphony Orchestra,** currently directed by Seiji Ozawa. During the summer, the BSO performs in the sylvan splendor of Tanglewood in western Massachusetts. But before the BSO took over Tanglewood's Berkshire Festival, the performers were not pleased with a winter season only. It didn't pay enough. So in 1885, Higginson founded the Boston Promenade, later Popular Concerts, currently the **Boston Pops.** His motive was ulterior: he feared his musicians might not return from summer stints in Europe if they weren't employed on a year-round basis.

The Pops is now a century-old Boston institution. Today, the Pops orchestra is not composed of BSO regulars. The musicians, the repertoire, and the traditions are different. At Pops concerts, chairs are removed from the main floor and replaced by small tables and tiny seats. Food and drink is encouraged, and boisterous festivity settles over the staid hall until the Pops' more elegant cousin returns in the fall.

For over fifty years, the guiding light of the Boston Pops was Arthur Fiedler, who took the baton in 1929 and singlehandedly shaped the Pops into the immensely successful group it is today. Fiedler was an idiosyncratic and vivacious man, both as a conductor and in his private life. He was a noted "sparkie," who loved to follow fire trucks, and he had an extensive collection of fire-fighting memorabilia. The current director, movie score master John Williams, is only slightly less flamboyant.

Another unique and exciting group that regularly performs at Symphony Hall is the **Handel and Haydn Society,** which began its illustrious career on Christmas Day in 1815 with a performance of Handel's *Messiah*. The *Messiah* performance has become an annual event, moving to Symphony Hall when it first opened in 1901. Today, the Society produces six Messiah concerts a year during the season, as well as separate concerts of other work between November and April. The Handel and Hayden Society is the oldest continuously performing group in the country.

A younger, yet well-established **Boston Classical Orchestra** performs in Faneuil Hall and the Old South Meeting House under the direction of distinguished conductor Harry Ellis Dickson. Established in 1979, this professional ensemble attracts capacity crowds for exciting performances by soloists and orchestra alike.

For summer classical outdoor listening, head forty-five minutes outside of Boston to Mansfield to hear the Pittsburgh Symphony perform at **Great Woods.** Great Woods attracts an extremely popular variety of singers and bands. Such well-known performers as Rod Stewart, Jimmy Buffett, Stevie Nicks, the Beach Boys, Gordon Lightfoot, and Tina Turner have graced the Great Woods stage. Although concerts take place outdoors, most seats are sheltered from rain.

Many of the musicians who perform at Symphony Hall were trained right here in Boston, some at the **New England Conservatory of Music,** 290 Huntington Avenue, which has been in existence since 1867. The NEC is an internationally known institution, where musicians can receive both undergraduate and graduate degrees in music. The main emphasis is classical, but new music, including jazz and ethnic music, is also taught. The school welcomes visitors, and wandering through the halls during the mornings when many students are practicing can be quite an exhilarating experience. (Call ahead first.)

> *William Haynes was a late-nineteenth-century Boston silversmith who, at the request of a BSO flautist, set out to design a high-quality flute to rival the European models. Today, the company, located just off Arlington Street, produces only four hundred instruments a year, all of them of such exceptional quality that there is a years-long waiting list to get one.*

The NEC also hosts over three hundred concerts a year, most of them during the academic school year. Concerts range from solo piano recitals to 120-voice chorus performances. Since most of the concerts are free and open to the public, they're certainly among the best musical bargains in the city.

Some of the concerts, especially the professional ones, are given in the NEC's **Jordan Hall,** another acoustically superior concert hall. Jordan Hall is also stage for a variety of acclaimed smaller Boston musical institutions, all of which offer performances throughout the year. Among these are the singing societies, like **Boston Concert Opera, Boston Musica Viva,** and the **Boston Cecelia Society,** and the performing groups, such as the **Boston Philharmonic** and the **Klezmer Conservatory Band** (a group that specializes in Yiddish and Eastern European folk music).

With such an abundance of working musicians, it's only natural that Boston should be the home of a strong related music industry as well. William Dowd and Hubbard harpsichords are made in the area, as well as Haynes flutes. Henry Kloss, who developed the Advent and KLH speakers, is also Boston-based, and in Cambridge you'll find **Mooradian Cover and Case,** owned by saxophonist, Ron Mooradian. He manufactures padded musical instrument cases to protect everything from a student's saxophone to a priceless string bass.

Students and other musicians go to **LaSalle Music, Inc.,** on Boylston Street for their electronic keyboards, guitars, and signal processors. Then there's also the **Rayburn Music Store,** at 263 Huntington Avenue in the Back Bay. It may seem like just another store, but it's also the home of Emilio Lyons, an affable Italian whose reputation as a fine instrument repairman is nationwide. Emilio's specialty is brass and woodwinds, but his real love is saxophones, and many famous American jazz musicians, including Stan Getz, Sonny Rollins, Woody Herman, and Phil Woods, will have no other hands but his on their "axes."

Another company, with a broader musical base, is **E.U. Wurlitzer, Inc.,** at 360 Newbury Street. Started in 1890 by German immigrant Ernst Ulrich Wurlitzer, a Kapelmeister and violin repair expert by trade, it has evolved into a $5 million company. The catalyst to growth was a farsighted manager who encouraged the company to carry Fender basses — among the first electric musical instruments. The '30s, '40s, and '50s saw Wurlitzer on the cutting edge of providing new electronic musical instruments east of the Mississippi, and that hasn't changed. They no longer sell violins, but anything else a musician needs is available. Visiting celebrities like Tony Curtis and Chuck Berry have stopped here for equipment.

The **Boston Music Company,** a hundred years old in 1986, is an even older institution than its counterpart, Wurlitzer. This store stocks virtually every piece of sheet music ever printed, and arguably houses the largest selection in the country. (It also stands among the top six outlets in the country for music boxes, and we don't mean only the simple ones. Have you ever heard a music box that plays over seventy notes? They have one!)

A visit to any of these establishments will bring you into contact with musicians — struggling and otherwise. It's a good bet that if they're not graduates of the classically oriented NEC, they're students at the **Berklee College of Music,** the next stop on our tour. Founded in 1945 by Lawrence Berk (and now run by his son Lee), Berklee is considered the Julliard of jazz education, the home of new music of every description. Berklee's strength lies in the quality of its practical training for professional musicians. After a grounding in classic theory and technique, students are taught by an internationally famous faculty. The school has become a forerunner in the study and development of electronic music as well. Raymond Kurzweil, whose digital synthesizer (manufactured by his company **Kurzweil Computers**) is revolutionizing popular music, is very much involved in the audio engineering and electronic music programs. Berklee also offers clinics conducted by a wide variety of renowned musicians, including Wynton Marsalis, Paul Simon, Chick Corea, and Barry Manilow.

The **Berklee Performance Center,** on the corner of Massachusetts Avenue and Boylston Street, is the college's performing space. Located in the former Fenway Theater (Boston's first movie theater), the Performance Center is yet another excellent hall, and is especially geared acoustically for modern music. The box office at the center is also an outlet for Ticketmaster, where you can purchase tickets to your favorite concerts in New York, Worcester, or right here!

Wintersauce Chorale, a sixteen-member singing group, now performs at John Hancock Hall. In the long New England tradition of fine choral music, Wintersauce chooses from an eclectic repertory of sacred, traditional, and contemporary music. Their season runs from December through early spring with three concerts; the Christmas performance is the best known. They mix jazz and classically trained musicians as well as guest performers into their productions, and are generally thought of as the best broad repertoire group in the city.

All these musicians get hungry, so the area between the NEC and Berklee is filled with small, moderately priced eateries offering everything from quick snacks (**Hatcreek Café** and **Soft Rock Café** serve light fare) to a full ethnic meal (try **Steve's** for an array of Greek food). There's also the nearby **Newbury Steak House,** an old favorite for grilled foods and salad bar in faded wood-paneled elegance. Contemporary music lovers and memorabilia buffs will have a blast at the internationally known **Hard Rock Café** on Clarendon Street. In the Ivy League tradition of Boston, you'll find the inscription "Musical Institution of Rock" above the doorway. At the Hard Rock, it's not just the American fare but the active, fun atmosphere that draws local and tourists alike!

After eating at the Hard Rock, you may feel like browsing through some records. Try the world's largest music store, **Tower Records,** at 360 Newbury Street. Your favorite rock stars, the classical greats, the European trend-setters, and fabulous jazz musicians are all awaiting you at Tower.

A tour of Boston's musical establishments would not be complete without mention of some of its churches, where great music is often a regular part of the program. We're not going to visit them in geographical sequence, but we want you to know where they are, so that you can avail yourself of some of the fine music they present. Musical performances that are not part of the regular church services are also listed in the local newspaper music calendars, or call for their schedule. If you see that something you like is going to be performed, you'll have the added delight of being able to listen to it in an uplifting environment. An added bonus is that most of the church concert offerings are free, or almost free.

Emmanuel Church, 15 Newbury Street: Emmanuel has developed into a city institution. Rector A. L. Kershaw and Mark Harvey, an accomplished jazz trumpeter and leader of the Aardvark Orchestra and Ribs Experimental Combo, see the church as having a special ministry to the community through the arts — music in particular. That ministry has expressed itself through the music of Haydn, Schubert, and Stravinsky, but most of all through the church's production of the works of Mozart and Bach, whose birthdays each year the church celebrates with concerts. Some of Bach's sacred music is performed as part of the liturgy every Sunday, and the church hosts chamber music and other performances throughout the year.

First and Second Church, at Berkeley and Marlborough Streets:

Several groups use the performance space in this church. Notable among them are Dinosaur Annex, Extension Works, Underground Composers, and the Baltic-American Society.

Trinity Church, Copley Square: Every Friday from early spring to late fall just past noon, the church hosts half-hour free concerts, mostly of organ music. The Christmas section of Handel's *Messiah* is presented during that season as well as a traditional candle-lit carol service.

Old North Church, 193 Salem Street: As well as owning the first church bells pealed in America, the Old North is also the repository of our country's first organ. The so-called Claggett Organ has since been rebuilt several times, but the case goes back to the 1736 original. (Although he didn't play the organ, as a teenager Paul Revere was a bell ringer here.) No secular music is performed here, but the organ and bells provide a spectacular accompaniment to weekly services.

The Church of the Advent, 30 Brimmer Street: The Harrison organ in this church, designed in 1935, remains a standard of beauty and clarity of sound, and is still one of the finest instruments of its kind in America. This Beacon Hill house of worship also has one of the finest choirs around, so a visit to High Mass is always musically rewarding.

The First Church of Christ, Scientist, Christian Science Center: This is the mother church for the Christian Scientists, and the organ, installed in 1952, is as imposing and impressive as the church itself. Built by the Aeolian-Skinner Organ Company, it has 13,595 pipes and is played from four keyboards with 200 draw-knobs. It is one of the largest organs in the world, and if you want to hear it, your best bet is to attend Sunday or Wednesday evening services. Otherwise you have to wait for the annual concert given on First Night, the citywide celebration of New Year's Eve.

St. Paul's Cathedral, at 138 Tremont Street, has a Chinese Choir that sings at their special noon service on Sunday. The church hosts occasional performances of outside groups such as the Handel and Hayden Society. The **Old West Church,** 131 Cambridge Street, has an organ that is reputed to be one of the ten best in the world. The Old West Organ Society meets there to play and give concerts on the organ, and the New England Conservatory has a strong connection with the church. Several local and international individuals and groups give concerts throughout the year at the Old West.

King's Chapel, at 58 Tremont Street, hosts noontime concerts every Tuesday, except in the summer.

Tour Sites

Berklee College of Music
1140 Boylston St.
Boston, MA 02215
266-1400

Boston Classical Orchestra
551 Tremont St.
Boston, MA 02116
426-2387

Berklee Performance Center
136 Massachusetts Ave.
Boston, MA 02115
266-7455

Boston Concert Opera
117 W. Concord St.
Boston, MA 02118
536-1166

Boston Cecelia Society
1773 Beacon St.
Brookline, MA 02146
232-4540

Boston Music Company
116 Boylston St.
Boston, MA 02116
426-5100

Boston Musica Viva
295 Huntington Ave.
Boston, MA 02116
353-0556

Boston Philharmonic Orchestra
17 Brigham Rd.
Waltham, MA 02154
536-4001

Boston Symphony Orchestra
Boston Pops
301 Massachusetts Ave.
Boston, MA 02115
266-1492

Christian Science Mother Church
175 Huntington Ave.
Boston, MA 02115
450-2000

Church of the Advent
30 Brimmer St.
Boston, MA 02108
523-2377

Emmanuel Church of Boston
15 Newbury St.
Boston, MA 02116
536-3355

E. U. Wurlitzer, Inc.
360 Newbury St.
Boston, MA 02116
437-1815

First and Second Unitarian
  Church of Boston
66 Marlborough St.
Boston, MA 02116
267-6730

Great Woods
Route 140
Mansfield, MA 02048
508-339-2333

Handel and Haydn Society
158 Newbury St.
Boston, MA 02116
266-3605

Haynes Flutes
12 Piedmont St.
Boston, MA 02116
482-7456

Hubbard Harpsichords, Inc.
144 Moody St.
Waltham, MA 02154
894-3238

Jordan Hall
30 Gainsborough St.
Boston, MA 02115
536-2412

King's Chapel
58 Tremont St.
Boston, MA 02108
523-1749

Klezmer Conservatory Band
1 Merrill St.
Cambridge, MA 02139
354-2884

Kurzweil Computers
185 Albany St.
Cambridge, MA 02139
864-4700

LaSalle Music, Inc.
1090 Boylston St.
Boston, MA 02115
536-0066

Mooradian Cover and Case
202 Hamilton St.
Cambridge, MA 02139
492-8930

New England Conservatory
   of Music
290 Huntington Ave.
Boston, MA 02115
262-1120

Old North Church
193 Salem St.
Boston, MA 02113
523-6676

Old West Church
131 Cambridge St.
Boston, MA 02114
227-5088

Rayburn Music
263 Huntington Ave.
Boston, MA 02115
266-4727

St. Paul's Cathedral
138 Tremont St.
Boston, MA 02111
482-5800

Symphony Hall
301 Massachusetts Ave.
Boston, MA 02115
266-1492

Tower Records
360 Newbury St.
Boston, MA 02115
247-5900

Trinity Church
Copley Square
Boston, MA 02116
536-0944

Wintersauce Chorale
P.O. Box 8008
Boston, MA 02114
523-4634

RESTAURANTS

Bangkok
177A Massachusetts Ave.
Boston, MA 02115
262-5377

Soft Rock Café
1124 Boylston St.
Boston, MA 02115
424-1789

Hard Rock Café
131 Clarendon St.
Boston, MA 02116
424-7625

Steve's Donut Shop
1110 Boylston St.
Boston, MA 02215
247-8134

Hatcreek Café
Eliot Lounge
85 Massachusetts Ave.
Boston, MA 02115
421-9169

Steve's Restaurant
62 Hereford St.
Boston, MA 02115
267-1817

Newbury Steak House
94 Massachusetts Ave.
Boston, MA 02115
536-0184

Key Notes

Since it would be impossible for you to run all over the city on a "jazz tour" or a "folk tour" — you couldn't conceivably get to hear everything you wanted in one evening — we've organized these nighttime tours as much as possible by geography. We serve up a sort of musical stew for you; a dash of rock, a pinch of reggae, and a splash of jazz mixed in with a solid soup base of piano bars. Feel free to pick and choose from this tasty menu and dive in wherever you have a special interest.

THE COMMON TO COPLEY

Pull out a jacket and tie for this tour, because it takes advantage of some of the better-dressed evening watering holes in Boston. Our first stop is at the venerable Copley Plaza Hotel, one of the few historic deluxe Boston hotels. The Plaza offers two opportunities to enjoy live music, depending on your appetite. The **Plaza Bar,** which has been compared to a British officer's club in India, is heavily paneled and cozy. Here, you can enjoy nightly cabaret-style entertainment. Corporate Boston tends to fill the seats at the end of a long day, so arrive here early (or very late). Across the hall is **Copley's,** where food as well as drinks are served. More like an Edwardian barroom, this less formal, noisier spot offers music with your supper from single piano to a livelier trio according to bookings.

The recently built Westin Hotel (one block west of the Copley), represents the best of modern hotel planning. It is linked to Boston's newest up-scale shopping mall, Copley Place (see page 121) by an impressive enclosed second-story bridge, and the lobby is reached by way of an escalator from the ground floor, past a waterfall of major proportions. Off the reception area is the **Lobby Lounge,** a vast and rather public space dominated by a cream-colored baby grand piano. In spite of the scale, the surroundings are very appealing: peach-colored and comfortable. The music is consistent and easy to listen to, and people-watching is a major attraction.

A few blocks down is the inimitable **Ritz-Carlton Hotel,** at Arlington and Newbury Streets. Recently remodeled and renovated, the First Lady of Boston has shed some of her dowager image and now provides first-rate jazz piano music nightly (except Sundays) in the downstairs **Ritz Bar.** The atmosphere is civilized, tasteful, and expensive, but for in-town jazz and good bar service, it's hard to beat. The armchairs and small tables help you feel you've been invited for the evening, but don't stay for more than a few sets.

At number 120 Huntington Avenue is the Colonnade Hotel, which houses **Zachary's Bar** and restaurant. The bar is off to the right, and the ultimate, old-world atmosphere is gracefully complemented by a jazz trio most of the week. If you want to sing instead of listen, keep going until you reach the **Lenox Hotel** at the corner of Boylston and Exeter Streets. **Diamond Jim's** is our stop here, a friendly "hands-on" piano bar where, depending on the night and the clientele, you can join in on anything from show tunes to mellow rock, and tie down your hunger with some hors d'oeuvres at 5 P.M. Before heading off to our final stop, we recommend you remove that tie you've been wearing up 'til now.

Division Sixteen, at 955 Boylston Street, is the place to be seen in Boston these days. This popular restaurant/bar in a renovated police station is noted for huge food portions as well as its young, ultra-hip clientele. The action continues on the pastel-colored art deco premises until early in the morning, with live jazz two nights a week from September to June, and loud radio the other nights. We have definitely begun this tour on the higher end of the age spectrum and ended it at the younger end, but age is relative; if you are young at heart, continue on to the next tour.

Head up Boylston Street toward the Public Garden and walk past the Four Seasons Hotel until you are across from the Common. Halfway through the block, down a large alleyway, you can join the hip professional set at **Zanzibar** nightclub. The broad music programming, with danceable hits ranging from the 1950s through the 1990s, attracts a diverse upscale crowd. The circular dance floor, surrounded by palm trees and bamboo furnishings, brings to light a tropical theme that includes swings along the rail upstairs. A second dance floor below, a billiards and dance floor upstairs, and easily accessible bars combine to make this coat-and-tie required club a Boston hotspot.

A few blocks away, at the Tremont House, you'll find two nightclubs in one hotel. At the **Roxy,** within a traditional ballroom made modern by the lighting and clientele, you'll find a unique nightclub atmosphere. After twenty minutes of dancing to popular tunes, the focus suddenly shifts to the stage where you can watch a live big-band music performance. Dancers and singers even grace the stage to offer a delightful respite from the busy dance floor. The upstairs can be reserved for private functions such as post-wedding receptions and individual parties. For a taste of the past, walk next door the **Jukebox.** This club specializes in music of the 1950s and 1960s, complete with memorabilia and a relaxed atmosphere.

KENMORE SQUARE

Boston is one of the rock and roll centers in the country. The Cars, Aerosmith, Peter Wolf, and J. Geils have put the city on the map. And Kenmore Square is the heart of Boston's rock and roll beat.

Kenmore Square, the popular Boston University hangout, is accessible by the Green Line and just a short walk away from Lansdowne Street, where it is easy to find a club to match your image. At 15 Lansdowne, **Citi** attracts an energetic, outgoing crowd. With a capacity of 1300, the large dance floor fills up fast, and a view is available from all sides. Video screens and neon lights make this place popular with college students and the young working crowd.

Next door — be careful not to wear a collar — join an eclectic group of people in a more casual atmosphere. **Axis** is well known for its diverse alternative music. Two live concerts a week range from funk to reggae to rock and roll. Nationally known acts attract rockers and kick-back bankers alike at this Lansdowne location. The permanent stage doubles as another level for cocktails and dancing. Upstairs, **DV8** offers changing art exhibits, billiards table, comfortable sofas, and multimedia performances.

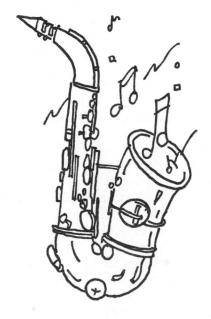

Continue down Lansdowne for one more original club on this street of diversities. The woman's torso entwined in neon light marks the entrance to **Venus de Milo,** a swanky euro-club that draws a late crowd. Inside, a combination of Victorian, European, and psychedelic decor create an international cosmopolitan flair. Dancing is fabulous, to watch or participate in, and this is the best place to catch a not-yet-popular trend displayed by a fellow guest.

Hard rock calls again however, and the **Rathskeller,** at 528 Commonwealth Avenue, is our next stop — affectionately and prophetically called "the Rat" by the locals. Depending on perspective, the Rat can seem cramped, noisy, and dirty, or exciting, new wave, and punk. Whatever your opinion, it is a good place to hear new talent on its way up. The Police, Talking Heads, and the Cars all performed here early on, and who knows who else will turn the corner to fame from a start in this club? It's open seven nights a week, with live music downstairs from Wednesday through Saturday.

Another choice, across the street, is the **Lipstick/Narcissus/Celebration** combination, an impressive undertaking for the over-eighteen crowd. The three distinct clubs are open access to all after an initial cover charge, and each has its own character. Narcissus, with its whole ceiling done in neon, is the largest of the three. Spreading over the first floor and the balcony, it has four bars and three dance areas, special lighting effects, and persistent high-energy dance music provided on occasion by live bands. Lipstick turns into a comedy club on Wednesdays, and on the weekends features a D.J. spinning the top 40. Wednesday at Celebration, on the ground floor, is heavy metal night, and the rest of the week offers music with a D.J. or live, sometimes nationally known bands. Strobes, border lights, and TV monitors pick up the action, and the activity on weekends has to be seen to be believed.

The **Paradise,** at 967 Commonwealth Avenue, is a good area concert club, hosting big-name talent along with local favorites in a live format during the week. Recently face-lifted to attract a more up-scale audience, the Paradise becomes a dance club on Friday and Saturday nights, which attracts a nicely mixed crowd.

FANEUIL HALL/GOVERNMENT CENTER

The area around Government Center and Faneuil Hall is as active at night for music as it is during the day for planning and high finance. Our first stop is high above the city at the **Bay Tower Room,** 60 State Street. By day a private club, the Bay Tower Room affords the public an unquestionably dramatic view of Boston at night. The city seems to float in a sea of lights thirty-three floors below, and the floor to ceiling windows give you the sense that you are peering down from your own private hot-air balloon. The music is relaxing until 9 P.M., when the atmosphere suddenly changes and dancing is available to the big band sound. You can eat here if you wish (it's pricey), or just enjoy a drink at the elegant bar while listening to the good piano music nightly from about 5:00 P.M. to 8:30 P.M.

Now back down, and into the carnival atmosphere of Faneuil Hall Marketplace. The **City Side** restaurant, at number 262, is a renovated warehouse with a "California modern" feel. The entertainment and clientele are as contemporary as the surroundings. Nightly except Friday there is live music from 9 P.M. 'til 1 A.M. — the only establishment in the marketplace that currently provides it. The sound is varied, from an a capella group to an ongoing commitment to rhythm and blues. The City Side is an up-scale dating bar that caters principally to the late-twenties professional set, but anyone at all can enjoy the music and dancing.

If you want a lively close to your evening, wander back over to **The Black Rose** (see page 66), which features live Irish entertainment nightly. But if you feel mellow, and want fewer people and less noise, the Bostonian Hotel's **Atrium Café** is your place to finally unwind. Yet another of the city's seemingly unending supply of white pianos provides the music, but the surroundings and the service make this small, glass-walled lounge an expensive but elegant oasis from the bustling humanity of the adjoining Marketplace. Sitting here, in the heart of the oldest part of Boston, imparts an eerie feeling if you close your eyes and let the sense of history as well as the music wash over you.

HARVARD SQUARE/CAMBRIDGE

No musical tour of Boston is complete without a pilgrimage to Harvard Square in Cambridge, the place where so many folk careers began back in the late 1950s and early 1960s. So we break our Cambridge exclusionary rule once again. Tulla's coffee shop is gone, as is the Club 47, but the memories of Joan Baez performing in Harvard Square live on. Some still recall the days when the shy Boston University student with the electrifying voice first performed. She went on to profoundly influence the history of folk and protest music in America.

The black-clad, poetry-reading, coffee-drinking folk music

folk who were attracted to the Square during that pre-Vietnam period have left a legacy not only of folk music, but of entertainment in general. Whereas then there were limited places in the Square to go to for music in the evening, now some of the liveliest acts in Boston are available in Cambridge — and not always indoors.

Harvard Square is still a mecca for performers, but many of them perform on the street. As long as the weather is warm you can be assured of free, often impromptu entertainment, particularly in Brattle Square just west of the MBTA Station. The sounds range from marimbas and wood blocks to violin concertos and jazz clarinet, but there is always a ready audience on this "Hyde Park Corner" of music, especially on weekend evenings.

Check out the activity here before going up to the corner of Church and Palmer Streets (behind the Coop) to visit **Passim's** (formerly called Club 47) at 47 Palmer Street. Bob and Rae Anne Donlin made their commitment to Cambridge in 1969, adding music to liven up their small coffee-house in 1971. They encouraged local folk groups then, and are still good friends with well-known performers like Ronee Blakley and Dave von Ronk. Nowadays the club is known for its changing lineup of national and local acoustic musicians, who perform nightly (except Sunday). The atmosphere is comfortable and unpretentious, and the intentional lack of a liquor license is compensated for by good teas, ciders, and coffees. This stop is a must if you want to relive the "old" Harvard Square.

The **Regatta Bar,** at the Charles Hotel, has become one of the most popular spots for fine jazz listening in the greater Boston area. Understated natural finishes, a friendly staff, and a blue-chip booking policy have all combined to turn the intimate two-hundred-seat club into a place to hear and be seen in elegant surroundings. Stan Getz, Anita O'Day, Herbie Mann, and Astrid Gilberto are a few of the nationally known performers who have appeared since the bar's opening. This is a place where fans of all ages can congregate comfortably because they share the common denominator of a love for music. In the summertime, the Charles Hotel sponsors "Jazz in the Square," a series of early evening outdoor jazz concerts that are open to the public. In the past, audiences have had the pleasure of listening to the talent of Rebecca Paris, Winetta Jackson, Christine Key, and Michael Metheny. The Charles Hotel is definitely the place for the most consistently good jazz in Boston.

To experience a community celebration of the constant renewal of life, join **Revels, Inc.,** for their annual Christmas Revels at the Sanders Theater in Cambridge. Costumed in traditional garb, the troupe performs ritual dances, processionals, carols, and drama for its audiences and encourages them to join in. The troupe welcomes spring and fall with similar festivities. Their aim is to encourage and support traditional music and dance.

In spite of what residents would have you believe, Cambridge is not only affluent Harvard Square. Massachusetts Avenue leads east back toward Boston and passes through Central Square, home to a much funkier music scene. Make your first stop at the **Plough & Stars,** at 912 Massachusetts Avenue. This is Cambridge's most serious neighborhood gathering ground, where carpenters and politicos rub elbows and hoist Guinesses with students, writers, and native sons. The Plough offers a variety of live musical groups with an emphasis on rock and roll and blues, but the overheard conversations often make the most exciting entertainment.

For a healthy dose of reggae, Latin, African, and other ethnic beats, try the **Western Front,** at 343 Western Avenue. Or, if jazz is your cup of tea, head in the opposite direction toward Inman Square, where **Ryles** offers some of the most authentic in the city. Nationally known jazz greats have been known to stop in at this club to catch the local talent and even take the stage for a set. Ryles, with both upstairs and downstairs rooms, is not a glamorous spot, but then again, you'll be concentrating on the fine music rather than the casual surroundings.

Back in Central Square, **Man-Ray** has attracted national attention for its 1950s kitsch atmosphere and determinedly new-wave clientele. The music is loud, electric, and progressive; there is occasional live music. Food is served from a perfect replica of a 1950s kitchen, complete right down to the suburban mom's menu. This is a favorite spot for local designers, artists, models, and students.

Finally, pay a visit to **Nightstage** at 823 Main Street, the area's newest contender in the first-class club category. Open only since October 1985, this spot was carefully designed with the sophisticated listener in mind. The stage is in the center, the room has every possible acoustic improvement, and the muted gray, beige, and mahogany decor form a subtle backdrop to the everchanging roster of well-known performers. Principally a blues and jazz club, they also bring in country and folk artists, the cover changing according to the act. No reservations, but tickets can be purchased in advance for the three-hundred capacity club.

At night your sense of hearing is augmented because sight is more limited and less distracting. But morning is coming soon, so rest and be prepared to put all your senses in play again, because play time it is. With Longfellow as our inspiration, we next give you, not "The Children's Hour," but The Children's Chapter.

Tour Sites

Axis/DV8
15 Lansdowne St.
Boston, MA 02215
262-2437

Bay Tower Room
60 State St.
Boston, MA 02109
723-1666

Black Rose
160 State St.
Boston, MA 02109
742-2286

Citi
15 Lansdowne St.
Boston, MA 02215
262-2424
Cover charge.

Copley's
Copley Plaza Hotel
Copley Square
Boston, MA 02116
267-5300

Diamond Jim's
Lenox Hotel
710 Boylston St.
Boston, MA 02116
536-5300

Division Sixteen
955 Boylston St.
Boston, MA 02115
353-0870

Jukebox
Tremont House
275 Tremont St.
Boston, MA 02116
227-7699
Cover charge.

Lipstick/Narcissus/Celebration
533 Commonwealth Ave.
Boston, MA 02215
536-1950
Cover charge.

Lobby Lounge
Copley Place
Westin Hotel
10 Huntington Ave.
Boston, MA 02116
262-9600

Man-Ray
21 Brookline St.
Cambridge, MA 02139
864-0400
Cover charge.

Nightstage
823 Main St.
Cambridge, MA 02139
497-8200
Cover charge.

Paradise
967 Commonwealth Ave.
Boston, MA 02215
254-2052

Passim's
47 Palmer St.
Cambridge, MA 02138
492-7679
Cover charge.

Plaza Bar
Copley Plaza Hotel
138 St. James Ave.
Boston, MA 02116
267-5300

Plough & Stars
912 Massachusetts Ave.
Cambridge, MA 02139
492-9653

Rathskeller (The Rat)
528 Commonwealth Ave.
Boston, MA 02215
536-2750

Regatta Bar
Charles Hotel
Charles Square
Cambridge, MA 02138
864-1200; 876-7777 for concert
   tickets
Cover charge.

Revels, Inc.
One Kendall Square, Bldg. 600
Cambridge, MA 02139
621-0505

Ritz Bar
Ritz-Carlton Hotel
Arlington at Newbury St.
Boston, MA 02116
536-5700

Roxy
Tremont House
275 Tremont St.
Boston, MA 02116
227-7699
Cover charge.

Ryles
212 Hampshire St.
Cambridge, MA 02139
876-9330

Venus de Milo
11 Lansdowne St.
Boston, MA 02215
421-9595
Cover charge.

Western Front
343 Western Ave.
Cambridge, MA 02139
492-7772

Zachary's Bar
The Colonnade Hotel
120 Huntington Ave.
Boston, MA 02116
424-7000

Zanzibar
1 Boylston Pl.
Boston, MA 02116
451-1955
Cover charge.

RESTAURANTS

Atrium Café
Bostonian Hotel
North & Blackstone Sts.
Boston, MA 02109
523-3600

City Side Restaurant
262 Faneuil Hall Marketplace
Boston, MA 02109
742-7390

JAZZ SPECIALTIES

Bennett Street Café
Charles Hotel at Harvard Yard
1 Bennett St.
Cambridge, MA 02138
661-5005
Summer jazz concerts in the
   courtyard.

Genji Restaurant
227 Newbury St.
Boston, MA 02115
267-5656
Sunday jazz brunch.

Hampshire House
84 Beacon St.
Boston, MA 02108
227-9600
Sunday jazz brunch.

Hyatt Regency
575 Memorial Dr.
Cambridge, MA 02139
492-1234
Sunday jazz brunch.

Skipjack's
500 Boylston St.
Boston, MA 02116
536-3500
Sunday jazz brunch.

Water Music, Inc.
12 Arrow St.
Cambridge, MA 02138
876-7777
Summertime jazz and classical
   land and sea concerts.

CHAPTER EIGHT

The Children's Chapter

Bostonians love children, their own as well as those of visitors, and the proliferation of parks, playgrounds, museums, and theater geared especially for youngsters is evidence of their fondness and respect. This is a city that boasts a fleet of Swan Boats, a display of dinosaurs, and a wondrous museum especially for small patrons. It even has a school especially to train nannies!

Our two tours are divided by age groups — the first for the five- to eight-year-olds and the second for those nine to thirteen. We also mention restaurants that welcome youthful clientele. Since each family's "touring" ability is different, we don't expect you to cover all the suggested activities in one day. Use the tour as a guide to your family's specific needs and interests. And don't forget that kids are pretty good at finding uncommon experiences of their own! (If you live in the Boston area or expect to be a repeat visitor, you should invest in the comprehensive and excellent guidebook *In and Out of Boston With (or Without) Children*, by Bernice Chesler.)

Kidtrek I: Ages 5 – 8

Recognizing that small children love to run, gallop, hop, skip, and in general work off a lot of energy, Boston is chock-full of excellent playgrounds. Playgrounds are not only great for stretching little muscles, but they're also a good place for meeting other kids, something that youngsters often miss while on vacation. All of these sites have pleasant grounds for an outdoor picnic.

199

Remember that urban playgrounds are not always well kept; be alert to broken glass and other hazards. We'll start off with a list of some of the best outdoor attractions in the city, in geographical order, beginning in the east.

Waterfront Park: Set right at the edge of the Boston Harbor, this play area affords a terrific view of the yachts and pleasure boats of Lewis Wharf and makes the most of its nautical theme. Wooden equipment for climbing, sliding, and hiding is grouped in a large boatlike structure that allows for maximum use of the imagination. In the summer, the fountain is turned on for wading. Parents can sit on the comfortable benches and enjoy the view while children pretend to be pirates and explorers. The only real drawback is the lack of bathroom facilities, but the nearby Marriott Long Wharf Hotel is fairly accommodating.

Boston Common Playground: For centuries, children have romped on the Common, although this particular area was not designated for their sole use until recently. Despite the rather limited facilities, children love this multiuse area, which is conveniently fenced off for safety. There is a geodesic jungle gym, slides at three different levels, and a large sand area, as well as the tables and stools for snacking. In the summer, the huge wading pool, affectionately (but no longer accurately) known as the Frog Pond, is filled with water and children happily splashing. It makes a lovely haven right in the center of downtown Boston, and the Common itself provides more than enough people-watching entertainment for the adults.

Public Garden Swan Boats: Across the street from the Common is the Public Garden, home of what is perhaps the oldest and most famous children's attraction in the city. The Swan Boat Rides on the Lagoon have been in continuous operation since 1877, when Robert Paget created them, adopting the swan motif from his favorite opera, *Lohengrin*. The rides were an instant hit in Victorian Boston, and they still are today. Bring along some bread to feed the well-bred and (well-fed) ducks as you circle the little lake. You'll be transported with quiet grace by collegiate boatswains who propel the swans with pedal-power. The pedaling builds strong thigh muscles, and is considered great summer training for autumn football players.

Make Way for Ducklings: According to local lore, a wild duck (dubbed Sally Mallard by her friends) once nested in one of the

Swan Boats and eventually hatched eight children. Sally and her offspring were immortalized in Robert McCloskey's book *Make Way for Ducklings* in 1941. Children familiar with this classic will get a thrill out of following the trail of Mother Mallard and her brood from the Charles River to the Public Garden and then riding on the boat that was their first home. In 1987 the city installed sculptures by Nancy Schon of the feathered family walking across the Common. If you cannot spot the statues near the entrance at Charles Street, look under crowds of children. Their little hands and bottoms keep the ducklings shiny and bright.

> *The bronze ducklings have also proven popular with vandals, regrettably. Two of the statues have been blowtorched or pried away, forcing the city to replace the figures. The last time this cruel stunt occurred, there was such an outcry that a duckling was returned anonymously. Unfortunately, it was the one that had been stolen the year before! Incidentally, the ducklings you should make way for are named Jack, Kack, Lack, Mack, Nack, Ouack, Pack, and Quack.*

Clarendon Street Playground: This small playground (on the corner of Commonwealth Avenue and Clarendon Street) is situated in one of the loveliest Back Bay neighborhoods. The ground cover is part grass, part sand, and there is a grassy hill that children love to roll down. A wide variety of large motor skill activities are provided by the swings, slides, bars, poles, and bridges of the wooden climbing structure, and the well-landscaped area is protected from too much sun in the summer. There is also a helpful parents' bulletin board that provides information on child care and other kid-related activities.

Esplanade Playground: There are several play areas for children along the Charles River, beginning at the Charles River Basin near the Massachusetts General Hospital. Here there are swings and a large wading pool, as well as a jungle gym and slide. Near the Hatch Shell is a fenced-in grassy playground with sandbox, swings, and animal-shaped climb-ons, as well as a pretend locomotive. Between the two lagoons is a modern climbing structure with a tire swing, slides, regular swings, and a ramp. Cool river breezes and some great opportunities for observing sports enthusiasts make this a good place for parents to relax while children play.

While we're still in the downtown area, we want to mention a few restaurants that are "stroller accessible" and not too expensive, and provide you with a change from the customary fast food establishments.

If you're near the top of the Common, a good place to go is the eighth floor restaurant at Filene's, the **Food Port.** Your meal will be wholesome, your table relatively private, and there are restrooms down the hall. Many of the older patrons enjoy having children around.

Near the Clarendon Street Playground you have two options. **The Travis,** 135 Newbury Street, is a determinedly old-fashioned cafeteria. Open from 6:45 A.M. until 4:45 P.M., they cater to people who want value for their money, and no frills. In good weather you can sit outside at the tables, or order a take-out sandwich and go down to the Esplanade.

In addition to ice cream and yogurt, **Dave's Homemade Ice Cream,** at 144 Newbury Street, carries pastries, soups, salads, and sandwiches that they serve throughout the day. In good weather you may sit outside.

Children's clothing stores are scattered throughout the city. One good location nearby is **Jacadi,** at 110 Newbury Street. They stock European classic clothing for children here, from infants to size ten. This is an attractive store with simple, affordable clothing. A companion store is **Veronique Delchaux,** which sells maternity clothes by French designers. Veronique is a good stop for working mothers who like normal clothing. If you and your daughter want matching dresses, you might walk down a few doors to **Laura Ashley** for identical feminine floral prints.

Our final recommendation on Newbury Street is **Carriage Square Maternity and Baby Boutique,** where assorted gift items accompany clothing by American designers and manufacturers. Just around the corner on Clarendon Street, at **Stork Time,** you can expect extraordinarily friendly service (they even give you quarters for the parking meters). Here you'll find a well-stocked store for expecting mothers and infants.

For a visual treat, the new and better **F.A.O. Schwarz** store on Boylston Street is full of some of the world's most interesting and colorful stuffed animals. Next door, the **Women's Educational and Industrial Union** has superior clothing for infants and young children. They also sell an intriguing variety of games.

Another location in Boston that caters to kids is Faneuil Hall Marketplace. At **Sharp Kids,** you are bound to find an innovative toy that will spark your child's interest. This store specializes in educational and scientific items to entertain all ages, from infants to teenagers. For the largest selection of stunt kites in New England, **Kites of Boston** in the marketplace features one-of-a-kind originals and custom-built kites for the novice and enthusiast. Other stores to soar through in the marketplace include **Tales with Tails,** where you can purchase stuffed animals with books to match, and **Kids Unlimited,** for children's clothes.

After exercising monetary restraint at all these shopping locations, you might be ready for the freedom of the outdoors. There are many outdoor activities that grownups will enjoy as much as children. Farther afield, the **Arnold Arboretum** in Jamaica Plain is an urban oasis that is especially nice for family outings. Leaf-collecting is a favorite activity here in the fall, and it's an especially scenic place to wander with a backpack or stroller (see page 55).

The **Franklin Park Zoo,** in Dorchester, is in the process of extensive and much-needed renovation. Parts of it are already finished, and the petting zoo is nice for small children. Among the major animal exhibits scheduled, the world-class tropical rain forest habitat is completed.

Another outdoor haven is the **Blue Hills Trailside Museum** in Milton, a short distance from the city (accessible by public transportation). Operated by the Massachusetts Audubon Society for the Metropolitan District Commission, this outdoor museum offers a terrific introduction to the natural history of the area. The exhibits are geared for young children, and there are guided tours available. A small collection of local wildlife, such as deer and geese is another attraction; berry picking is a popular summertime activity.

If you are traveling by car, you may wish to visit the **Stone Zoo** in Stoneham, about twenty minutes north of the city (call for directions). The Stone Zoo has resident wildlife, including giraffes, gorillas, polar bears, sea lions, and a tropical aviary. It's a favorite stop for elementary school expeditions. Another favorite kidtrek outside the city is **Drumlin Farm** in Lincoln, run by the Massachusetts Audubon Society. Farmyard animals, hayrides, beautiful views, and pumpkins in season are all part of this lovely country outing.

Children are especially difficult to entertain when it's time to move indoors. Luckily, no place in the city provides more to do, see, touch, and experience indoors than the world-famous **Children's Museum.** Plan to spend at least two or three hours at this remarkable place, and don't expect to spend it just waiting for the kids. The Children's Museum is a participatory treasure house that will surely change any notion that museums are stuffy, staid, or boring.

Ongoing exhibits include a two-story Japanese house that was transported in pieces from Kyoto, Boston's sister city, to give Boston children an experience with life in Japan. The "We're Still Here" exhibit presents the ongoing culture of the Native American, including a wigwam that the children may explore. "Mind Your Own Business" is not a put-down: it explores you and your body, how it works, and its continued health maintenance. The after-school program features events such as break-dancing contests and science demonstrations. The Club House has activities geared to children in their teens.

Of special interest to very young children is the Playspace, an enclosed area on the second floor reserved for infants and toddlers up to age five. Playspace provides exploratory activities for preschoolers in a safe and stimulating environment and allows a parent time to stay with his or her younger children while older offspring continue to explore the museum. Some favorite attractions in Playspace are the climbing castle, the funny mirrors, and the gas station where the children can "gas up" the climb-on car. There's a changing/nursing area for infants and an excellent parents' resource room that provides materials for art activities, staffed by helpful personnel. Check out the bulletin board and parents' resource book for more information about local kid-related activities.

When you leave the museum, stop in at the excellent gift shop on the first floor. But don't neglect to pay a visit to Recycle, on the second floor, where barrels of "stuff" recycled from local factories stand waiting for some creative imagination to transform them into wonderful rainy day projects. For a dollar or two, you can fill a grocery bag with spools, plastic bits, molded rubber parts, and various other "whats-its." You can also buy paper in all shapes and sizes. Pick up a little of everything in case you need to spend a rainy day in a hotel room with nothing to do.

For information on special programs both in and out of the Children's Museum, call the What's-Up Line (426-8855).

If it's spring or summer, you might also want to stop for a snack at the **Milk Bottle,** just outside the Museum. Built in 1934, this giant milk bottle–shaped hut was brought to its present location in 1978. True to its shape, the Milk Bottle serves dairy treats as well as sandwiches and salads for outdoor consumption. If you want a more substantial meal, **Matt Garrett's** at 300 Congress Street has an extensive menu for adults and a limited one for children. On the weekends children eat free from their menu when accompanied by two adults.

Another major indoor attraction in Boston is the **New England Aquarium,** just a short walk from the Children's Museum. Before you go inside, though, stop at the outdoor pool, where a family of harbor seals cavort and play all year long. You can also walk behind the aquarium to enjoy a striking vista of the harbor.

Once inside, just follow the spiral pathway around the main tank up to the very top. Each level of the path has a special exhibit along the outer perimeter, while the inside of the spiral provides a series of windows into the main tank. This tank, the largest cylindrical saltwater tank in the world, is home to a huge variety of species, from tiny shellfish crawling along the bottom to the huge swordfish swimming ominously in circles along the edges. The heavy glass makes it seem as if the creatures are within reach, and kids get a thrill coming face to face with a real shark.

Along the way, you'll want to make a special stop at the Edge of the Sea exhibit, a re-creation of a New England tidal pool where children can actually pick up starfish, horseshoe crabs, and periwinkles, and experience the habitat close up, with the aid of a well-informed "guide" to answer questions. Don't forget to take in the half-hour dolphin show on the museum's floating theater docked alongside the wharf — this show is a real treat. The museum also sponsors daily whale watching trips from May 1 to October 13. Sightings occur on virtually every trip, and Boston's outer harbor is a pleasure to explore.

A free indoor attraction is the **Boston Public Library,** where the children's department offers a picturebook film series, showing films of favorite children's books. Many local branch libraries offer storytelling hours several times a week. Call for dates, times, and selections.

The **Puppet Showplace** Theater in Brookline offers shows, on weekends during the school year and midweek in summer, as well as special shows during school vacations. The productions change constantly, but are always offered at 1 and 3 P.M., and are recommended for audiences over five years of age. Nearby is the **Children's Book Shop** at 237 Washington Street, where your child might while away a rainy afternoon snuggled into one of the store's "reading holes" browsing through the excellent collection of books.

A particularly interesting activity schedule is offered by the **Children's Workshop** in Cambridge. The shop, which sells a line of quality children's toys, has everything from creative movement classes to preschool art and music activities, as well as cooking, crafts, and special performances geared to preschool kids by local area artists. The store occasionally hosts a "sticker day," during which hordes of children come in to trade stickers and see what's new in the fabulous world of stick-on art.

Another interesting small exhibit is at the **Perkins School for the Blind,** in Watertown, where a tactile museum displays a changing exhibit of things to feel and explore. Not only is the exhibit fascinating for children, but the lessons it provides about the extensive world of the blind is an education for everyone. Tours of the facilities, with information about Helen Keller, can be arranged with a phone call.

For a good source of listings, and for information on a wide variety of activities, shops, and services that might be of special interest to families, pick up a free copy of the Boston Parents' Paper, *available at just about every stop on this tour. It's one of the best resources in the city for visiting or newly arrived families.*

Kidtrek II: Ages 9 – 13

Trekking through Boston with school-age kids can be tricky. Figuring out activities for different-age children is often difficult, especially if your eight-year-old wants to go skating while your eleven-year-old insists on boating. We can't promise to settle family disputes, but we can offer you a wide range of activities, both active and passive, indoors and outdoors, so that you and your family have as many choices as possible.

This tour follows no particular order, since the attractions are scattered throughout the area. We suggest you intersperse these sites with other activities, choosing the ones that appeal to your family and fit in with your specific itinerary.

A good place to start a family tour of the city is right at the top, in the **John Hancock Observatory** in Copley Square. The 360-degree view from this site is impressive to anyone, regardless of age, and it's fun to try to pick out landmarks or watch the planes taking off from Logan Airport to the east. There's no extra charge for the use of the telescopes, the multimedia film exhibits, or the dioramas. The elevator ride itself is worth the price of admission.

For the best view of Boston, head for Cambridge to the **Hyatt Regency** hotel. It welcomes families with facilities that include a swimming pool, bicycles (small sizes and those with booster seats on the back), and a special children's program called Camp Hyatt. Children can stay in a second room at half the rate of their parents, and receive free painter hats at check-in. If parents want to join their children in play activities, there is a small fort on the top floor of the parking structure with monkey bars to climb around on. On Friday and Saturday evenings there is an activity room where children can be supervised while coloring and playing games so that parents can have the night off. The Hyatt Regency's value of family patronage will make your stay enjoyable for all.

One of the most fascinating little-known attractions in Boston is the **Mapparium** at the Christian Science Center on Massachusetts Avenue, a several-long-block walk from the John Hancock Building. This unique stained-glass reproduction of the world (as it was when the Mapparium was constructed between 1932 and 1935) makes you feel as if you were literally standing in the middle of the earth. A glass bridge carries you out into the center of the huge domed building, where you can look up into the thirty-foot diameter sphere. You gain a unique perspective staring up into the world from this unusual angle, especially when you look at the relationship between the landmasses and bodies of water.

The Mapparium took almost a year to finish, and was created from 608 panels of glass, illuminated by 300 electric lights located outside the sphere. Since it was viewed as a work of art more than a realistic geographical rendering, the political boundaries have not been changed since its completion. An interesting effect of the room is that sound waves, bouncing off all that impervious glass, create a thrilling echo. You can hear someone whisper all the way across the room.

After exiting from the worldly view of the Mapparium, walk over to the corner of Newbury Street and Massachusetts Avenue, and enter **Tower Records,** the largest music store in the world, located at the base of the building designed by renowned architect

Frank Gehry. You name it, they've got it at this store: from jazz to hard rock — records, tapes, and disks. Both you and your children will find your favorite artists, as well as discovering a few new ones.

Another strongly recommended visit is a trip to the **Museum of Science**. Located on a plot of land that straddles the Charles River between Boston and Cambridge, the Science Museum provides interactive exhibits that are so much fun, your kids won't even realize what a rich educational experience they're having. One of the children's favorites is the *Tyrannosaurus rex* in the West Wing. This particular specimen arrived at his current home in a rather unusual style. Due to the transportation problems involved in moving him to the museum through traffic, the ancient fellow was air-lifted in along the river, dangling from a helicopter. His highly publicized arrival made him a celebrity to Boston schoolchildren, a position of importance he still holds. If you put a coin in the box at the dinosaur's feet, he'll oblige with a friendly roar of thanks.

Other popular attractions include the wave machine, the space capsule replica, and the music board, which lights up with different colors as different sounds are piped through it. In the "Human Body Discovery Space," there are hands-on medical exhibits where you can ride a bike and see a skeleton on the next bike mimicking your every move. Younger children will appreciate the Discovery Room, where they can participate in activities, from drawing and magnet projects to putting together real animal skeletons. There's an egg hatchery, where children can see chicks hatching out of their shells, and a fascinating telephone exhibit that traces the evolution of the talking machine. Another attraction is the museum's Charles Hayden Planetarium, which offers shows to children five and older all year long (check for times and price, as the admission is separate). The only Omnimax Theatre in New England uses the state-of-the-art film technology to give you the 360-degree feeling of being *there*, whether *there* is in the human body, the Great Barrier Reef, or outer space. It takes you places where most of us will never be able to venture.

As you walk toward the Esplanade, you'll see two old tugs, the *Luna* and the *Venus*, which served the Boston Harbor for half a century, guiding boats into the narrow ports and leading them forth again. In 1936, the *Luna* served as the queen of the tugboat fleet that successfully maneuvered the *Queen Mary* into New York Harbor on her maiden voyage to the United States. A book about her exploits, *Little Toot*, by Hardie Gramatky, was published a few years later and remains a children's classic. Your kids will enjoy a visit aboard the *Luna* or her sister ship, both of which have been retired and are being restored to their humble glory, and are open to the public free of charge.

The Esplanade also offers opportunities for boating, skating, and cycling. Skates can be rented for a nominal sum at Charles Street South by the Wang Center. In the wintertime, you can rent ice skates and skate along the Public Garden Lagoon.

Skimming along the Charles River in a sailboat or rowboat is a delightful way to enjoy a fine day. **Community Boating** operates a sailing program for children ages ten through seventeen for one dollar during the summer vacation. They also provide instruction in rowing and windsurfing. The facility is open for adults eight months of the year for a nominal fee. For places to eat, it is a short walk over to Charles Street. See Book Routes in Chapter 4 for a description of restaurants in the area.

Perhaps the best thing to do on the Esplanade is to camp out for an evening with the Boston Pops at the Hatch Shell. Usually they perform at Symphony Hall, but on selected dates, they weave their musical magic on the Esplanade (call for information; see page 184). Bring a blanket to sit on, and food and drink. The show, which is geared toward families, with a program of popular and classical favorites, is conducted by the inimitable John Williams or Harry Ellis Dickson. On the Fourth of July the concert is augmented by a spectacular fireworks display set off from a barge in the middle of the river, and the *1812* Overture is played to the accompaniment, at the appropriate moment, of a real cannon going off. The Esplanade Concerts also produce summer performances of the Boston Ballet and other popular attractions. Get there early to stake out a good spot. And take note of the oversized bust of long-time Pops conductor Arthur Fiedler near the footbridge named after him.

The Children's Museum will delight your older children too, but they may be more interested in the **Computer Museum** on Museum Wharf (attached to the Children's Museum). The Computer Museum is not just a bank of computers for junior whiz kids. The sixty interactive hands-on units allow children (and adults) to paint pictures, compose music, and create their own programs without any training. You can "fly" a plane on a program that realistically simulates flight, or watch the latest in animated video technology. There is a thirty-minute show of the state-of-the art computer animation and twenty-five historic robots in their own theater. There's even a computer that will alter the features of your face!

This is the only museum of its kind in the world (it was created by Kenneth Olsen, the founder of Digital Equipment Corporation) and is especially valuable because it provides a living repository of vintage computers and robots, from the largest vacuum tube computer ever built to today's desktop wonders. The Museum store carries educational and fun gifts such as high-tech jewelry, posters, books, and games. They even have a chocolate floppy disk and robot building kits. Occasionally there is a workshop for children and their parents to make a robot together.

Outside the Museum and halfway across the Congress Street Bridge is the **Boston Tea Party Ship Museum.** Although not the actual site of the historic party that bears its name, this is a replica of the ship from which 102,000 pounds of tea were tossed in December of 1773 by a band of angry Bostonians protesting the oppressive British tea tax (see page 9). It helps to remember, as you and your family toss a chest of "tea" overboard in commemoration of that event, that tea was considered as valuable as gold back then. Think, too, of New England winters — the citizens, who were disguised as Indians to protect their identity were probably pretty chilly on that December night!

Although it is not in Boston, it is worth a trip to Brookline to visit the **Museum of Transportation** in Larz Anderson Park. The exhibitions, which change on a regular basis, can be viewed in the carriage house that originally sheltered show horses belonging to Larz and Isabelle Anderson. Special shows, such as "Cars Made in New England" and "Future Cars of the Past," feature automobiles that were ahead of their times. The museum is only open Wednesdays thru Sundays in warm weather, and call for times in the winter. (While in Brookline, you might want to pay a visit to **John Fitzgerald Kennedy's Birthplace,** on Beals Street. A good family eatery nearby is **Edibles,** on Harvard Street, where homestyle cooking and terrific sweets are served up cafeteria-style.)

Now it's out to Charlestown for a tour of the **Charlestown**

Navy Yard, where the famous USS *Constitution* is berthed. The Navy Yard is a grand place to get a sense of the maritime history that was so crucial to the development of the city and the country. The USS *Constitution,* better known as "Old Ironsides," won the first major battle against the British during the War of 1812, since her wooden hull, which measures up to two feet in thickness, deflected British cannon fire as if it were iron. This famous American landmark served as the flagship of the fledgling American Navy and was never outrun, outmaneuvered, or demasted.

Old Ironsides fell on some hard times during the first half of this century, when she was ordered out of commission and left to rot in an abandoned navy berth. But the schoolchildren of America rallied to her aid fifty years ago, collecting their pennies and sending them to her rehabilitation fund. The ship was completely overhauled again for the Bicentennial, and today Old Ironsides is back on active duty: her assignment is to show modern visitors what it was like on a nineteenth-century fighting vessel. The sailors on board are well trained and receptive to questions, and full of interesting naval lore. They'll tell you the story of the ship's crew, sounding as proud of her battle record as if they had been one of the four to five hundred men and boys to do battle on her decks themselves!

Old Ironsides is not the only attraction at the Naval Yard. At the other end of Pier One is the USS *Cassin Young,* a WWII/Korean War destroyer that saw plenty of action in the Pacific, and is also open to the public. Just behind the *Young* is one of the first dry docks in America, where historic ships were restored.

Both ships, fascinating as they are, tell only part of Boston's glorious naval history. The **USS *Constitution* Museum,** located in the old pump house that controlled the water in the dry dock, presents the history of these old fighters with a hands-on exhibit that children adore. There's also a computer-simulated 1803 ocean crossing and a splendid display of gifts by an appreciative American public to Isaac Hull, successful military leader of the War of 1812. And the Commandant's House, directly behind the pier, is open to the public, so you can inspect the living quarters of the navy families who lived there from the beginning of the eighteenth century until just a decade ago.

At the other end of the city is a very different kind of historic attraction. The I. M. Pei–designed **John Fitzgerald Kennedy Mem-**

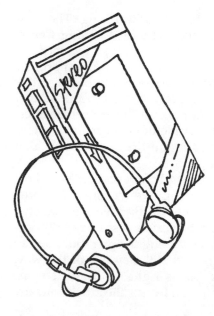

orial **Library** out on Columbia Point in Dorchester is a thrilling sight, rising like a white phoenix from the edge of the harbor. It also provides a rare insight into the life and times of a great American. The pictorial and multimedia exhibits are an exciting way for youngsters to get to know both. The library also has an impressive collection of Ernest Hemingway memorabilia.

Back in Boston proper, head to the downtown docks, and contemplate the Boston Harbor. Due to their great variety of landforms, vegetation, and historic structures, each one of the more than thirty Boston Harbor Islands has a unique character. Remains of ancient campsites prove that Indians frequented these islands more than six hundred years ago, and colonial farms were established on them as early as 1630. In the eighteenth century, guest houses and resorts were plentiful here, but by the late 1800s the city was using the islands for public purposes such as prisons, poorhouses, and sewage treatment facilities.

The Harbor was also integral to the city's defense, as the fortress remains on Governor's, Castle, and Long Islands attest. Today, the Harbor Islands are protected by state legislation, and are carefully maintained for sightseers. **Boston Harbor Cruises** and **Bay State Cruise Lines** offer cruises to the harbor's feature island — George's Island —where it is possible to spend the afternoon swimming, picnicking, and exploring the Civil War prison, Fort Warren. From there, boats leave for the inner and outer islands. There are free water taxis during the summer to eight other islands, maintained by the Friends of **Boston Harbor Islands.** If you are in the mood for a day-long version, try **Bay State Cruises** to Provincetown, Martha's Vineyard, Nantucket, and Hyannis — it could prove a fun experience as well as a way to beat the traffic.

For a great family day-long excursion, sail the Northeast

waters that are becoming famous for whale watching. The **New England Aquarium** and **Massachusetts Whale Watching Center** both sponsor day-long excursions from May through October.

The educational tour program department of **Massport,** the state mandated port authority, offers private tours of the active fireboat, the *Howard Fitzpatrick,* which is anchored in the harbor. The tour program also offers regular tours of the airport facilities. Sometimes the group is shown the inside of an airplane, if one is available, but there is always a trip to the fire station that takes groups along the roads by the runways.

By the way, if you're pier-hopping before or after your boat ride, but especially early in the morning, we recommend a brief trip down Commonwealth Pier to the Fish Pier, where the city's fresh fish supply comes in by the ton everyday (see page 82). Visitors are not encouraged to walk freely along the pier, but you can get a good glimpse of the activity and still stay out of the way. Some ships have fish-processing plants right on board, so that fresh fish literally goes off the boat and onto the trucks already cleaned and packaged for sale.

On a rainy day, you might want to explore some of the area's historic houses, especially since there are several that particularly appeal to children. The **Paul Revere House** in Boston's historic North End is the most famous house in the city. Your family might be amazed to discover that the Revere family raised sixteen children in this tiny saltbox structure! There may have been as many as eight siblings living in one room at a time. The sparse nursery, with its white plaster walls, pine wainscotting, and painted wood floor might make today's offspring grateful for their modern conveniences (a fact you shouldn't hesitate to point out). The rest of the house is fascinating too, providing an insight into the private life of the man who helped change the course of history one fateful night in April of 1775.

The new **State House** on Beacon Hill is a house of an entirely different sort, but if you go inside and get a copy of *Under the State House Dome,* the new children's guide, you'll find it a fun little tour. Most of the artwork and writing in the book was done by children. The Governor's office, the Senate Chambers, and the Sacred Cod, the symbol of the House of Representatives, are described in lively detail.

> *There are a number of walking tours especially designed for children. **Boston by Little Feet** is a guided tour geared for eight- to twelve-year-olds, while Boston Walkabouts provides an excellent way for your family to "do" the Freedom Trail, the well-marked route that leads visitors past some of Boston's most historic sites. Boston Walkabouts provides a well-detailed cassette of the Freedom Trail, available in French, German, Japanese, and English, to help you on your way. The **Historic Neighborhoods Foundation** offers various tours, such as the cherished* Make Way for Ducklings *tour, which follows the paths and adventures of the ducklings in the popular children's book.*

As long as you're downtown, your children will probably appreciate a brief stop at **Jack's Joke Shop,** the oldest shop of its kind in America. This venerable Boston institution is filled with a maniacal collection of jokes, costumes, books, and an oddball assortment of things humorous (or not, depending on your sense of the absurd). Some of the humor may not be age-appropriate, so close supervision is recommended. Jack's is owned and operated by Harold Bengin, whose father-in-law opened his doors in 1922 at the same location.

With so few stores that carry comic books, take heart and head for **Newbury Comics,** at 332 Newbury Street, for new and used comic books and related novelty items. Also on Newbury at 247, is the **Last Wound-Up,** which has replicas of toys that wind up, music boxes, and toy banks.

Boston for children is not just about places. There are a wealth of cultural activities available, ranging from dance classes at the **Boston Ballet School** and classes in painting, drawing, jewelry design, and ceramics at the **Brookline Arts Center,** to special children's performances of the **Boston Ballet Company** and **Boston Youth Symphony Orchestra.** (Check the local newspapers for a special listing section for children's events. The *Boston Globe's* Calendar section, which is in every Thursday edition, is a good resource, as well as the *Boston Parents' Paper*, available free throughout the city.)

Two programs are worth a special mention. The **Wheelock Family Theater** and the **Boston Children's Theater** both offer performances between November and May that are especially geared for quality family entertainment. Wheelock Family Theater, the resident company at Wheelock College, which specializes in teacher training, offers a fairly sophisticated range of classes and productions of children's classics, both old and new. Their productions make use of multiracial, intergenerational casts. In the summertime, the Boston Children's Theater runs a stagemobile, which rides like a gypsy wagon through the city, putting on performances at parks and playgrounds, and in winter and during the school holidays it stages weekend performances at **New England Life Hall.**

And, finally, what delights a child more than a festival, held out in the open air and in an ethnic neighborhood full of delightful things to see, do, and eat? Check our list in the back of this book and the newspaper for special celebrations.

In addition to playgrounds for the young, seasonal outdoor sports are readily available for fitness and fun, and spectator sports are a staple of any Bostonian's diet. Any youngsters not totally worn out by the history, culture, fun, and frolic provided in this chapter can work off any excess energy they still have in the next one.

Tour Sites

Arnold Arboretum
The Arborway
Jamaica Plain, MA 02130
524-1717

Blue Hills Trailside Museum
1904 Canton Ave.
Milton, MA 02186
333-0690

Bay State Cruises
723-2800
See page 222.

Boston Ballet Company
19 Clarendon St.
Boston, MA 02116
964-4070

Boston Ballet School
19 Clarendon St.
Boston, MA 02116
542-1406

Boston Children's Museum
Museum Wharf
300 Congress St.
Boston, MA 02109
426-8855
Admission fee; lower price on
Friday evenings.

Boston Children's Theater
652 Hammond St.
Brookline, MA 02146
277-3277

Boston Harbor Cruises
227-4320
See page 222.

Boston by Little Feet
See Boston by Foot, page 215.

Boston Pops/Boston Symphony
Orchestra
301 Massachusetts Ave.
Boston, MA 02115
266-1492 or 266-2378 (CON-CERT)

Boston Public Library
666 Boylston St.
Boston, MA 02115
536-5400

Boston Tea Party Ship Museum
Congress Street Bridge
Boston, MA 02109
338-1773
Admission fee.

Boston Walkabouts
See page 215.

Boston Youth Symphony
Orchestra
301 Massachusetts Ave.
Boston, MA 02115
267-0656

Brookline Arts Center
86 Monmouth St.
Brookline, MA 02146
566-5715

Charlestown Navy Yard
Charlestown, MA 02129
542-5672
See also USS *Constitution*
Museum.

Children's Book Shop
237 Washington St.
Brookline, MA 02146
734-7323

Children's Workshop
1963 Massachusetts Ave.
Cambridge, MA 02139
354-1633

Community Boating, Inc.
21 Embarkment Rd.
Boston, MA 02114
523-1038

Computer Museum
300 Congress St.
Boston, MA 02210
423-6758

USS *Constitution* Museum,
    Visitors Information
Boston Naval Shipyard
Charlestown, MA 02129
242-0543

Drumlin Farm
5 Great Rd.
Lincoln, MA 01773
259-9500

Franklin Park Zoo
Blue Hill Ave.
Dorchester, MA 02121
442-2002

George's Island
Call Metropolitan District
    Commission
727-5215

Hatch Shell
The band shell located on the
    Esplanade opposite Clarendon
    and Berkeley Sts.

Hyatt Regency Cambridge
575 Memorial Dr.
Cambridge, MA 02139
492-1234

Jacadi
110 Newbury St.
Boston, MA 02116
262-4049

Jack's Joke Shop
197 Tremont St.
Boston, MA 02116
426-9640

JFK's Birthplace
83 Beals St.
Brookline, MA 02146
566-7937
Admission fee.

JFK Museum and Memorial
    Library
Columbia Point
Dorchester, MA 02125
929-4523

John Hancock Observatory
Hancock Place
Boston, MA 02116
247-1977
Admission fee.

Kites of Boston
Faneuil Hall Marketplace
Boston, MA 02109
742-1455

Last Wound-Up
247 Newbury St.
Boston, MA 02116
424-9293

Mapparium
Christian Science Mother Church
1 Norway St.
Boston, MA 02108
262-2300

Massport
Educational Tour Programs
Logan International Airport
East Boston, MA 02128
561-1800

Metropolitan District Commission
  (MDC)
20 Somerset St.
Boston, MA 02108
727-5215

Museum of Science/
Hayden Planetarium
Science Park
Boston, MA 02114
723-2500 or 742-6088

Museum of Transportation
15 Newton St.
Brookline, MA 02146
522-6140
Admission fee.

Newbury Comics
332 Newbury St.
Boston, MA 02116
236-4930
Other locations in the Boston
  area.

New England Aquarium
Central Wharf
Boston, MA 02110
742-8870
Admission fee.

New England Life Hall
225 Clarendon St.
Boston, MA 02116
266-7262

Paul Revere House
19 North Square
Boston, MA 02113
523-2338

Perkins School for the Blind
175 N. Beacon St.
Watertown, MA 02172
924-3434

Puppet Showplace
32 Station St.
Brookline Village, MA 02146
731-6400

Sharp Kids
Faneuil Hall Marketplace
Boston, MA 02109
227-1150

State House
Beacon St.
Boston, MA 02133
727-3676

Tower Records
360 Newbury St.
Boston, MA 02115
247-5900

Walter D. Stone Memorial Zoo
149 Pond St.
Stoneham, MA 02180
438-3662
Admission fee.

Veronique Delchaux
112 Newbury St.
Boston, MA 02116
424-6800

Swan Boats
Public Garden
522-1966
"Swan season" is May to October.
Admission fee.

Wheelock Family Theater
Wheelock College
200 The Riverway
Boston, MA 02215
734-5200

Tales with Tails
Faneuil Hall Marketplace
Boston, MA 02109
227-8772

RESTAURANTS

Dave's Homemade Ice Cream
144 Newbury St.
Boston, MA 02116
262-5737

Matt Garrett's
300 Congress St.
Boston, MA 02210
350-6001

Edibles
329 Harvard St.
Brookline, MA 02146
232-8835

Milk Bottle
Children's Museum
Museum Wharf
Boston, MA 02109
426-7074

Travis
135 Newbury St.
Boston, MA 02116
267-6388
See Historic Boston, Chapter 1,
  for restaurants near the USS
  Constitution.

Additional Resources

Massachusetts Whale
  Watching Center
508-747-1251
New England Aquarium Whale
  Watching Hotline
973-5277

EMERGENCY NUMBERS

Police, Fire, Ambulance
911

Poison Information Center
232-2120

BABYSITTING SERVICES

Alternative Care
Boston: 451-5250
Brookline: 734-0010

Parents in a Pinch
Brookline: 739-5437

Minute Women
Boston: 227-1889
Brookline: 277-5588

HARBOR CRUISES

Bay State Cruises
20 Long Wharf
Boston, MA 02110
723-2800 (information); 723-4027
(reservations)
For whale watches.

Boston by Sail
65 Lewis Wharf
Boston, MA 02110
742-3313

Boston Harbor Cruises
1 Long Wharf
Boston, MA 02110
227-4320
For harbor cruises and whale
watches.

Massachusetts Bay Lines
398 Atlantic Ave.
Boston, MA 02110
542-8000

Water Music, Inc.
12 Arrow St.
Cambridge, MA 02139
876-8742

RECOMMENDED READING

The 1988 Boston Area Children's Yellow Pages. Reading, Mass.: Addison-Wesley, 1988.

Chesler, Bernice. *In and Out of Boston With (or Without) Children*. Chester, Conn.: Globe Pequot Press, 1982.

Kales, Emily and David. *All about the Boston Harbor Islands*. Captain George's, Inc., 1983.

Maynard, Mary, and Dow, Mary-Lou Maynard. *Hassle-Free Boston: A Manual for Women*. Brattleboro, Vt.: The Stephen Greene Press, 1984.

Norton, Bettina A. *Neighborhood Trivia Hunt* Series. Boston: Ban Publishing Company, 1985.

Summerchild in Boston. Boston: The Advent-School, 1988.

Westman, Barbara. *The Beard and the Braid.* New York: Barre Publishing Co., 1970.

Westman, Barbara, and Kenny, Herbert. *A Boston Picture Book.* Boston: Houghton Mifflin Company, 1975.

Boston Parents' Paper
P. O. Box 1777
Jamaica Plain, MA 02130
522-1515
Available at most stops on the tours in this chapter.

CHAPTER NINE

The Sporting Life

Bostonians have three major obsessions: crazy driving, politics, and sports. If there's a common denominator there, we don't know what it is. But in sports, it probably has to do with die-hard loyalty and a love of the underdog. Heart-warming comebacks and frenetic last-minute skirmishes are the staple of a Boston sports fan, probably because the big home teams — the Red Sox, Celtics, Bruins, and Patriots — have found themselves in so many tight situations over the years.

But faithful fans have been rewarded with a great deal of memorable, if not championship, playing. The Celtics stand on top in terms of actual winning records. Since 1960, they've been World Champions sixteen times. The Bruins have made it to the Stanley Cup Playoffs seventeen times, although they've won only twice. The Red Sox won the American League pennant in 1967, 1975, and 1986, although the last time they actually won a World Series was in 1918. And the New England Patriots, after years of fumbling, actually made it to the Super Bowl in the 1985–86 season.

Although the professional sports arenas in Boston are small, you can almost always get tickets to a game. Before any sports event, even a playoff, there are always industrious people outside the stadiums selling tickets. (The one exception is Celtics tickets, perhaps the hottest item in the sports world.) Unfortunately, although scalping is illegal, it's about as pervasive as illegal parking in the city. Try the authorized outlets first, though: you'll often be able to get seats.

In this chapter, we'll take you on a guided tour of the places and people that make up the Boston sports scene. We'll look at spectator sports first, concentrating on the various arenas of play for the professional teams. Then we'll cover the major participatory sports by category, giving you some general ideas about where to go to indulge in your favorite activity, and what to expect from your fellow sports fanatics when you do. The Tour Sites and Resource section at the end of the chapter gives more detailed information on most of the major sports institutions in the city.

Cheering Them On

This tour can be accomplished entirely by public transportation — no surprise when you consider that a team can't have a following if its fans can't easily attend the games. Hop on the MBTA's Green Line and get off at North Station, a stone's throw from **Boston Garden.** Home of the Bruins ice hockey team and the Celtics basketball team, the Garden (as opposed to "the Gardens," meaning the Public Garden) is surely one of the sacred cows of the city. It has been recently renovated, but it always emerges unscathed in its old unrepentant shape to welcome hundreds of thousands of fans who couldn't care less if the building was built out of dry twigs, as long as they can see their beloved teams play.

The Garden houses a railroad station, offices, a few bars and eating places, and an arena. Yet it still manages to convey a sense of intimacy when you're sitting in the stands. Since it first opened its doors in 1928, the Garden has been home to scores of great hockey and basketball players, and it really feels as though their spirits still linger in the yellow-tiled hallways that seem to curve endlessly around the playing area. The championship banners and retired numbers of all the stars hang from the rafters, giving the appearance of a medieval banquet hall.

The floor of the Garden is unique. It was built during World War Two when short wood was all that was available, so it's parquet, just like the floors of the elegant drawing rooms on Beacon Hill. But the bolts that hold it together have begun to pop up slightly, creating irregularities that can wreak havoc with a bouncing basketball. The Celtics, of course, love to play home games, because they know exactly where the funny spots are. The ice rink, too, has its idiosyncracies due to the uneven flooring, but the Bruins, like the Celtics, don't mind.

It's not architecture, however, but the personalities of the two home teams that lend the Garden its unique flavor. No two teams could be more different, both in their approach and in the kinds of fans they attract. The **Boston Celtics,** for instance, have been called a "Yuppies' team." In the past, basketball was the poor relation of Boston sports. Despite an impressive record, there was no loyal local following. Even in the 1950s and 1960s, when the Celtics won eleven straight titles, you could walk into the Garden any night and not find a crowd.

But Larry Bird and his teammates have changed all that, and a ticket to a Celtics game is now worth its weight in gold. Back in May of 1984, Bird saved the championship for his team by popping in a bank shot from the corner 1:07 seconds before the buzzer, wresting the Eastern Conference Championship from the Philadelphia 76ers in an improbable come-from-behind victory that still has fans grinning. "The Bird" has become a Boston institution despite his Indiana roots, and his appearance on a Boston street is likely to draw bigger crowds than the mayor himself.

If Larry Bird epitomizes the winning appeal of the team, president and former coach Red Auerbach is its anchor. He's been with the club for over thirty-five years and can be seen at every game in his box at center court facing the Celtics' bench. A game is officially over after he walks across the court with a cigar stuck in his mouth, looking for all the world like a poker player who just came up with a full house.

Visiting players can often be found staying at the Westin Copley Place hotel or at the Marriott Long Wharf on the waterfront; after the game, you'll have a good chance of spotting them at **Clarke's,** at 21 Merchants Row. But the best place to feel the Boston sports spirit is at **Champions** in the Marriott Copley Place. Filled with memorabilia of Champions Corporation President Michael O'Meara and sports attorney Bob Woolf, there are sports photos, signs, players' jerseys, bats, balls, hockey pucks, and just about anything else you can think of related to sports. With grilled chicken sandwiches and hamburgers as the most popular dishes, this is definitely the bar and restaurant for sports enthusiasts. The dance floor is popular on the weekends, and they even serve nonalcoholic beer. Down at **Fred P. Otts** in North Quincy Market, a fun-loving atmosphere is encouraged through lip-sync contests, dirty dancing, and a constant disk jockey. Besides, you can beat the summer heat here at the only Faneuil Hall Marketplace bar with an air conditioner!

The **Boston Bruins,** on the other hand, are a hard-hitting bunch, and their fans tend to be more blue-collar, although no less knowledgeable or enthusiastic than the Celtics' fans. Just as hockey seems to spawn more physical altercations than basketball, so hockey fans seem to come into physical contact with one another more often than their hoop-happy counterparts. There is often as much action in the stands as there is on the ice.

For the Bruins, the past is more magical than the present. Years ago they were the preeminent sports team in the city; every kid in Dorchester and South Boston wanted to grow up to wear the black and gold. Bobby Orr, Phil Esposito, and Pie McKenzie were the heroes back then. Then the sport lost popularity, and the team seemed to fall on hard times.

Nowadays, the Bruins are playing the kind of swift and merciless game of hockey that won them fame in the first place. True fans know everything there is to know about their team, including the Canadian national anthem (because so many players hail from up north). And most fans would be fairly well qualified to get out on the ice and make the referee's calls themselves, although their objectivity would be seriously in question.

After the game, the team members can often be seen at the **Kowloon Restaurant** on Route One in Saugus, since many of them live on the North Shore. But the die-hard fans can be found in the North Station restaurant, **Sports Café,** right in North Station beneath the Garden.

Across the street from the Garden at 166 Canal Street, you can dress casually and hang out with a hard-core sports crowd at **Fours Boston.** With seven televisions, you can sit almost anywhere in this bar (downstairs or above) and still be able to watch live sports with fellow fans. Sports celebrities often meet before and after games at the **Dockside Restaurant,** in the shadow of the Custom House. Steak tips and pizza are the specialties here. For some moderately priced seafood in a warm atmosphere, step into the **Oyster Club Raw Bar and Grill** at 200 Portland. After games at the Garden, the place gets packed from door to door, but the upstairs/downstairs restaurant has some tasty dishes that are worth the wait.

Return to the "T" and take the inbound train six stops to the Copley station. (Taking the "T" is actually a spectator sport in itself, as any Boston commuter can attest. Not only do you get to watch the other passengers, you also have free entertainment. Some of the stops have recently commissioned artworks (see page 171), and almost all have become favorite practicing studios for budding Boston musicians. The acoustics are challenging, but the audience is captive, and appreciative listeners have been known to make financial contributions if there is a particularly long wait for a car.) But the reason we've brought you up here at Copley is so you can use your imagination; picture yourself standing at the finish line of the **Boston Marathon,** right in front of you on Boylston Street.

It's hard to classify the Boston Marathon as either a participatory or spectator sport, because it tends to be both. Running is easily the most popular individual sport in the Boston area, and the Boston Marathon, a long-standing tradition, inspired enthusiasm even before jogging became a national pastime.

First run in 1897, the marathon was modeled after the ancient Greeks' twenty-six-mile course. The marathon has been run continuously on April 19th, or the Monday on which Patriot's Day is celebrated, since its inception in 1897. (Patriot's Day is a local holiday marking the battles in Lexington and Concord during the Revolutionary War.)

Marathon superlatives are remembered by avid runners in the same way that Celtics fans remember Larry Bird's corner lob. The fastest man's time (2:07.51) was set by Ron d'Castella in 1986. The fastest woman's time (2:22.09) was set by Joan Benoit in 1983. Two world wheelchair records were set in 1989. Philippe Couprie of France (1:36:04) won the man's wheelchair category, and Connie Hansen of Denmark (1:50:06) placed first in the woman's division. In 1989, 6458 persons entered the Marathon; 5104 completed the course.

The first woman to run the race was Kathy Switzer, in 1967. She was bodily thrown out; women have been officially allowed to enter the race only since 1971, and Nina Kuscsik was the first legal entrant. It's interesting to note that Joan Benoit's winning time in 1983 broke not only the women's record, but the records of a great number of male runners as well!

The Marathon starts in the town of Hopkinton, on the town green, and finishes in front of the John Hancock Tower in Copley Square. (It used to end at the Prudential Tower, but changed when the John Hancock Insurance Company decided to underwrite a major portion of the $60,000 race purse in 1986.) The course is ideal, with gently rolling hills and lots of straightaways, except for Heartbreak Hill, in Newton. At six miles from the finish, Heartbreak Hill presents most runners with a natural wall when their reserves of energy are often at their lowest. The fact that the incline is steep doesn't help, of course, and many a runner has been known to give up before reaching the top of the hill — hence the name. But the Hill has never stopped eighty-one-year-old Bostonian John Kelley. The 1989 race was his fifty-eighth, and in true, tenacious Yankee fashion, he intends to run it 'til he dies.

The Boston Marathon was criticized recently because it didn't offer substantial financial rewards for winners. The international runners were beginning to pass Boston by in favor of the big money races, such as New York and Los Angeles. But the city was quick to realize that it couldn't afford to allow the revered Boston Marathon to fade into obscurity because of a little matter of a few dollars, and local businesses — and even the towns along the route — came up with competitive prize money.

If you want to run in the Marathon, contact the **Boston Athletic Association** for information on qualifying times, eligibility, and how to register. If you want to watch, just get an early place along the route (which is printed in all the local papers before the event). Hopkinton is a favorite because of the intense excitement and anticipation surrounding the entrants as they limber and psych up for the race. (It takes half an hour before the mass of runners can all pass the starting line, and the times are computed accordingly.) But Wellesley College, Heartbreak Hill, and any spot along Commonwealth Avenue, Beacon Street, or Boylston Street in Boston are also exciting vantage points. Don't be shy about handing out cups of water, which most runners will gratefully accept. Any verbal encouragement you can offer will be equally appreciated. The atmosphere along the route is friendly, and everyone roots for each participant, knowing what a supreme effort it takes just to complete the course.

The quintessential runners' hangout is the **Eliot Lounge,** where marathoners have traditionally gone after the race to rehydrate and celebrate their relative victories. In 1972, bartender Tommy Leonard ran the Falmouth Road Race on Cape Cod and became friendly with four-time marathon winner Bill Rodgers. Leonard invited Rodgers to the lounge after the 1975 race, which Rodgers happened to win. When the media asked Rodgers what his plans were after the race, he told them he was going to the Eliot Lounge to have about ten "Blue Elephants" (a drink made with blue curaçao). The Eliot now serves a runner's pasta dinner a few nights before the marathon in addition to its après-race celebration, but don't be surprised if you can't get in the door for the few days before and after the race. Either way, pause and look down at the cement sidewalk outside the door. Bill Rodger's bare footprint is immortalized there — Boston's answer to Grauman's Theatre in Hollywood.

Back underground again, catch any *out*bound Green Line car, as long as it's *not* marked Arborway. Continue to Kenmore, and then walk the rest of the way to **Fenway Park,** home of the **Boston Red Sox.**

Fenway exudes the same quizzical and slightly offbeat charm as the Red Sox themselves. If you're a real fan, you'll love both in spite of their quirks. The park, situated a block west of Kenmore Square, was built in 1912, and its unique many-sided shape is not an accident. The land next door, now populated by a series of disco clubs, was not available for sale at the time, so the builders simply used what space they could get. Still, the small size of the stadium (capacity 34,182) makes for very special baseball viewing, and Fenway is considered one of the best ballparks in the country from a spectator's point of view. Fenway manages to handle two million fans a year in spite of its size, making it second only to Yankee Stadium, which is twice as large. The novelist John Updike, a dyed-in-the-wool Red Sox fan, calls Fenway Park "a lyric little bandbox of a park. Everything is painted green and seems in curiously sharp focus, like the inside of an old-fashioned peeping-type Easter egg." Small as it is, the park now has private suites, built atop the left- and right-field stands in 1983. More recently, 610 stadium club seats ("The 600 Club") were constructed above the grandstand with new broadcast booths and a press box high above the club. A color videoboard with a black and white messageboard lights up above center field.

The park was rebuilt in 1934 by Tom Yawkey, late husband of current owner, Jean Yawkey. Mrs. Yawkey can sometimes be seen in her box to the left of home plate, along with an omnipresent vase of fresh flowers.

Boston's baseball history goes back even before the Sox, to the Boston Pilgrims, who entered the American League in 1901, the first year of operation. They played at a Huntington Avenue field where Northeastern University now stands. The name Red Sox was adopted because of the color of the players' stockings. The team moved to Fenway in 1912.

The most obvious feature of Fenway Park — and baseball's most notorious landmark — is the left-field wall, better known as the Green Monster. Thought to be an asset because it is such a short reach for a home run, the Wall has actually been a nemesis for the home team. It's been called baseball's Lorelei, luring right-handed hitters with the promise of an easy 315-foot homer, only

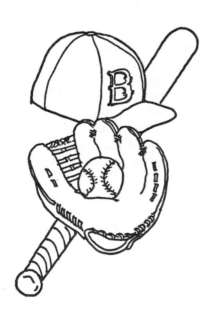

to dash their hopes against the padded green 37½-foot-high cement. In any case, the left side of the field is the place to sit, as much of the action seems to be directed in that area.

The Sox have a pretty luminous list of players in their Hall of Fame, including Carl Yastrzemski, Ted Williams, Luis Tiant, and Johnny Pesky. (In his early years, even Babe Ruth was a Red Sox.) After the game, fans hang out at the **Cask 'n Flagon, Copperfields,** and **Who's on First,** all in the vicinity of the ballpark. And, if you're lucky, you may even run into some players at **Daisy Buchanan's** or **Friday's.** Don't be shy about asking for autographs. The Sox are happy to oblige their fans even if they have lost the game.

You can't get out to the **New England Patriots** football stadium by the "T," although buses do run during the season. That's because the Pats now play out at Sullivan Stadium in Foxboro, forty-five minutes south of Boston. This sixty-one-thousand-seat arena has all the advantages of a college stadium despite its size. There are no tiers, poles, or pillars to block the view, and the sight lines are terrific from everywhere in the house. The stadium also boasts the largest TV screen in New England, a Diamond Vision Board by Mitsubishi, which has thirty-six thousand cathode ray tubes, as opposed to your home set's *one*. Live half-time shows have been replaced by videotaped performances of old games, highlights, replays of the current game, and, of course, commercials.

The stadium was named for the Sullivan family who built it in 1971, and who owned the team until 1987. The Patriots are now owned by Victor Kiam, nationally known for his electric shaver commercials. Founder Billy Sullivan is as much of an institution as the team, and his family's idiosyncratic adventures on and off the field are a part of Patriot lore. Billy's son Patrick often sat on the benches with the players and was actively involved in the game, sometimes engaging in dramatic altercations with referees on the field.

One of the biggest Patriot's traditions is the tailgate picnic before and after the game. The tradition began with the New England Ivy League teams, and is still a staple of any college football weekend, but the Pat's fans are the only major leaguers who really seem to follow suit. Probably one factor is the traffic congestion on Route 1 two hours before and after game time. Cars start arriving in the huge Foxboro parking lot long before the game is scheduled to begin, and fans unload meals that range from the elaborate to the mundane. Tablecloths, candelabra, and champagne are not unusual, nor is a beer-and-hot-dog feast. After the game, hot chocolate and coffee are often served in the same manner, and it's usually 6 or 7 P.M. before the parking lot finally empties out.

The team was originally called the Boston Patriots, and they played wherever they could find space in Boston — mostly on the college fields, and even in Fenway Park. They were first members of the American Football League, and joined the National Football

League in 1970. Since that time, they have racked up an impressive number of losses, including a miserable no-win season in 1984.

All that changed during the 1985–86 season, when the team advanced from behind to the AFC championship playoff against the Miami Dolphins, and then won the title in a thrilling display of skill in the Orange Bowl. Suddenly, the Patriots were a team to contend with, a fact that some loyal fans still seem unable to believe. The 1986 Super Bowl was a major event for Boston, and some twelve thousand fans went to New Orleans to see the Patriots play the Chicago Bears, who won Super Bowl XX handily.

With such great teams as the Celtics, Bruins, Patriots, and Red Sox, the dedicated Boston sports fan is one-of-a-kind. Perhaps nowhere else in the country will you find such die-hard fans and renowned athletes as in the New England area. To recapture all of those past sports glories and moments of excitement, you can't miss the **Sports Museum of New England** across from WBZ radio station on Soldiers Field Road in Brighton. Championed by former Celtics great Dave Cowens, who is chairman of the board, this museum is the first of its kind in the region. The facility includes an archive with photos, artifacts, and memorabilia of the region's great athletes, a library room, and video production facilities. You can flip through a catalogue of sports films and videos, and then choose some for your own personal viewing or press a button on the video jukebox to watch a great moment in sports history. The most popular exhibits are life-sized sculptures by Armond La Montagne of Bobby Orr and Larry Bird, complete with uniforms and poised for sports action. In 1991, the Sports Museum is expected to move to the historic **Customs House Tower** in downtown Boston.

Tour Sites

See pages 243–249 for a complete list of Tour Sites, Restaurants, and Resources for Sporting tours.

Moving On

What is the magic element about Boston, the element that differentiates it so clearly from other cities its size in the United States? Surely one such element is the use of the Charles River and the land alongside it, which provides the city with an open public playground through all the seasons. Boating takes place on it, and running, cycling, and skating take place beside it. The Charles is Boston's backyard, and a splendid place to be during the day. Eighty miles long from start to finish, it's the only river in America whose mouth is maintained by dams lower than the adjacent tidal ocean.

BOATING

Boaters in Boston fall into two major classes: sailors and oarsmen. (Power boating is considered cheating to most dyed-in-the-wool Bostonians.) Although sailing takes a certain amount of training, luckily there are several opportunities available for instruction. Perhaps the most popular water sport institution in Boston is the **Community Boating School.** The boathouse where the school is located dates from 1940, when Helen Osborn Storrow (see Chapter 2) left money for a public boating establishment on the River near her Back Bay home.

Today, the program is cooperative: experienced members teach new members how to sail. The membership fees are gratifyingly low, and instruction rates are also modest. You can get complete instruction in basic technique from qualified teachers, and have plenty of time on the water to practice. During the summer, there are children's classes. From April to November, the river is full of white wedges of sail tacking unevenly about the basin between the Museum of Science and the Massachusetts Avenue Bridge.

The name of **Boston by Sail** says it all. The company offers sixty-minute daytime and ninety-minute sunset cruises around the city from May to mid-October. The boats sail from the Boston Waterboat Marina, behind the Long Wharf Marriott. There you can also learn how to operate a power boat, and sailing lessons for kids are offered in the summer.

The upper reaches of the Charles are dotted with other boat-houses, most of them college-owned. Many offer sailing for students, but the college boathouses are really dedicated to the noble sport of crew. And don't call it rowing. Rowboats bear absolutely no resemblance to the sleek, nearly weightless shells that skim the water with otterlike speed.

The absolute pinnacle of crew-mania in Boston occurs on the third Sunday in October, when the annual Head-of-the-Charles Regatta attracts thousands of fans to the area to compete in that prestigious race. Crew teams from colleges and clubs all over the country bring their shells to Cambridge to race the difficult three-mile course between the Boston University Boathouse and the Christian Herter Center in Allston. They race single file, with the winner judged on elapsed time, and the sight is a marvel to behold on a crisp October afternoon. The best seat in the house is on the Weeks Footbridge near the Harvard Business School, but get there early for a view. Picnicking along the banks of the river is encouraged, but you'll have to arrive before the hordes to commandeer a good spot.

Traditionally, the crew of a winning boat tosses the coxswain overboard after a win. The losing team is supposed to hand over their tee-shirts to the winners, and the object of the season is to see how many tee-shirts the team can collect. The phrase "give him the shirt off my back" allegedly comes from this ritual.

The shells, which can accommodate from one to nine people, are designed to move along the water as fast as the oarsmen and -women can propel them. Most college crews practice in the early morning and late afternoons, and you can see them hard at their oars, working in perfect synchronization as the lightweight coxswain shouts orders to the eight-member team. The oldest intercollegiate crew meet in the United States is the Harvard–Yale competition, which has been held every year since 1854.

SWIMMING

Swimming in urban rivers is not a good idea in this day and age, although Massachusetts, with its reputation for an ecology-minded populace, deserves some credit for environmental consciousness. In the summer of 1985, after a decades-long clean-up effort, the Metropolitan District Commission (MDC) declared the Charles River once again safe to swim in — but only near Forest Grove in Waltham. Some day it may become possible to swim again in the Charles River Basin, but until then, there are a number of nearby beaches that get plenty of use in the summer (see the list at the end of this chapter).

The MDC also has nineteen area pools — two of them right on the River — admission is only 25 cents under age fifteen; 50 cents for adults. The MDC swimming pools have wading pools for young children alongside them, although sometimes the layout of the pools is such that adults can't easily go back and forth from one pool to another. Several local hotels also have pool memberships available to area residents and nonguests. The **YMCA** and **YWCA** in Boston and Cambridge have pool times available for family swims, as well as for lap swimming at a nominal fee. (See Tour Sites.)

We'd be remiss to discuss swimming in Boston without at least mentioning the "L" street Brownies, a group of people "of a certain age" who make it a habit to dive into the Atlantic Ocean off Carson Beach in South Boston even in winter. There is an annual picture published in the local paper of these hearty souls, dressed in only bathing suits and caps, nosing their way into the frigid January surf like happy seals!

RUNNING

The Marathon isn't the only game in town for runners, and on the other 364 days of the year, you'll find plenty of company if you want to go out for a jog. In this town, even Mayor Ray Flynn is an avid runner and does a respectable five or six miles a day. The favorite route for Boston joggers is on the Esplanade, along the river past the Harvard Business School up to Watertown Square, and all the way back down Soldiers Field Road and Storrow Drive to the Museum of Science Bridge, for a total of over 17 miles. (You can cut across on any of several other bridges if you can't make it that far.) The Esplanade trail is special, though, because it has fitness stops along the way where runners can stop and stretch, increasing their aerobic and anaerobic conditioning. Running maps are available from several sources; most have distances clearly marked.

Even if you choose to run on the sidewalk, Boston provides a scenic and fairly level course. However, runners are cautioned to beware of traffic at all times; Boston drivers have a reputation for ignoring small distractions such as traffic lights and pedestrians. There are several runners' clubs that will provide information on the running scene in Boston, including where to run and when, and a listing of runners' events such as road races and field runs.

> *"It's unnatural for people to run around city streets unless they are thieves or victims. It makes people nervous to see someone running. I know that when I see someone running on my street, my instincts tell me to let the dog out after him."*
> — *Mike Royko, newspaper columnist*

CYCLING

If you prefer your aerobics with wheels under you, Boston is an ideal city for cycling. In fact, biking is a great way to get to see the city, since Boston can easily be traversed — and you don't have to worry about finding a parking place! Bicycles are as much a part of the Boston scenery as the college students who use them, but the young are by no means the only citizens to avail themselves of pedal power. Back in Victorian Boston, bicycles were considered the only form of dignified exercise other than promenading, and the Commonwealth Mall used to be filled with ladies and gentlemen dressed to the nines, pedaling at a stately pace atop their high two-wheelers. Today, there is still a club for people who have preserved those gangly relics, and some members can even ride them, though they're a lot more difficult to maneuver than low-slung modern bicycles. There are many bike trails with either scenic or historic significance, and they range from short hops to extended day trips around the area. There are also a number of cycling organizations to help you on your way with everything from rentals to maps (see page 247).

The Esplanade is a favorite place to ride for the same reasons it's a good place to run. There's a well-marked bike path named after Boston physician Paul Dudley White, a heart surgeon who was one of the early pioneers of preventive exercise. White, who was President Eisenhower's physician, was himself an avid cyclist, and in his memory the city renamed its bicycle path, with its smooth paving and ever-changing scenery. Another advantage of the path is that the Esplanade connects to the city at several points by ramped footbridges (good for wheelchairs, too) so that you don't have to risk life and limb crossing major thoroughfares like Storrow Drive. If you are feeling particularly adventurous, you can travel the entire 17.7 mile circuit between Science Park and Watertown Square, along both sides of the Charles River. For a map of this and other Boston-area bike paths, call the **Metropolitan District Commission,** or send them a self-addressed, stamped envelope. The **State Transportation Library** also offers the *Boston-Cape Cod Bikeway Map* and the *Massachusetts Bicycle Map*.

Perhaps the best resource for serious cyclists is the **Boston Area Bicycle Coalition,** a nonprofit organization dedicated to improving the cycling environment in and around the city. Their newsletter, called the *Spoke N' Word,* covers everything from commuter survival and cycling traffic laws to the latest week-long excursions up to New Hampshire and Vermont.

SKATING

Skating is another pastime with a long history in Boston. Roller skating was all the rage in Victorian Boston between 1860 and 1890, and entire family expeditions were devoted to idyllic trips along the Charles River or through the Public Garden and Common. Roller skating was even favored by the ever-so-proper Boston Brahmins. Even the local ministers recommended it from their pulpits as a suitable family activity.

Today, although the old metal key-skates have been replaced by shoe skates with high-performance plastic wheels, skating along the Esplanade is still a favorite family sport. The flat, smooth pavement of the paths make them ideal for even the most novice skater, and experts can really strut their stuff. As a matter of fact, on a warm spring day the riverfront near the Hatch Shell often turns into an impromptu skating exhibition center as serious skaters pirouette and pike with consummate skill.

There are also good skate rental outlets near the Esplanade, and most of them will have maps available should you want to venture elsewhere on skates.

There are plenty of opportunities for ice-skating at indoor and outdoor locations throughout the city, but mostly in winter. One of the finest is the Lagoon in the Public Garden, where skaters have been gliding for a hundred years. Skating on the Lagoon is free and quite safe: the ice is thoroughly checked before it's opened to the public. One side of the bridge is reserved for figure skating and on the other, hockey sticks are allowed, so there is no danger of the two types of skaters getting tangled. The best place in the city to watch skating in winter is definitely from the main dining room of the Ritz Hotel across the street, where everything seems to take on a timeless burnished glow when seen through the huge picture windows.

If the Charles River seems an enticing spot for ice skating, be warned: it's almost never frozen enough to support weight (in spite of the fact that every winter finds some college students dragging out a zany array of objects to sit in the middle of the river until they are retrieved or sink beneath the semifrozen surface).

Indoor skaters usually flock to the **Skating Club of Boston,** considered to be New England's finest competitive training center. The club is not usually open to the public, but there are times available for general skating, except in June when the whole operation closes for a month. There are also public skate-dancing sessions, which are as much fun to watch as they are to participate in.

Another great opportunity to watch terrific skating is at Harvard University's annual Evening with Champions. Held the first weekend in November, this event raises money for the Jimmy Fund, a children's cancer fund, and is considered one of America's foremost exhibitions of figure skating.

Perhaps the best family skating opportunities, however, are at the network of MDC rinks located throughout the greater Boston area. There are twenty-two of them, and in season, all have times set aside for inexpensive public skating. The rinks are covered, but not enclosed, so dress warmly. One of the most popular is the **Stephen Steriti Rink** in the North End, where you not only get to skate, but get a terrific view of Bunker Hill and the USS *Constitution* as well.

RACQUET SPORTS

Underneath the Estabrook Memorial Clock in the **Longwood Cricket Club** is an inscription that translates from Latin to read, "This corner of the earth beyond all others delights me most." That may seem like overstatement to some people, but they are people who clearly do not take their tennis seriously.

The name Longwood Cricket Club is actually a misnomer, for the club is not in Longwood, nor is cricket played there. Longwood was the name of Napoleon's exile home on St. Helena. In 1840, David Sears named his six-hundred-acre Brookline estate after it, and the name was appropriated in 1877 by a group of cricketers who used to play their game on a corner of Sears's property. With the 1878 installation of the nation's first grass tennis court, the club and its purpose were forever changed. But the club retained the name Longwood Cricket Club because tennis was thought at the time to be a "sissy" sport. (City toughs would pass by and yell out "love" in a falsetto voice, irritating the players and throwing off their serve.)

Today, Longwood has twenty-eight grass and fourteen clay courts. The clay stadium courts were added in 1970 amidst much grumbling from old-time members. "If God hadn't meant tennis to

be played on grass," groused *Globe* sportswriter Bud Collins, "humans would have been born with rubber-soled feet." For one week every year, when Longwood hosts the U.S. Pro Tennis Championship in July, it does seem as if certain humans were born, if not with rubber-soled, at least with winged feet, for some of the best tennis in the world is played on the clay courts. It's interesting to note, by the way, that Longwood also hosts the annual Rogers Bowl Tennis Tournament in September, whose contestants are all over age seventy.

Longwood may be *the* place in Boston to play tennis, but it's not the only place. A number of private clubs in the city have hours during which the public may play for a fee, and most have reciprocity with other clubs around the country (check if you already belong to a club back home). The MDC offers a number of public (clay and asphalt) courts throughout the city, and two of the best are beautifully located, on the Common and the Esplanade.

There are other racquet sports that have even more social cachet than tennis these days. The **Boston Racquet Club** is devoted solely to racquetball and is strictly a private club. Even if you can't play, there is a restaurant here where the public is welcome and you can mingle with the players.

Squash is the fastest-growing racquet sport in the city. It is a game so fast and furious, it makes tennis look like croquet. Squash seems to suit Boston's aggressive professionals, with its quick footwork, finesse, and one-on-one format. Says **Harvard Club** squash pro Mo Khan, "In forty-five minutes you can get the best workout of your life, and that suits the lifestyle of Bostonians just fine."

Mo Khan's position in this city is unique, as tied to Boston politics as it is to Boston sports. Khan was playing an exhibition match in Pakistan during his stint in the Pakistani Air Force when John F. Kennedy saw him play. Kennedy, an avid squash player, was so impressed by Khan's game that he invited him to the White House when Khan came to the United States. After Khan got out of the service, he applied for pro positions in several American cities, but it was Kennedy's influence that got him the coveted Harvard Club job that he has held, as undisputed king of the sport, for over twenty-five years. Khan's influence has been instrumental in making Boston a squash city, not only for the locals, but on an international level. When he came to the Harvard Club in 1963, there were 125 squash players; by 1985, there were over 700. Each autumn, the city is host to the national and international squash open played in a Plexiglas-enclosed box in the rotundas of the Boston Cyclorama (see pages 153–154).

Both racquetball and squash can be played at a number of the city's athletic clubs where you are welcome on a one-time basis for a fee. Most clubs will arrange games, or you can wait around the courts and be pretty sure of scaring up some quick competition. The area Y's have some good playing courts as well.

Tour Sites

Boston Area Bicycle Coalition (BABC)
P.O. Box 1015, Kendall Square
Cambridge, MA 02142
491-RIDE

Boston Athletic Association (BAA)
17 Main St.
Hopkinton, MA 01748
435-6905

Boston by Sail
65 Lewis Wharf
Boston, MA 02110
742-3313 for reservations.

Boston Common or Charles River Esplanade
727-7090 to reserve a tennis court.

The Boston Garden
150 Causeway St.
Boston, MA 02114
227-3200

Boston Racquet Club
10 Post Office Sq.
Boston, MA 02109
482-8881

Community Boating, Inc.
Charles River
21 Embankment Rd.
Boston, MA 02114
523-1038

Fenway Park
24 Yawkey Way
Boston, MA 02215
267-9440

Harvard Club
374 Commonwealth Ave.
Boston, MA 02215
536-1260

Longwood Cricket Club
564 Hammond St.
Brookline, MA 02146
731-2900

Metropolitan District Commission
   (MDC)
General Information
20 Somerset
Boston, MA 02108
727-5215

Skating Club of Boston
1240 Soldiers Field Rd.
Brighton, MA 02135
782-5900

Sports Museum of
   New England
1175 Soldiers Field Rd.
Boston, MA 02134
78-SPORT

Steriti Rink
Commercial St.
Boston, MA 02109
523-9327

Sullivan Stadium
Rte. 1
Foxboro, MA 02035
508-262-1776

YMCA
316 Huntington Ave.
Boston, MA 02115
536-7800

YWCA
140 Clarendon St.
Boston, MA 02116
536-7940
Also located at 7 Temple Street,
   Cambridge (491-6050).

RESTAURANTS

Cask 'n Flagon
62 Brookline Ave.
Boston, MA 02215
536-4840

Champions American Sports
   Lounge
Marriott Copley Place
110 Huntington Ave.
Boston, MA
262-5776

Copperfield's
98 Brookline Ave.
Boston, MA 02215
297-8605

Clarke's
149 Merchants Row
Boston, MA 02109
367-1297

Daisy Buchanan's
240A Newbury St.
Boston, MA 02116
247-8516

Dockside Restaurant
183 State St.
Boston, MA 02114
723-7050

Eliot Lounge
370 Commonwealth Ave.
Boston, MA 02215
262-1078

Fours Boston–The Sports Bar
166 Canal St.
Boston, MA 02114
720-4455

Fred P. Otts
29 North Quincy Market
Boston, MA 02109
227-9373

Friday's
26 Exeter St.
Boston, MA 02116
266-9040

Kowloon Restaurant
Rte. 1
Saugus, MA 01906
233-9719

Oyster Club Raw Bar and Grille
200 Portland St.
Boston, MA 02114
523-7435

Ritz-Carlton Hotel
15 Arlington St.
Boston, MA 02116
536-5700

Sports Café
120 Causeway St.
Boston, MA 02114
723-6664

Who's On First
270 Newbury St.
Boston, MA 02116
236-1566

Additional Resources

BEACHES

All of the following are accessible
  by public transportation:
Carson Beach (South Boston)
Constitution Beach (East Boston)
Revere Beach (Revere)
Savin Hill Beach (Dorchester)
Tenean Beach (Dorchester)

RESOURCES FOR PEOPLE WHO LIKE TO BE FIT
(whether resident or tourist)

Fit Corp.
Two locations:
133 Federal St.
Boston, MA 02110
542-1010
6th Floor, Hilton Hotel
40 Dalton St.
Boston, MA
262-2050

Fitness to Go
44 Travis Dr.
Chestnut Hill, MA 02167
964-9565

Joy of Movement
Two locations:
542 Commonwealth Ave.
Boston, MA 02115
266-5463
561 Boylston
Boston, MA 02116
536-3377

Room to Stretch
355 Congress St.
Boston, MA 02210
451-3551

Squash Club
15 Gorham St.
Allston, MA 02134
731-4177

Vitality
151 Tremont St.
Boston, MA 02111
482-6669
The magazine for your wealth,
health, and happiness.

CYCLING ORGANIZATIONS AND BIKE PATH INFORMATION

American Youth Hostels, Inc.
1020 Commonwealth Ave.
Boston, MA 02215
731-5430

State Transporation Library
10 Park Plaza
Boston, MA 02116
973-8000

OTHER SPORTS CLUBS

Appalachian Mountain Club
5 Joy St.
Boston, MA 02108
523-0636

Massachusetts Volksport
   Association
3 Arthur Ave.
Hamilton, MA 01982
508-468-2104

Boston Center for Adult
   Education
5 Commonwealth Ave.
Boston, MA 02116
267-4430

Sierra Club
3 Joy St.
Boston, MA 02108
227-5339

Cambridge Center for Adult
   Education
42 Brattle St.
Cambridge, MA 02138
547-6789

RENTALS

Beacon Hill Skate
45 Charles St.
Boston, MA 02114
523-9513

SAILING

Boston Harbor Sailing Club
72 East India Row
Boston, MA 02110
523-2619

Boston Sailing Center
54 Lewis Wharf
Boston, MA 02110
227-4198

SPORTS TICKETS

Boston Bruins Tickets
227-3200, 227-3206, 742-0200

New England Patriots Tickets
426-8181

Celtics Tickets
523-6050

Red Sox Tickets
267-8661

TRADITIONAL AREA RACES

Sasson Championship, 10K
Fourth Sunday in March
Boston

Boston Milk Run, 10K
Second Sunday in April
Boston

Youville Hospital, 10K
Fourth Sunday in March
Cambridge

Elizabeth Grady 10K Boston
   Classic
Third Sunday in April
Boston

Run for Peace, 10K
First Sunday in April
Cambridge

Boston Marathon, 26.2M
April 19 (Patriot's Day)
Hopkinton to Boston

Charles River Run, 7M
First Sunday in May
Boston

Women on the Run, 2M & 5M
Third Sunday in May
Cambridge

Freedom Trail Race, 8M
First Sunday in October
Boston/Cambridge

Tufts Health Plan 10K for Women
October 12 (Columbus Day)
Boston/Cambridge

Bostonfest Marathon
Third Sunday in October
Boston

Boston Medical Center, 10K
Third Sunday in October
Boston

Jordan Marsh Road Race, 5M
Thanksgiving Day
Boston

Manufacturers Hanover Corporate
   Challenge, 3.5M
July
Boston

Governor's Cup Road Race
September
Boston

WBCN Road Race, 10K
October
Boston

TRADITIONAL AREA WALKS

Walk for Hunger, 10K
Sponsored by Project Bread
May
Boston

March of Dimes Walk America
   Walk-a-thon, 18M
April
Boston

Volksmarch 10K
June (includes 25K Bikefest)
October
Ft. Devens

Stride Boston Fitness Walk and
   Expo
September
Boston

Epilogue

So, now you have it. Boston A to Z: art galleries through zoological gardens, antiques through zinnias, and architects through zealots. It's been challenging to limit our stories, keep in the essentials, and uncover uncommonness wherever we looked. Far more erudite books exist about this wonderful city, compiled by meticulous scholars and researchers, and we recommend every one of them. But whether you're an armchair traveler, tourist, student, or resident who is eager to enjoy the city's best and brightest — we feel proud to have offered you this book. It is our gift to the city of Boston, which has given us so much pleasure for so many years, and which has never asked anything from us but our loyalty. No matter how much or how little time you have to spend here, we hope you will share that loyalty with us, and help salute that very old, ever new, ever astonishing "hub of the solar system" (that's what Brahmin Oliver Wendell Holmes called it) . . . Uncommon Boston!

In the Vicinity

A Geographical Listing

If you happen to find yourself in a particular section of Boston — whether you're staying with friends in the area or you have a few hours to spare between meetings — here's a handy guide that lists sites mentioned in the tours, arranged by geographic area. Since the tours in this book are primarily by subject or topic rather than location, this list will also help you create a tour of your own. Use the regular index in the back of the book to locate the page(s) where detailed discussions of the site appear. And please note, restaurants and shops are *not* listed here, so refer to the tours and the lists after each tour for those. Happy touring!

BACK BAY

Ames-Webster House
Arlington Street Church
Baylies Mansion
Berklee College of Music
Berklee Performance Center
Boston Architectural Center
Boston Common
Boston Public Garden
Boston Public Library
Burrage Mansion
Church Court Condominiums
Church of the Covenant
Christian Science Mother Church
Clarendon Street Playground
Copley Plaza Hotel
Copley Society
Copley Square Park
Emmanuel Church
First Baptist Church
First Church of Christ, Scientist
First and Second Unitarian Church
Fisher College
Four Seasons Hotel
Gibson House
Goethe Institute
Harvard Club
Horticulture Hall
Hotel Vendome
Institute of Contemporary Art
John Hancock Observatory
Jordan Hall
Mapparium
Marriott Copley Place
New England Conservatory of Music
New England Historic Genealogical Society
New Old South Church
118 Beacon Street
150 Beacon Street

Park Plaza Hotel
Public Garden Swan Boats
Ritz-Carlton Hotel
Sheraton Hotel
St. Botolph Club
Symphony Hall

Trinity Church
267 Commonwealth Avenue
Westin Hotel
Women's Educational and
  Industrial Union

BEACON HILL

Boston Athenaeum
Boston Common
Black Heritage Trail
Bulfinch Pavilion and Ether Dome
Central Burying Ground
Charles Street Meeting House
Church of the Advent
85 Mount Vernon Street
45 Beacon Street
George Parkman House

Houghton Mifflin Company
Little, Brown & Company
National Society of Colonial
  Dames
Nichols House Museum
Old West Church
State House
Society for the Preservation of
  New England Antiquities
Women's City Club

CAMBRIDGE

Blacksmith House Bakery and Café
Botanical Museum
Children's Museum
Harvard Cooperative Society
Harvard Lampoon Castle

Houghton Library
Longfellow House
Mount Auburn Cemetery
Out of Town Newspapers
Widener Library

CHARLESTOWN

Boston Marine Society
Bunker Hill Monument
Charlestown Navy Yard

USS *Cassin Young*
USS *Constitution*

DORCHESTER

John F. Kennedy Museum

DOWNTOWN

Bedford Building Clock
Bostonian Hotel
Boston Music Company
Boston Racquet Club
Brattle Book Shop
Colonial Theater
Faneuil Hall
Filene's Basement
Globe Corner Book Shop
Hotel Meridien
King's Chapel Burial Ground

National Park Service
  Headquarters
Old Granary Burial Ground
Old South Meeting House
Old State House
Omni Parker House Hotel
Park Street Church
Post Office Square
St. Paul's Cathedral
Wilbur Theatre

FENWAY/KENMORE

Boston University Bookstore
Boston University School of Fine
  Arts
Fenway Park
Isabella Stewart Gardner Museum

Massachusetts College of Art
Massachusetts Historical Society
Mugar Library
Museum of Fine Arts
Wheelock Family Theatre

NORTH END

Copp's Hill Burial Ground
Old North Church
Paul Revere House

Pierce/Hichborn House
St. Stephen's Church

WATERFRONT

Bay State Cruise Lines
Boston Design Center
Boston Fish Pier
Boston Harbor Cruises
Boston Tea Party Ship and
  Museum
Children's Museum
Christopher Columbus Waterfront
  Park

Computer Museum
Harbor Walk
Milk Bottle
New England Aquarium
Rose Fitzgerald Kennedy Garden
Waterfront Park

Boston Festivals —
A Small Sample

Chinese New Year
January or February
Chinatown
267-6446 (Events line)

Annual Valentines Festival
February
536-4100

Black History Month
February
536-4100

New England Boat Show
Early February
Hynes Auditorium
262-8000

Annual New England Spring
   Flower Show
March
Bayside Exposition Center
536-9280

Saint Patrick's Day Parade
March
South Boston
725-3912

Boston Kite Festival
April
Franklin Park
725-4006

Paul Revere's Ride Re-enactment
April 19
Hanover St.
10 A.M.

Memorial Day Parade
May
Copley Square
536-4100

Annual Dragon Boat Festival
Late June
Esplanade
426-2237

Bunker Hill Re-enactment and
   Parade
June
Charlestown
241-9511

Cambridge River Festival
June
Various Cambridge locations
498-9033

Dorchester Day Parade
June
Dorchester
725-4000

Boston Annual Harborfest
  Celebration
July
Waterfront
536-4100

Boston Pops Annual Fourth of
  July Concert
Charles River Esplanade
Hatch Memorial Shell
266-1492 or 727-5215

Chowderfest
July
New England Aquarium
227-1528

Harborfest Fireworks Concert
July
Charlestown Navy Yard
227-1528

Independence Day Oration and
  Parade
July
Faneuil Hall
725-3911

August Moon Festival
Mid-August or September
Boston Common
725-3914

Faneuil Hall Marketplace
  Birthday
Celebration and Parade
August
523-1300

Columbus Day Parade
October
Between East Boston and North
  End
725-3911

Head of the Charles Regatta
October
Charles River
864-8415

Veteran's Day Parade
November
Commonwealth Avenue–Back Bay
725-3912

Christmas Tree Lighting
First week in December
Prudential Center
236-3581

Re-enactment of the Boston Tea
  Party
December
338-1773

First Night New Year's Eve
  Celebration
December 31/January 1
536-4100

Index